Dharma
Family Treasures

Dharma Family Treasures

Sharing Mindfulness with Children

Edited and illustrated by

Sandy Eastoak

North Atlantic Books
Berkeley, California

Published by
North Atlantic Books
P.O. Box 12327
Berkeley, California 94712

Cover art by Sandy Eastoak
Cover design by Paula Morrison and Legacy Media, Inc.
Book design by Paula Morrison
Typeset by Catherine Campaigne
Music scored by Seward McCain
Printed in the United States of America

This is issue #48 in the *Io* series.

Dharma Family Treasures is sponsored by the Society for the Study of Native Arts and Sciences, a nonprofit educational corporation whose goals are to develop an educational and crosscultural perspective linking various scientific, social, and artistic fields; to nurture a holistic view of arts, sciences, humanities, and healing; and to publish and distribute literature on the relationship of mind, body, and nature.

Library of Congress Cataloging-in-Publication Data

Dharma family treasures : sharing Buddhism with children / edited by Sandy Eastoak. —2nd ed.
    p. cm.
Originally published: Dharma family treasures. 1994
Includes bibliographical references.
ISBN 1-55643-244-5
    1. Buddhist children—Religious life.   2. Parenting—Religious aspects—Buddhism.   3. Religious life—Buddhism.   I. Eastoak, Sandy.   II. Dharma family treasures.
BQ5436.S53   1997
    294.3'75'083—dc21   96-50985
                                            CIP

1 2 3 4 5 6 7 8 9 10 / 01 00 99 98 97

Master: I have no tolerance for those who use their children as an excuse for not practicing.

Hermit: I have no tolerance for those who use their practice as an excuse for not parenting.

Beggar: When we fully immerse ourselves in parenting as our practice, we answer the question, Of what use is it merely to enjoy this fleeting world?

    O sincere trainees, create no Dharma orphans. Quickly is dew gone from the grass. Quicker still are children grown.

For my family

Contents

Sandy Eastoak

❧

Introduction

This book began in 1985, when Michele Hill and Deborah Hopkinson realized that "the issue of family involvement with lay Zen in America was perhaps the most important and controversial subject we would ever take up." During their ten years experience in editing *Kahawai: A Journal of Women and Zen,* they had heard considerable rumblings from the impact of parenthood on women's practice.They sent out questionnaires to inquire about interest in a book on Zen practice for families. Over and over parents stressed their need to learn how other parents were adapting practice and basic concepts to the rhythms and readiness of their children.

Soon after, Michele attended a retreat with Thich Nhat Hanh at Plum Village in France: "It was the first time I had experienced a setting where children were welcomed as equal participants in Buddhist practice, listening to talks, leading tea ceremonies, walking and doing sitting meditation with adults." This experience helped focus the book. The manuscript was called *Simple Treasures,* reflecting the purpose of introducing children to the Three Treasures of Buddha, Dharma, and Sangha—and the hope of integrating practice into family life by simple means.

As the book swam in the ocean of life, it encountered a powerful crosscurrent. The optimistic tone of the book began to sound a little too rosy. The ideal image of quiet ritual and gentle acts of compassion clashed with what we and our children actually said and did on any ordinary day. It obscured the live tangle of angers, hopes, fears, disappointments, frustrations, joys, and sorrows of children and parents joined in the complex struggle toward growth and understanding. Practicing mindfulness with children isn't simple, and that's the truth.

❧

A new image guided further work on the book: the lotus, ancient symbol of spiritual process. Rooted in the mud of deluded existence, the lotus bud grows on the strong stem of daily practice, and rising above the water, blossoms into enlightenment.

The root of our practice as parents is a complex of dilemmas: How do we find time to meditate? How do we apply the precepts to the needs of a toddler? How do we clean up our own karma so the pain we experienced as children is not passed on? How do we make parenting our vehicle for enlightenment? How do we do no harm but only good to these small beings? How does our practice honor our commitment to be the best parents we can?

As the stem of our practice, we need a social context that honors parenting as a spiritual path. Where do we find support for our efforts to solve our root dilemmas? How do we get recognition that the problems we are struggling with are not obstacles to spiritual practice, but *are* spiritual practice? How do Buddhist traditions guide us? How do we find or create guidance where the tradition is lacking? How do we dare suggest the tradition may be lacking? Where can we practice communally *with* our children? How can we establish children's programs and family practice days within our sanghas? How do parents and children function in the sangha? How does the sangha function in the passage of the generations?

The blossom of our practice as parents is an independent relationship between our children and the path of wisdom. How can our children develop a dependable refuge? Where can we find stories, songs, poems, simplifications of basic teachings, interpretations of sutras, and rituals to guide our children? How can our children find their own way to the wisdom that beckons us? By what means will the mindfulness of their lives not be limited by the extent of our understanding, but grow and flourish beyond us?

The lotus of Buddhist parenting grows in the soil and weather of contemporary global mind. Although both parenting and Buddhist practice are timeless activities, there is something afoot on earth right now that we have to face directly to be either responsible parents or mindful trainees. The earth is undergoing a great crisis. In the next generation or two, human life will be either transformed or gone forever, taking with us most other life forms. As parents, as Buddhists, we must awake to the enormity of life's longing for itself that we experience in our children, a dragonfly, a pine.

Enlightenment is nothing other than ordinary life, but this is not an ordinary time. Our practice and our parenting cannot be ordinary. Traditionally Buddhism focused on spiritual growth without taking much notice of current events and social causes. Today engaged Buddhism is growing urgently. Inner and outer work are becoming interwoven.

In parenting and other activities, I experience a conflict between business as usual and a state of emergency. My senses and my heart tell me this is an emergency, yet, like a schooling fish unable to break from the group direction, I keep on with business as usual. I want my children to enjoy all the wonderful things of childhood — birthday parties, scout meetings, field trips, art projects, games, county fairs. And I can't shake the feeling that we have to do something else — go stand in front of the bulldozers, never use the car again, go door to door telling about tree devas.

The connection between mindfulness and the fate of the earth is immediate and total. If several generations ago parents had asked these questions about spiritual practice and childraising, the earth would be reasonably healthy today. We would not be wondering if any of our children will live to see grandchildren. Today our task is more than cleaning up our family karma, honoring parenting as a spiritual path, and giving our children access to a wealth of spiritual teaching. Now we need to practice on the razor's edge between panic at the danger we face and joy in the ordinary beauties of life begetting life. It is somehow that line linking panic and joy that can save us.

As I worked on this book, I splashed in muddy water. While I explored the most inspiring ideas about practicing Buddhism at the very source of the future, I inflicted on myself and my family a workload that devoured my time and patience. This paradox is common to both Buddhist practice and general efforts at world-saving. *Being present with our children and modeling stillness and simplicity is our real work.* We can't lock them in the closet so we can meditate or send them to boarding school so we can go clean up the ocean. We can't tell them all the beautiful things about the Buddha while we rush frantically from peace meetings to sesshins to ballet lessons.

Here's a koan it may take several lifetimes to solve: How do we make loving our children, Buddhist practice, and healing the earth coincide? *Without rushing!* Our children, our practice, our earth—each requires our full energy and lots of empty, goalless time. And each requires no separation whatsoever from the other two.

❀

Over time, the book became a merging of complex concerns with simple teachings. Sharing the treasures of Buddha, Dharma, and Sangha with our children becomes our practice. Simultaneously, we understand that we practice as a *dharma family.* We are embedded in the great web of dharma that is the universe. And particularly for us, as we help Buddhism find its specifically North American, British, or Australian form, our dharma family is the trees and birds, mosses and fungi, fish and mammals, rocks and waters of our home. As we focus with our children we are aware of the enormity of life beyond our focus. In this way our family practice answers to the needs of our place and time, and embodies the compassion that is the essence of Buddhism.

It is possible that the paradox between our need to secure a future for our children and the requirements of nonattachment, when experienced in intimacy with our natural dharma family, will yield a particularly vital form of Buddhism. Then our efforts to include children in our sanghas will have inestimable benefits.

Discussing these hopes, one mother joyfully imagined the Buddha climbing back in the window of his home, returning to his wife and son. Perhaps we begin a journey with the family treasuring Buddhism. Perhaps farther on, Buddhism will also treasure the family.

Meanwhile, this remains a radical book. It challenges our usual patterns of thought and behavior. It very clearly asks for changes in our parenting, in our meditation centers, in the very way we think about Buddhism. So it shouldn't feel like any other book, but should bother us a little.

Each author's original style has been retained to give the reader the benefit of diverse personalities, traditions, and experiences. Some apparent inconsistencies result. Students of one teacher will talk of five precepts, those of another, ten. Dharma is capitalized by some authors but not by others. Just as some people, depending on the direction of their spiritual journey, cannot in good conscience write about God, but can write about god, so Dharma does not mean quite the same thing as dharma. As Buddhism is inherently a fluid, nondogmatic religion, subtle nuances of religious perception are valid and precious.

Similarly, the meaning of "strength" and "weakness" of writing style is not for Buddhist parents what it is for academics. The intellectual need of a mom seeking a moment of guidance between mopping a spill and defusing sibling rivalry is different from her need on the following evening when the kids have miraculously fallen asleep early.

The texture of a parent's life is quite uneven. Intelligence and foolishness, order and chaos, wisdom and pettiness, love and anger, serenity and uproar alternate abruptly in an unpredictable kaleidoscope of experience. At best, it teaches us to make allies of our rational and irrational sides. Otherwise, the world breaks down.

The structure of this book respects both texture and necessity. It is meant to be picked up and put down as time and circumstance allow, following the thread of one's needs, in any order. Poems extend the meanings of essays from the rational surface of our thoughts to the nonrational layers of our psyche. Stories enable us to share with our children by reading aloud. Together, the stories and poems nourish that part of ourselves most fully capable of *meeting* our children.

The first section introduces the experience of parents as children affect their practice. The second validates these experiences as a spiritual practice equal to any. The third shares ways of including children in practicing at home and in the sangha. The fourth gives basic teachings in simplified and story forms. The fifth integrates family practice with native being.

Throughout, some of the material is written for adults and some for children. There are materials for preschool and school-age children and for adolescents and young adults. Some of the poems and stories are ageless. Some materials have been written by children.

Paula Gunn Allen wrote in *The Sacred Hoop* that "The mythic narrative as an articulation of thought or wisdom is not expressible in other forms. . . ." While not a mythic narrative, this book is more than an anthology. The ideas of a diverse and deeply committed group of people are gathered in a form that is itself a story. Its intent is the nourishment of parent and child engaged in answering courageously a question our society cannot yet quite hear.

The topic of parenting and practice is far deeper and more vast than any of us appreciated when we began. Our experiences ranged from the somewhat chilly "adults-only" attitude of some meditation centers to the attentiveness traditionally given to children in Jodo Shinshu temples. Our practices ranged from long-time priesthood to peripheral wondering. We held in common a commitment to bringing forth the truth in our lives with our children.

At first, most of us wrote pretty close to what we'd read or heard about practice and parenting, which was neither much nor imaginative. Each time I spoke with a contributor, our thoughts sparked, our ideas danced. Each question bred deeper questions. Gradually we coaxed each other out onto limbs where we began to name the unheard. In that space we could feel how only just beginning we are.

What we have been able to articulate so far strokes the surface of a topic whose shadowy mass we only dimly perceive. Parenting as a path of practice looms like a great uncarved block. The challenge of learning its secrets beckons us, whispers promises of great compassion and healing. In this challenge and its promise, we are not alone.

While this book is written specifically for Buddhists, about Buddhist experiences, with Buddhist concepts and terminology, its fundamental questions are universal. This is especially apparent as we understand that our desire to share our practice with our children is not that they light incense and sit on zafus as they grow up, but that they stay acutely in touch with the most urgent questions of our collective being and find their own wise and compassionate answers.

Here we join company with all parents everywhere. The questions discussed above—linking spirituality with survival—are the questions that parents of every religious persuasion are currently grappling with. While Buddhists with mindfulness practice ask for children's programs, Catholics with children's programs seek mindfulness practice. All are working to integrate spirituality, parenting, and protection of our children's future. Ultimately these are inseparable for parents of any faith.

One of the hopeful phenomena today is the crossing of racial and sectarian lines. Within Buddhism there is growing collaboration. I am optimistic that as Japanese and African Americans and Zen and Tibetan and vipassana and caucasians and Jodo Shin and Vietnamese all talk together and share experiences, we can create a Buddhist family practice that works in North America.

At the same time, we need to cross lines farther out into the world. We share with people everywhere—Christians, Muslims, Hindus, Baha'is, Jews, Native Americans, Zoroastrians, Pagans, agnostics, and atheists—the difficulties of living in a time of crisis for family values. Perhaps Buddhist efforts to raise children mindfully can benefit all—if we expand our practice through a process of inter-learning with all the variety of parents we encounter in our daily life. On earth today, the challenges and hopes of mindful parenting are universal.

Together may we take refuge and rescue all beings.

Part One

✿

Parents Practicing

John Tarrant

Dream, dream

She sleeps to dream,
and what can she dream of who is hardly
gathered into being?

Breasts, sunshine, fountains
running with milk,
the rose as large as her face.

Sun, moon and great beings
bend over her
and follow her days.

Since birth her head has a furrow
ploughed on the contour;
it is filling in now.

Her hands rise
as if around a violin.

To watch her sleep
is to sit at the fire in winter
lost in the light
that I have always believed
was promised.

Mel Weitsman

❀

Taking Care of Daniel

I have the great good fortune to be able to take care of our little baby, Daniel. That's a big part of my practice right now. For this month, I'm being mother while Liz is going to nursing school. I've always appreciated mothers' practice, and for me it's really a wonderful kind of practice to be a mother and be on a baby's schedule. Daniel is like a little monk. One time after his bath, Liz put his towel over one shoulder and said, "He looks just like a little monk." He's also a teacher for me because he has such undisputed purity. I'm like his anja, his attendant. I have to be very attentive. If I let things slip by, he gives me the business. I can't make many mistakes, and I have to do everything right on time. If I start wandering, he lets me know, but he's very good and very patient with me. I'm patient with him, too, so we get along very well; and he only gives me a problem when I'm not paying attention. In between feedings and changing diapers, I can talk to people and do whatever work I have to do. I am pleased that when I am interacting with someone he always finds his place, so I seldom feel that his presence is intrusive. It's harder to go someplace, of course, because he needs his afternoon nap and his bottle. I haven't had such a strict schedule since I was at Tassajara, so for me it's like monastic practice.

Even though, to my knowledge, it has never been recognized as such, mothers' practice is somewhat like monastic practice because you're on a very strict, continuous schedule. The problem is that mothers and children usually practice together alone, whereas in monastic life, people practice together with a lot of support. In the past, mothers and children had an extended family situation like those in "less developed" countries do at present. But in America, people feel autonomous in their homes, and often there is great loneliness. Mothers and children don't have the support they have had in other times and places, and a great deal of the time, there's anxiety caused by pressure to do something else. It's hard to feel justified settling into just bringing up somebody. Actually, it's a great accomplishment and very fulfilling, but it's hard these days to see it this way.

The thing about this schedule is that I can't linger anywhere. When something is called for, I must just focus on that activity. When the baby is crying and needs something, I just stop what I'm doing and respond. I have to pay attention just to the baby's need. When the telephone rings, I have to ask Daniel to be good and turn my attention to the caller. Someone knocks on the door, and I have to be attentive to the person knocking. And the baby has to take his place in the rhythm of my life; and he does.

We sometimes tend to think that a baby has his demands and that's that. But a baby knows instinctively how to cooperate with the situation at hand, if you allow that. Daniel is very interested in my life, and when he is included as an observer, he is very good and his presence is a positive factor. If I see the changes he makes in my life as something going wrong, then my mind starts to move. This is a very important point. Many sources instruct us: when you sit in meditation, don't let your mind move. Letting your mind move means being caught by discrimination or judgment. This means something has gone wrong. Something wrong means being caught by right and wrong. So just willingly to let go and respond gives me some freedom. If I say, "Oh, oh, this is wrong," my mind starts to get into a judgmental mode. Then everything starts to go wrong, and I begin finding blame. There's no longer nonstop flow. The ball is no longer bouncing on the stream.

For me, this form of practice is just to take care of what comes up and allow my life to be endlessly interrupted. As soon as I take the attitude of being bothered, the calmness of mind vanishes. It's like the razor's edge. I can walk it very well, and it becomes a broad path, if I am truly attentive. This is the power of zazen. This is how I feel I can practice zazen, moment after moment in my life.

Mushim Ikeda

❀

Talking to Joshua

To be a mother is sweet,
And a father.
It is sweet to live arduously,
And to master yourself.

O how sweet it is to enjoy life,
Living in honesty and strength!

The *Dhammapada*

One summer morning, during a three-month meditation retreat, I was assigned to sweep the sidewalk in front of the temple. The teacher, a strong-willed Korean monk, had declared "no talking," and in the "silence" which we humans so often fill with chatter, I discovered a world rich with sensation: the fly that suddenly buzzed at the window, the hiss of a candle flame, the breath circling through my body all felt equally alive and wonderful.

Using a heavy push broom, I worked my way down the sidewalk. A large black beetle, startled, leaped from a crack in the cement and scrambled across my path beneath the upswung broom. The sky went black, my body melted, there was an electrifying split-second in which I was simultaneously looking down at the beetle, and gazing up into a great darkness. Then, as if in a dream, I lifted the broom and saw the beetle stagger about, right itself, and run off. My heart was pounding, and tears of relief filled my eyes.

All beings want to live and be happy. A potent and inescapable truth had inscribed itself into every cell of my body. My life and the beetle's were equal expressions of Life itself. We were distinct, yet we were one. We were vulnerable to one another, having changed roles and forms countless times in previous existences. We were intimate.

All beings want to live and be happy. From this realization emerges the first Buddhist precept: Not to kill, but to cherish all life. It has been said that the precepts, which some people first view as restrictions or commandments, are actually koans, unsolvable riddles that we must nevertheless answer in each moment. Possibly the greatest koan of my life was put to me in the unlikely setting of a Seventh Day Adventist Hospital in Seoul, Korea, where a kindly American doctor informed me that I was pregnant. My head shaven, dressed in the gray garments of a Buddhist nun, I had in my knapsack a few clothes, a small amount of cash, and the return half of a round-trip ticket, U.S.-South Korea. The situation was clearly impossible.

"Do you intend to keep the baby?" the doctor asked.

To my own astonishment, I answered immediately and without doubt. "Oh, yes!" I said. A second later I thought, "I must be crazy. How can I do this?" And again the answer came strong and clear: "You can do this because now you are a mother." To step forward, to join lay life, to embrace the human future, this was to be my spiritual path for many years. Yet unlike the decision to begin monastic Zen training, this decision came easily, perhaps because I was not making it alone. Tiny but definite as a candle flame, my son had joined me. We would make our way together.

❧

Practice continued. I joined a household of Buddhist meditators, worked, and sat daily. When I was five and a half months pregnant, I traveled to the Mount Baldy monastery in the San Gabriel Mountains outside of Los Angeles to join Joshu Sasaki Roshi for the December Rohatsu sesshin. I knew that once my baby came, my opportunities to sit in the meditation hall would be limited; I wanted to "see the old man" and celebrate Buddha's Enlightenment.

During sesshin, all students lead the monk's life, waking at 2:30 a.m. and proceeding through various rounds of sitting, chanting, formal meals, work, and so on, to a schedule timed to the minute. Each student met privately in a face-to-face interview with Sasaki Roshi several times a day. In this simple fashion, the seven days passed, with the last night being a time of continuous practice in honor of Shakyamuni Buddha's effort.

Obviously an exception to the rule, I was well accommodated by the supportive staff. I slept in a private room, usually the infirmary, fairly close to one of the outdoor porta-toilets, and meditated in the "second zendo" across the path from the main zendo. I was by myself for long hours, joined occasionally by a member of the kitchen staff or other monks and nuns whose duties necessitated a departure from the main schedule. I could leave the zendo whenever I needed to use the toilet or rest, an unusual freedom that made the retreat feel very vast and spacious, almost playful.

Soon after the sesshin began, a heavy snowfall blanketed the mountain, piling up on the zendo roof, covering the path, and weighing down the branches of the pine trees. After the evening sitting ended, I would wait for the main zendo to empty, then carefully trudge down the icy path through the forest. The full moon lit my way; each step and my koan and the precious burden of my lively unborn child became one with my visible breath. The entire snow-covered world felt silent and pregnant, alive with a minute circuitry of energy. Over time, I felt a friendly relationship developing between myself and the meditators in the main zendo; I could hear the sticks clapping, bells ringing, and shuffling of feet from their building, and sometimes I stood outside and watched the black-robed figures doing walking meditation in the snow.

Joshua sat within me. Each morning in the sutra hall he would respond vigorously to the drum and gong accompanying recitation of the *Heart Sutra*. During zazen he napped or turned in his warm, tidepool world. Meditation was a joy for me. Despite the intense cold and the snow, I felt like a gardener in spring, watching a seed sprouting, pushing through soil into the sunlight, and growing leaf

9

by leaf toward its flower. I spoke to my son, conversations that were long and companionable, wordless and profound.

"How do you manifest Oneness with baby?" Sasaki Roshi asked. His round face glowed with happiness and maternal pride; the tiny sanzen room was warm and womblike, within the larger body of the snowy mountain. The koan was intimate; I felt it rumbling and turning inside me, opening into the future where, moment by moment, I would demonstrate my practice through more than a thousand days of breast-feeding, diaper-changing, and the demands of single-mothering. Sasaki Roshi's enthusiasm was unwavering; he demonstrated with simplicity and clarity the quintessential Zen ability to seize my situation as the perfect situation in which to practice, as I believe he would if I had come to him saying that I had cancer, AIDS, no money, a great deal of money, or whatever. The ability to accept and love one's difficulties—that was the key.

❀

Joshua is three and a half years old. I talk to him every day, and he talks to me. I remember vividly a Dharma talk by Samu Sunim in which he said: "The difference between us is that when you talk, I listen, but when I talk, you talk." I want really to listen to what Josh has to say, and when I do I see how much we have in common. Unlike me, he does not have to make grocery lists, get the car repaired, balance the checkbook—the logistics of adult responsibilities. Yet his world, so filled with mystery, monsters, and gigantic emotions, is not far from my own.

Riding in his carseat to morning preschool, he is quiet, thinking. "Mom," he says, "I don't want you to become an old woman and die."

"Do you feel worried about that?"

"Yes, I do."

"I understand how you feel," I tell him. "Sometimes I feel that way too. But try not to worry so much. Mom will take care of you for a long time."

He gazes out the window, his small, round face serious and preoccupied. Working on his koan, I guess. We have come so far together, he and I, each step an adventure. I doubt that there is a definitive "how to" guide in this often stormy journey, although there are many valuable resources—other parents being at the top of the list. My effort has been to provide my son with a wide variety of experiences, and to talk with him as his consciousness begins to open and connect to the larger world. Visiting Buddhist hospices, viewing studios of artist friends, hiking at Point Reyes, recycling containers, and growing cherry tomatoes on the deck of our Oakland apartment are all ways of planting seeds for his future, though the values he chooses will be his own, and may differ radically from mine.

We recently returned from a Rohatsu sesshin celebrated under John Tarrant Roshi's guidance. It included three small children, who ate, bathed, played, and argued with one another as their parents came from and went to the zendo. A childcare coordinator enlisted the help of several practitioners to do childcare during the day, and the tenzo (kitchen head) went to the trouble of setting up a separate tray for the families at each meal, taking into account the children's special needs. The teacher, whose daughter was one of the three children, prepared for his teishos (Dharma talks) and a precepts ceremony in a living room littered with toys, acorns, books and sleeping bags, with the kids singing, laughing, tumbling and crying around him. My partner, Joshua's daddy since Josh was one year old, drove to the rural site in order to support my practice, enabling me to sit in the zendo during the early morning and after dinner periods in addition to the periods when childcare was provided by the sangha. Well-loved and welcomed by all, the children quickly set up their own environment, including an area between the couch and the wall that was the "children's zendo," the main rule being that one had to be quite noisy there.

This was the second Rohatsu with the California Diamond Sangha I have attended with Joshua and, as he did last year, he asked to go to the zendo in the morning after breakfast. Entering quietly in his pajamas, he offered incense, rang the bell, and made a bow. We sat together for a number of minutes, walked around the room, and left.

"You must educate baby!" Sasaki Roshi told me as I sat before him in December, 1988. I took his words greatly to heart, and since that time I can truly say that my entire practice has been oriented toward providing a spiritual education for Joshua, an environment in which he can directly experience the wisdom and love that come from practice. Although Buddhism naturally plays a large part in our family life, there are other more modest means that are important to us, including Josh's multicultural preschool co-op and the wider community of friends and relations who have helped and encouraged at every turn.

We are all, fundamentally, made from our mothers' bodies and their love. Each night before going to bed, my son sits on my lap and presses his ear against my chest, listening to who I am, remembering. I gaze into his face, listening to his breath, remembering the night after he was born. Quiet and wakeful, we looked at one another for a long time. I felt as though his newborn body were the gateway to an immense tunnel filled with a crystalline ladder spiraling backward in time, containing the genetic and karmic essence of all our ancestors, and extending back to the first life form. How it shone! At that moment I understood the rightness of human life continuing itself, and despite the darkness that surrounds us, our capacity "to enjoy life, living in honesty and strength." I was contained within my baby, and he within me, a resonant abode of many voices.

Allan Hunt Badiner

❀

Communal Pursuit of Happiness

We are aware that our joy, peace, freedom, and harmony are the joy, peace, freedom, and harmony of our ancestors, our children, and their children.[1]

The first thing I do when I return home is pick up my baby daughter, India, and hold her in my arms. Whatever I do next—greet my wife Marion, pour something to drink, or just sink into a chair and catch my breath—my arm remains wrapped around her, holding her snugly to me. It is clear she can feel how glad I am to be reunited with her. Her little mouth widens into a wide, ecstatic grin of delight—while my mouth does the same until we are both wearing bright expressions of sheer joy. There we sit, breathing and smiling together, for what seems like countless time.

Reflecting on this deeply rewarding experience, it is easy to see that joy is not an individual matter. When India smiles, I feel happy, and my smile gives her great pleasure. The Buddha's teaching on interdependence feels particularly evident at these times. When India is unhappy or crying, there is no way I can really be happy. My practice becomes making her happy.

While my joy and pain are shared with India, they are also shared with her unborn children—the seeds of whom have been physically present in her body since her own conception. When she and I are communing in rapture, it seems as though my deceased father is also smiling within me. Perhaps his mother too is checking in on the excitement. Both the roots and fruits of the

13

family tree enjoy this refreshing shower of love, despite differences in time and space.

Sometimes I see my mother living in the motions and expressions of my daughter. When she is crying, the pain of the generations seems to be crying along with her. I remember being aware of my mother's unhappiness. When I experience joy with my daughter, it feels as if that joy also touches my mother, and nourishes and heals her.

At times in my own childhood, my parents made me unhappy and caused me to suffer deeply. In order to forgive them, I remember that they suffered as children too, and they didn't know how to transform themselves. They carried the suffering with them and passed it on to me even though they didn't consciously want to. Awareness is the only sword that can cut through this vicious circle.

To notice that our joy, peace, freedom, and, in fact, our very happiness in this life are *not just our own* is an awesome realization. We best live our lives in such a way that both our children and our ancestors can feel free within us to grow and change. When we liberate our parents within us, we liberate ourselves and our children. For them to be at peace, we must be at peace with them. For us to be peaceful, they must be at peace. Now it is clearer to me how my daughter's unborn children are able to make my grandmother happy, or how my great-grandfather could torment my future grandchildren. It happens within me!

Occasionally we bring India with us when we sit in the zendo. Most of the time she is able to stay quietly perched against a shoulder enjoying our calm bodies and the deeper rhythm of our breathing. When the bell is invited to sound, the baby becomes totally still and transfixed. Her eyes slowly rise to find my face, and just as our eyes meet, her face ignites into an ebullient smile. Her wild effervescence summons the notion to my mind that her future daughters and sons, and their children too, are in touch with this moment.

My wife and I have been wondering how, as India grows older, we might encourage habits and behaviors that will support this multigenerational love. We want to be aware when our child is happy or not, and we want her to be aware of our feelings too. The key must be awareness—without which there can be no happiness. The joy that we share with her is possible only when we are aware that India is really there, and that we are truly seeing her. To protect her joy, and our own, I envision engaging her in a practice of mindfulness, so that she will be deeply aware of those around her. I plan to breathe and smile with her regularly.

The pursuit of happiness is not as personal an enterprise as we may have thought. Happiness is not found for oneself, but for the whole chain of being in both directions of time, of which we are but a temporary link. If I practice well and often, the benefits will be enjoyed by many generations. When I breathe slowly and mindfully, I am cultivating the seeds of happiness that lie within countless generations of beings far into the future and back into the past. As Thich Nhat Hanh likes to remind us, the past and the future dwell right here in the present moment. The joy born of mindfulness touches the past and shapes the future right now.

Notes

[1]The third of the Five Awarenesses, see *Plum Village Chanting Book* (Berkeley, CA: Parallax Press, 1991), p. 133.

Laurie Jackson

❀

Saints Never Need Children

On March 27, 1990, my younger sister Nancy was killed in an avalanche while climbing the world's seventh highest mountain in the Nepalese Himalayas. Oddly enough, it was she who guided me to the idea of mothering as practice. I say it was odd because in her life Nancy was not particularly spiritual and said that she never wanted to have children. She moved largely in male circles, as a chemical engineer during the week and a mountain climber the rest of the time.

At first it was just the grief and the reminder of our vulnerability, the short time we have on this earth, that made me think seriously about what I wanted to do with my life and what I wanted to give to my children, who were three years and fifteen months old at the time. After a lapse of four years I began to meditate again, and found to my surprise that I had a much deeper connection to spirituality, as well as more focus and discipline. I suddenly understood the meaning of a spiritual path.

However, I was thwarted by not having enough time or energy. I was always exhausted and often found it difficult, if not impossible, to sit and meditate. I was impatient with the constant interruptions inherent in mothering, and saw my children as impediments to practice. It had been an easy decision to stay home and be a full-time mother. I had felt very comfortable and satisfied with meeting my children's physical and emotional needs, and had made this my priority. So I was unprepared when the conflict arose between the demands of caring for them and the time I needed to pursue my spirituality.

Then one day while I was meditating I heard my sister's voice say, very clearly, "Hi Laurie," and felt a rush of wind through my body. Soon after I had a vivid dream in which I was climbing with Nancy. We stopped in a cabin to rest, and she told me that before she died she had had a baby, and asked me to raise that baby. I was very resentful because I wanted to go on with her, but I reluctantly went back to get the baby. It was not until later that I understood the meaning of this dream.

The year before, when I was in Seattle for Nancy's memorial service, I was walking in a small park on the shore of Puget Sound. I saw a newspaper clipping lying on the ground and picked it up. It turned out to be a five-year-old review of Tsultrim Allione's book *Women of Wisdom*. The dream and hearing Nancy's voice motivated me to find and read this book about Tibetan Buddhist women saints. In the introduction the author relates her mothering experiences and suggests that a path is needed to help women be spiritual within the context of our daily lives. I suddenly realized that mothering could be a great opportunity for spiritual growth instead of a distraction, and that Nancy had been guiding me toward this understanding.

The idea that my children could be an integral part of my practice and path, especially during the years when they are small and totally dependent, helped me see my situation in a much more positive way. Being able to meet my spiritual needs while caring for my children would resolve my dilemma. I did not know how to accomplish this, however. About this time I found my way to the Zen temple in Ann Arbor, which is an hour away from my home.[1] The Buddhist concept that practice is more than just meditation, but rather is continuous mindfulness throughout one's daily activities, gave me a way to begin.

At first my goal was very idealistic: I wanted to give my children a perfect role model of a joyful, mindful, present, loving, patient, playful, etc. etc. etc. mother. Yet I was so clearly light years away from being this kind of person that I quickly became discouraged. I saw the path as being black and white: either one was an enlightened mother or one was not, and I certainly was not. Whenever my children misbehaved I felt somehow that if I were only farther along the path, more developed spiritually, they would not act like that. I thought that a path for mothers must be a separate and distinct entity from other paths, since being a mother was so different from anything I had ever experienced.

I searched for a book that would tell me how to be an enlightened mother. Although I did not find much literature directed specifically to mothers, I did find brief accounts of other women's spiritual experiences relating to mothering. Some encouraged me, others intimidated me. For example, I was reassured by Tsultrim's story in *Women of Wisdom,* for she had been a Buddhist nun before becoming a mother, yet reached a point where she was unable to meditate for a while. I was heartened to hear from the priest of my Zen temple, Sukha Murray, that after the birth of her first child she too was discouraged about her practice. Her teacher, Samu Sunim, told her, "Karima [the baby] is your practice." When I read about Jan Chozen Soule yelling at children just two hours after returning from retreats, I actually felt relief.[2] All of these contacts showed me that my frustrations and difficulties were not unique. Nevertheless, when I read accounts by women who found giving birth to be an overwhelmingly spiritual experience I burst into tears, feeling that I had failed my children from the moment of their birth (both my children were born by Caesarean section, the first after three days of labor). Descriptions of practices other mothers were doing with their children also upset me, as I felt my children were missing so much.

During this time I struggled to maintain my formal daily practice. Before having children I had meditated off and on for sixteen years, and for me practice had always meant sitting quietly and going into a state of deep meditation for at least thirty minutes. Once I had children I found that more often than not I was too tired to sit and meditate, or I was too agitated, or I had no time, or I was interrupted too often. If I tried to meditate during the day, it usually ended with a child sitting in my lap or having to go potty or fighting with the other one. By evening when the children were finally in bed, I was often sleepy or too overwhelmed by all I wanted to accomplish in my time without them to concentrate. I have never been a morning person, and it seemed that whenever I managed to get out of bed earlier than usual, my children would hear me and get up too.

Throughout this period I attended formal sittings at the Temple every other week, occasionally managed to get away for overnight retreats, and did as much reading as I could. Gradually, instead of seeing how different a mother's path is from other paths, I started to realize how similar it is. A sentence in a book called *The Way of the Mother* struck me. The author, writing from a Christian perspective, said, "My hope when I reflect on myself as mother is simply to be there."[3]

This hit home. After all, isn't the fundamental goal of Buddhist practice simply to be there in each moment? And is this not, after all, where I fail miserably? I have always been task-oriented. Even though I am not working outside the home, I still get caught up in all the things I have to accomplish, and focus on them instead of the children. It is hard for me to take time just to play with them. It made sense that learning simply to be in the moment is one's task, regardless of whether one is a monk, a laborer, or a mother. Once one has the perspective that mothering is a spiritual path, the teachings can be applied to that context as well as any other.

Next, I began to broaden my definition of formal practice. I learned that when I am agitated vigorous prostrations will calm my mind when struggling through a sitting meditation will not. When I am sleepy, chanting or walking meditation are possible where sitting meditation is not. Beads can help me focus my mind. If I do not have long to practice, I can just do ten or fifteen minutes. My goal is still to be able to get up in the morning and have a long stretch of uninterrupted time when I am fresh, but in the meantime this is what is possible.

I also try to practice informally during the day by chanting or repeating my practice while I am doing activities such as cooking or laundry. This is hard for me, as I am easily distracted, but my ability to concentrate is slowly improving. When I remember, I stop and take three mindful breaths as Thich Nhat Hanh suggests, especially when I am getting frustrated or angry. When I am feeling impatient, I repeat the first part of the Ksanti Paramita—May I be patient!—over and over.

Gradually I am coming to see that this path, like any other, is a process. Change, much less enlightenment, will not happen overnight, no matter how much I want it for the sake of my children. I have learned that some kind of daily formal practice is necessary, and that sitting with a group keeps my daily practice going. Attending sittings at the Temple every other week gives me the opportunity to have quiet, deep meditations and gets me back on track if I have slacked off in my practice. I am much more able to do the continuous, informal practice if I keep up my daily formal practice.

The Buddhist teachings are also important. Even if I only read a page or two a day it helps keep my focus on my spiritual life. I feel fortunate that Sukha, the priest of the Ann Arbor Zen Temple, has two school-aged children. Her dharma talks are very practical and are often related to raising her children, which helps me apply the teachings to mothering. When I ask Sukha for advice, she understands my situation and is able to give specific advice based on techniques she herself has tried. The Temple is also supportive of families, offering monthly family services and a week-long summer camp, and including children in special events such as Buddha's Birthday and the Liberation of Life Service.

The next step is to incorporate some practice and rituals in my daily life with my children, to give them a sense of the sacred. This is difficult, because my husband and I have very different ideas about spirituality and what we want to give our children. This has been a source of conflict between us. He is comfortable doing nothing structured and I strongly want us to do something together. In addition, because feelings were never discussed in my family while I was growing up and I kept all my spiritual experiences to myself, I am uncomfortable with being the one to initiate rituals. However, we are making progress. Recently we started having a moment of silent or spoken gratitude before dinner, and my husband has agreed to attend a family service at the Temple to see how he feels about taking our children regularly.

I have also discovered that I can overcome my discomfort and include my children in practice instead of being interrupted by them. Last night my three-year-old would not go to sleep, my husband was at work, and I desperately wanted to meditate. I decided to go ahead and do chanting and a walking meditation, even though I felt somewhat shy and embarrassed about doing these in front of my daughter. She sat next to me while I chanted, then followed me for twenty minutes during a walking meditation. I was thrilled — not only was I able to do some practice, but also I had overcome what was in my mind a big hurdle. It just happened without planning and making a big deal of it.

I am learning to accept the ups and downs, and have faith when the stretches of not practicing come, that I will return. Often, I find I have reached a new level of understanding when I start up again. It was after one of these stretches of not doing any sort of daily practice that I added chanting and prostrations to my daily practice.

I now have goals I can live with: to give my children a mother who is working to become more spiritual, loving, and open; to be impatient and angry less often; and to live in the present. I want them to sense that life has meaning, that every thought, action, and moment are important. I try to focus on gratitude for what I have learned and am able to give my children now, and to learn from women who are farther along without letting myself feel inadequate.

I understand now that no matter how enlightened I am, my children will still behave like children. They will still go through all the testing and impossible behavior that is part of their development. What practice gives me is a longer fuse. When I am focused on the present I can deal with their behavior in more creative ways —

make them laugh, distract them, or be patiently firm—and avoid yelling or swatting bottoms. Practice will not make them perfectly behaved children, but it does make me a better mother.

Mothering has stresses that are unique to it. It also has unique joys and benefits: spending all one's time with beings who live completely in the moment and who are totally honest and open provides a wonderful practice environment. What better situation could there be for practicing patience, understanding unconditional love, mastering one's reactions, or overcoming the slothful habit of sleeping too much? Choosing not to attend retreats or sittings because children need us is a powerful lesson in putting others' needs before our own. I am constantly awed and humbled by my children's total acceptance, need, and love for me as I am. No matter how irritable I am they forgive and forget, do not hold grudges, and want to be with me. Their love is much more unconditional and accepting than mine, and I have much to learn from them.

In *How to Raise a Child of God,* Tara Singh said that children bring us to God, that "the child is entrusted to the parents and the reward is the growth of the parents. He grows physically and you grow spiritually. As you grow you have more to give to the child." Saints, he added, never need children, but worldly people do.[4] I certainly needed children to bring me to a spiritual path. Mothering has been a great catalyst for my growth. Responsibility for these lives gave me the impetus to make personal changes when I was not motivated just for my own sake. It made me see myself and my life from a different perspective.

In the same way that society at large must come to accept full-time mothering as a legitimate and essential occupation, Buddhists need to recognize mothering as a real and solid spiritual path. Women should not be made to choose between mothering and following a path, nor should they be made to feel that mothering is an inferior path. On the contrary, perhaps it is a path with more built-in challenges and opportunities than others.

Development of a path for mothers could give us much in the way of support. It could help us learn to apply Buddhist teachings to mothering and to be understanding and patient with ourselves. It could also provide a context for sharing ideas about how to keep going. Temples and mothers need to develop less rigid standards of formal practice that acknowledge and allow for interrupted sleep and nursing babies, and that accept that mothers may be unable attend formal sittings or long retreats during certain of their children's developmental stages. Mothers need to be encouraged to do what they can instead of struggling to meet ideals that are unrealistic for them. In short, temples must try to accommodate mothers, children, and families.

Joen Snyder, a mother who is ordained and was "totally fanatical" about practice while her children were small, has said,

> Zen Buddhism is very young in this country, and it seems that in the first few years of practice we became very excited and wanted to forget everything and submerge ourselves in this beautiful clear lake we found. We wanted to swim across and back again, practice our laps. And we didn't want to stop—no interference. No children allowed, no pets allowed, no husbands allowed. But at some point— and maybe that's the true beginning of practice—we realized that stopping and taking care of all these difficult situations is *it*, that that's the path! *That's* the path of compassion, of wisdom.[5]

Recognition of mothering as a path, by Buddhist communities as well as mothers themselves, is an important step.

Notes

[1] The Zen Buddhist Temple within the Buddhist Society of Compassionate Wisdom, under the direction of Venerable Samu Sunim.

[2] Jan Chozen Soule, "Taking Realization into Everyday Life," in Ellen Sidor, editor, *A Gathering of Spirit: Women Teaching in American Buddhism.* Cumberland, RI: Primary Point Press, 1987.

[3] Carol Wallas La Chance, *The Way of the Mother: The Lost Journey of the Feminine* (Rockford, MA: Element, 1991), p. 102.

[4] Tara Singh, *How to Raise a Child of God,* Second Edition. (Los Angeles: Life Action Press, 1987), pp. 112 and 323.

[5] Sandy Boucher, editor, *Turning the Wheel: American Women Creating the New Buddhism* (San Francisco: Harper & Row, 1988), p. 339.

Barbara Gates

❧

Snakebird in the Potty

Encircling my three-year-old daughter Caitlin with a protective arm, I look into her face. Her chin tilts as she looks up at me, her dimple deepens, her eyes glint dark. Although danger from the catastrophic fire in the Oakland hills is now over, my bedroom windows three miles below are still gray with soot. The sudden devastation has jolted us in the Bay Area into a new awareness of mortality, not only our own, but that of the houses we live in, of our city, of the earth itself. For me, as a mother, this has particular power. Through pregnancy, birthing, and these early years of child rearing I have already been haunted by the fragility of life—both Caitlin's and mine as her caretaker. Here, safe, on the bed with her now, I bask in the nurture of presence, mine with her and hers with me.

The day after this cataclysm, Caitlin and I clean out my dresser drawers. We empty everything on the quilt and rummage through scarves, shawls, even a lace fan handed down to me through generations in my family. As Caitlin unfurls each scarf, waves each handkerchief, I tell her the story of the foremother who passed it to me. Caitlin holds up a frayed silk scarf. "That was your great grandmother Helene's. She used to play the piano with me." "Did I know her, Mama?" "No, Sweetpea. She's been dead for a long time." Caitlin cuddles closer and brings her face near mine. "But people don't really die, do they, Mama?"

Caitlin's question speaks to me as if I had asked it myself. Exploring death with Caitlin, perhaps I will overcome some of my own fear and find more peace in the cycles of life. With the touch of the frail scarf, the echo of the stories I've told of our lineage, the view of the decimated hills, we clasp hands.

❀

Such a moment of looking and not turning away, of surrender to what is before me—all of it no matter how frightening or painful—is as complete and as open to possibility as many I have had sitting on the meditation cushion. Presence is indeed my practice as a mother.

Although I now find few hours for formal meditation, I continue to glean wisdom from past years of sitting, from my practice as a mother, and from my work. Recently, I have been editing a book-in-progress by the vipassana meditation teacher Sharon Salzberg. Sharon writes:

> There is a quality of mindfulness which is active, connecting and full of love. It's based on the ability to let go and be empty. We can call this active quality presence. When we can let go, there's nothing impeding our loving connection and we are fully present in a way that is a gift for ourselves and others. Sometimes we are awakened into presence at the thought of death. Our priorities may shift radically and we are truly here in our relationships, not withholding something to see what happens later. This is what we call metta or love.

Before I became a mother I'd always been a dreamer, unaware of much that surrounded me. I would leave the refrigerator door open, crash into people in the market, step in dog messes and jay-walk between cars on busy streets. And I'd felt tied to the unrecognized forces driving me from within to burst without consideration into other people's lives.

Now the tingling sweetness of Caitlin inspires me to cultivate awareness. I know how she thrives when she's truly heard and seen. I know her vulnerability to life's jangling knocks and jolts. And I know her mortality. So, when I cook her meals, when I answer her questions, or cross the street holding her hand, awareness begins to permeate my life. Each moment in my practice as a mother, as ephemeral as it is, encompasses the universe.

Just as in meditation we learn to allow the fleeting moments to arise and pass away, a child teaches us to surrender to change. In tiny ways every day I am doing "mortality" practice: learning to let go so that Caitlin's ever changing nature may unfold.

Until recently, if I wanted to move Caitlin to a new activity, I simply plucked her up from wherever she was, and physically introduced her to whatever I had in mind. I would pick her up from a chair and plunk her on the potty, or pick her up at the top of the steps of our Victorian, carry her all the way down, across the flagstones and into her carseat. In a series of revolts several weeks ago, she let me know that she was no longer the toddler I thought she was. When I began to strap her into the carseat, she jumped out of my arms, sailed out of the car, and jostling me aside, ran back across the flagstones, tumbled up the steps, to the very top. Then she turned and started down, shouting, "I'm doing it now myself." Likewise, when I'd already undressed her and put her on the potty, she wriggled off, pulled up her pants over one buttock and dashed back across the room to her crayons, while chastising, "Mama, you shouldn't of done that to me!" When, and if, she went to the potty, it was going to be in her own time, and in her own way. So, she reminds me to loosen my mindset on who she is, and if I miss a beat in my attention to who she is becoming, she rings the bell!

In the midst of the tangles of daily life, my practice with Caitlin can connect me to the jaggedness of my own feelings. The other day, in the rush and tension of a visit from out-of-town relatives, I lay next to Caitlin for her nap. I felt her warm little self tucked against my beating heart. As I relaxed into the loveliness of contact, all of the grating busyness of my day welled inside of me. A tear slid down my cheek, wetting Caitlin's arm. Abruptly she sat up, her small hand cupping my chin. "Mommy, why are you sad?" she asked. I didn't know what to answer. Finally I said, "I feel like

I have *sooo* many things to do I can't do them all, and the ones I do get all mixed up." "Oh," she said, then paused and snuggled back down next to me. "We'll feel better after our nap!"

❦

I am told that after the female octopus lays her eggs, she stops eating and focuses all of her own life force on blowing highly oxygenated water over her eggs to keep them alive. When the eggs hatch, the mother, totally exhausted, dies. This is the way I have sometimes felt, that I will give all of my life energy as a mother, and then die.

The unrelenting demands on a mother can call up many painful and unwanted feelings. At these times, when stretched to the very limits of my energy, I may be suddenly confronted with the darker aspects of who I am. This can be frightening.

On such a day last month, I felt I would collapse if Caitlin didn't go down for her nap. Exhausted from a night of broken sleep, I had been battling with dirty dishes, garbage, and unmade beds while Caitlin, shrill and banging, poured the shavings from the pencil sharpener all over my newly swept floor, pulled me under a blanket with the dog, leapt off the couch onto my back. I did not crave sleep for myself so much as a break from the attention to someone else's needs. Like the mother octopus, I had even forgotten to eat. When none of my lullabies, backrubs, or pleading could get Caitlin to sleep, something ferocious broke from me. I grabbed her by the arms and shook her, shouting, "Caitlin, you've got to nap!" She started to cry and yet I persisted, pinning her little thrashing body to the bed. But the powerful undercurrent of my love for her allowed me to see my own unexpected rage, and I started to cry too. I wrenched myself into the other room.

Flinging myself onto the couch, I grasped my taut jaws in my hands. I closed my eyes and trembled with the heat of pent up pressures. Then, for a moment I could smell my own fear. Gradually, I began to cradle my own face, and the muscles loosened. I could hear Caitlin crying for me from her room. In a rush of sadness I felt our sweet, brief meeting of lives. "I refuse to clash like this," I thought.

When I returned to Caitlin, her sobbing subsided. I held her tender in my arms, and slowly she fell asleep. I am so grateful that mother love—the commitment to awareness—stopped my rage and gave me a mirror to see how off-kilter I had become. I now know how crucial it is that I attend to my own needs and equanimity of mind as well as Caitlin's. What a fearsome teaching of the middle path!

Of course, Caitlin herself is my best teacher. She shows me many helpful outlooks, like the spirit of nonjudging. As she somersaults through our life together, she stops suddenly to inquire into what she calls her "treasures"—a twig, a ball of dry mud, a piece of silver foil, a dead snail.

Recently Caitlin has begun to use the potty. She leaps up after a poop and leans down over the bowl. With a yelp, she calls me. "Mama, I made a mountain" or "Mama, it's a pond with little boats sailing in it." The other day she insisted that my husband Patrick join her in the bathroom. "But Daddy, come see. It's a Daddy and a Mommy and three little Caitlins." And, indeed it was, so he reports. Yesterday Caitlin's creative pooping transcended the ordinary mountains and boats. "Mama, Daddy," she cried, "I made a snake with feathers. It's a snakebird!"

The presence Caitlin teaches me at the potty is fundamental—to be with whatever comes, even if some might perceive it as ugly. She is neither disgusted by her poop, nor afraid of it. In fact, she is curious, nonjudgmental, and imaginative. What a way to greet life!

Watching Caitlin at the potty, I think not only of my own poop, flushed ignored and unappreciated down the drain, but of all the "poopy" thoughts that come up in meditation or daily life. Do I welcome the excremental spewings of my own mind? Do I include them in my awareness? Do I castigate myself for having them, psychologize them into something else, deny them entirely? As the mind spins its stories, mightn't I at least appreciate Trungpa Rinpoche's apt metaphor for distasteful thoughts—"manure for Bodhi!"?

✿

Beginner's mind is another gift from child to mother. The other day Caitlin and I went to an exhibition of some wild and colorful jewelry made by a friend. The earrings were particularly whimsical, little people in bright regalia, limbs dangling akimbo. When I stopped to talk with the artist, Caitlin's amazed cry interrupted us. She waved a jaunty clown earring. "This lady has three legs!" After my artist friend laughed and commented, we returned to our conversation. Another amazed cry: "Mama, this one has two legs!" The magic of two legs! I had forgotten.

✿

From an early age, Caitlin has awakened Patrick and me to our connections—to the creatures and people of our neighborhood, to the moon, sun, and stars. As a baby she would sit in her highchair at the kitchen table and perched with an expansive view through the many windows, she would keep track of all of the local goings on. She felt and expressed her tie to everything and everyone. From her first word "bird" for the hummingbird in the window feeder, she went on to learn everyone's names and to herald the cats on the fence, the parrots in the loquat tree. "Celia, " she often calls to our neighbor on the right. "What are you planting in your garden?" To Bart and Amy behind us she shouts, "Are you making dinner?" As if they could hear her through closed windows and across two yards. Yet inevitably, they see her waving and wave back.

Caitlin truly sees and wonders about the people we pass in the streets, the people who have become non-people to me. "What's that boy's name?" she'll ask. "Where is that lady going?" Caitlin is only beginning to distinguish between family and strangers. Her questions remind me of the oddness of disconnection, of how lonely it feels to ignore our neighbors or to act as though the people we pass in the street don't have names and moments of sadness or tenderness just as we do.

The other evening, after visiting with friends and their toddler son Nathan, we stepped outside onto their porch. Caitlin pointed into the night. "Mommy. Daddy. Is that our moon? Is that Nathan's moon too?" I didn't know how to articulate what I wanted to express. The words stuttered out, perhaps a bit pat. "It's our moon, and Nathan's moon. It's everyone's moon. And we all belong to the moon as well." Probably my words didn't matter so much as the spirit of her question. We all looked up, and together we felt the tug in our hearts towards the moon in the night sky.

In asking her questions about the universe, about life and death, Caitlin reconnects me to my own childhood questioning, to my own witness to the great forces we do not understand and cannot control. On the day after the calamitous fire, as I sit on the bed with Caitlin, I caress the blue silkiness of my grandmother's scarf almost as if it were a fragment ripped from the cosmos. Again and again Caitlin's questions inspire me to stretch my mind to include what I hardly dare approach on my own. "Why did Great Grandma Helene die?" "Why couldn't someone save those people from the fire?" Caitlin pleads. I can sense her indignation at injustice, her fear, her awe.

As we explore together, I keep looking into her questioning eyes and through them I reach into my own consciousness. A memory from my childhood spins into awareness. Forty years before, in the back seat of a car driving towards the mouth of the dormant volcano Mt. Etna, I had asked my Grandmama Helene almost the same questions. While my mother and Granddad Leonard talked and laughed in the front seat, we in the back stared out at the eerie slopes littered with rubble and volcanic ash. Grandmama Helene drew me close and told me about volcanoes and earthquakes, about the churning and heaving of the earth, and about how this volcano had erupted long ago killing many people and devastating their homes. Sitting now with Caitlin, I remember the almost unbearable fear I felt as the car circled up towards the mouth of the volcano, that Mt. Etna might suddenly erupt again and destroy my family.

When I myself was five, just holding Grandmama Helene's familiar hand, with its thin piano-playing fingers and bony knuckles, let
me ask about death, and even further, about the birthing and dying
of the earth. I can't remember Grandmama Helen's words, but I do
remember that the safety provided by her presence allowed me for
an instant to encompass the vastness.

Now, as I hold Caitlin's hand and meet her questioning eyes, I
can see the rubble of volcanic ash from Mt. Etna extending into the
rubble from the fire in the Oakland hills, where the burnt-out chim-
neys rise like headstones for all of humanity. "Couldn't anybody
save their houses?" Caitlin asks. "No, Sweetpea. They couldn't."
Tenderly I touch the tip of my finger to her cheek, rose with life.

Diana di Prima

❀

Narrow Path into the Back Country

for Audre Lorde

1
You are flying to Dahomey, going back
to some dream, or never-never land
more forbidding & perfect
than Oz. Will land in Western airport
noisy, small & tacky, will look around
for the Goddess, as she stands
waiting for baggage. Well, we carry
pure-land paradise within, you carry
it to Dahomey, from Staten Island.

2
we endure. this we are certain of. no more.
we endure: famine, depression, earthquake,
     pestilence, war, flood, police state,
     inflation
ersatz food. burning cities. you endure,
     I endure. It is written
on the faces of our children. Pliant, persistent
     joy; Will like mountains, hope
that batters yr heart & mine. (Hear them shout)
And I will not bow out, cannot see
your war as different. Turf stolen from
     yours & mine; clandestine magics

we practice, all of us, for their protection.
That they have fruit to eat & rice & fish
till they grow strong.
(Remember the octopus we did not cook
Sicilian style/West African style—it fills
your daughter's dream)   I refuse
to leave you to yr battles, I to mine

my girl
chased white coyote, sister to my wolf
& not thru mesas.

3
how to get the food on the table
how to heal
what survives this whirlwind:
people and land. The sea
tosses feverish; screams in delirium.
To have the right herb drying in the kitchen:
your world & mine/all others: not the Third
this is Fourth World going down, the Hopi say.
Yet we endure.

4
And more, we fly to light, fly into
pure-land paradise, New York
Dahomey, Mars, Djakarta, Wales
The willful, stubborn children carrying seed
all races, hurtling time & space & stars
to find container large & fine enough
fine-wrought enough for our joy.
For all our joy.

Part Two

A Valid Path

Diane di Prima

To Tara

Rosebud, or fat baby cougar bending
Over the page, rising like breath, a
smile, a grace, in passage, like the swans
waking at midnight in a watery garden

She raises slow plump arms, she spins
Solemn as conch, the ritual
Winks, among cypresses

Mushim Ikeda

❧

Beyond a Fixation

My first Zen teacher used to tell us of a Korean practitioner who left his family in order to become a monk. When his son grew older, he went to the temple to seek his father. The monk was sitting in the meditation hall; when his son entered, he refused to turn from the wall and recognize his child. The son left, and the father continued to dedicate himself to his practice until he reached enlightenment.

Because the basic forms of Zen practice were developed in an Asian monastic context, certain deeply rooted models and attitudes may have traveled to the West within the forms. The historical Buddha's renunciation of his wife and son can be held up as an example of spiritual nobility, and children thus can be regarded as karmic burdens, distractions for the serious meditator. These attitudes are seldom overt, and are usually only dimly perceived in a certain chilly irritability in the atmosphere of a practice center, the difficulty of implementing childcare during retreats, or the regard of special food, toys, heating, and so forth for children as indulgences inappropriate to "hard training." In their extreme and undoubtedly misunderstood form, these attitudes can result in abuses such as locking young children into rooms while their parents meditate out of hearing range. As Western Zen evolves beyond a fixation on enlightenment as an end justifying any means, we can learn from our painful mistakes and wholeheartedly welcome children into our practice, cherishing their freshness and vitality, and teaching by example rather than rules a deep respect for meditation and its way of life.

John Tarrant

❀

Han Shan's Carousel

My daughter's first words were "Mummy," "Daddy," and "Dojo." Over the past few years, Roberta and I have been traveling to sesshin with her. I didn't want to be the kind of teacher who goes off and leaves his family at home. So, through carting diapers to Perth and Sydney, and preparing talks while my hair is being pulled, it's come to me that the best way to convey the Dharma to my daughter is to immerse her in the attention that, through zazen, we've learned to give to breath, the rain, the garden, the person in front of us, the world. Being in retreat feeds this kind of attention, but intrinsically it has nothing to do with retreat. Complete attention is itself a kind of love and is one of the true gifts that we can give to one another.

In the Hua Yen vision of the universe each thing contains each other thing, its Buddha nature shining out of it. We are all held in the great matrix, parts of each other, and a family is a fragment of this net. One thing we've found is that having young children around seems to deepen the retreats. The children circle in their own bright dream while we, the meditators, circle in ours. Their ancient voices, the freshness of their view of things, and the splendid, primary colors of their toys—the presence of the children is like a single hibiscus flower on the altar. Among the dark robes and black cushions it begins to sing, it recovers for us the pleasure of walking this arduous way of ours, and we know by experience how awareness honors the things of our lives, so they come forward to greet us and we are never lonely again.

There was an old and great Chinese master named Han Shan

who left the worldly world, went into his hermitage and shut the gate, never expecting to open it again. It occurred to me that having a child was like this gate closing so that something else could open, a kind of before and after division of my life. After Sarah things are more constricted, even sleep is not guaranteed; everything demands more attention and, like that little hut in the mountains, is more infinite. My monastery lies in daily things, persuading Sarah to get dressed, taking her to preschool on the way to work. And I began to know in the cells of my body that it is the commonplace life, fully inhabited, which contains eternity. What Han Shan is doing today is teaching his daughter letters on the keyboard. So I wrote some of my own Han Shan poems. Here are three of them.

Han Shan in Santa Rosa

She walks down the hall carrying
her doll, the present widens
and she is the first treasure and the last,
not as the trees are,
mossed with winter rains,
not as my enemy is
who leads me secret alleys
into tranquility, and not
as dolphin, field or star,
but in a sweet intensity of heart
more personal than I thought
my heart could bear
in outward voyage.
She has and is a light which is
to feed her, clean her, hide and seek
and swings and books,
so she has joined us to the world
and to each other
in a density that, fragile, seems
beyond unjoining.

In this garden we suffer and become
our own work.
I become her left hand and her right.
Fog enters from the Pacific.
The trees are near.
I can't remember the road I came on.

Han Shan at Gorrick's Run

Black boughs rigged with spider silk
sail into light
as I walk into 500 lives of walking;
walking over brick and stone, walking
into moonlight laid before me like a palace,
walking home, walking to exams,
walking downstairs to be introduced
to a dark haired woman, walking to zazen,
walking in the rain with my collar turned up, walking
to comfort a baby, walking while full of the unsteady light
of fever, walking under the stars,
walking under plum blossoms to accompany the woman
in labor, walking while confused, hesitant,
lost in memory and mist, walking
while singing, walking with a dear companion,
walking with purpose and without,
and the chestnut does put out fingertip
pale fires of green in winter's midst;
birdsong, stored like honey,
pours from the cliffs of comb, the sun calls it,
calls my daughter's hand
with its sensitive heft
to rise and I take it.
This is the two shilling piece
I lost at the wharf as a boy,
and this is the meaning of winter entire
with its cold, cold toes.

Frost crunches like toffee,
mist gathers its hem and rises, moss is green
on the path with its wavering clubs.
I go into the hermitage and draw the gate.
I have books and silence
but there is some deeper view.
The heart doesn't hoard the scraps of the day,
the forest is calm for mile on mile
and the real naturally appears:
On the floor by the heater
the small girl sings and dresses her doll.

Han Shan's Twenty Years

Han Shan
declines to be a noble man
for his riches are many.
Rain on the roof brings thoughts
of twenty years ago.
He checks on his sleeping daughter.

Amie Diller

❀

Practice at the Hearth

American Buddhists are now mature enough to reassess the relationship between monastic practice and lay life. The assumed superiority of monastic practice is being challenged by dedicated lay practitioners, many of whom are creatively bringing Buddhist practice into their family life.

When the Buddha left his wife and child, his action was radical in a culture where people lived and died in the same village, if not the same house. Everyone lived in an extended family network where their identity depended on being a part of the whole rather than on being an individual. People were utterly intertwined with extended family, caste, and village relationships. Even the spiritual life was prescribed for most, and the life of a sadhu, or wandering spiritual seeker, was not actually condoned until after a person had fulfilled their social obligations and entered their twilight years. In this context the Buddha's home-leaving was a radical and liberating move.

Over the years Buddhism developed along a split of monastic and lay practice. Buddhist texts were likely to extol the virtues of monastic practice to the point where one Zen teacher wrote of how a courtesan who put on a monk's robe in jest was liberated from past karma. Household life was seen as counterproductive to the spiritual seeker, and most lay practitioners gained merit by donations to their local temple. Now we are in a process of examining Buddha's teachings with a willingness to keep what creates Buddhas and shed what is encrusted tradition.

Because we inherited centuries of a patriarchal, monastic Buddhism, parents especially find themselves torn between doing formal practice and taking care of their families. I have heard the angry frustration of young mothers unable to free themselves of children to attend retreats, struggling with the sense that they are not "really practicing." They express repeatedly that they do not feel that their practice is validated. As some people choose the monastic path and others choose to practice in families, we must drop our judgments that one path is superior and validate each as a Dharma gate.

Traveling through Asia, I was impressed with how free-flowing and integrated Buddhism is in the daily lives of people. It makes a tremendous difference when Buddhist practice is taking place in a predominantly Buddhist culture. There, Buddhism is for many simply their daily religion. Families chant their sutras, have Buddhist weddings and funerals, and flow in and out of monasteries for education, spiritual renewal, and retreats. This lay population supports the work of the monks and nuns who practice full-time meditation. Both sides are acknowledged as necessary parts of the whole system. In the United States there is not the same financial or cultural support for monks. The majority of serious meditation practitioners live in families and work in the marketplace, doing their daily meditation at home or with a small neighborhood group, using weekends and vacation time for longer retreats. Yet these people often feel that they are not engaged in the "real" practice, a view which I found deeply embedded in myself.

For twelve years I lived a life devoted to formal Zen practice, mostly in residential Buddhist communities. I spent several years living in a Zen monastery, diligently pursued a university degree in Buddhist studies, was ordained as a Zen priest, and became a resident priest in a New England Buddhist center. When I found that I was pregnant, even though I embraced the pregnancy and child-to-be, there was an inner voice which took me to task for betraying my practice. I fantasized about sitting sesshins with my newborn resting quietly in my lap, nursing her during kinhin, and participating in work period while she slept quietly. I imagined packing her up and bringing her with me on the pilgrimage I had planned to Japan. As I spoke of these things to my friends who were already parents, they had the grace to refrain from saying more than a quietly muttered, "There, there, dear. We'll see."

I gradually became cut off from the Buddhist world I had known. While others were participating in monthly retreats and rising at 5 a.m. to work diligently on their koans, I was bedridden, throwing up, and growing a baby. I felt where once I had been engaged in the exciting and extraordinary event of Buddhism rooting in America, I was suddenly relegated to that most mundane ordinariness of all, motherhood. My concept of Zen practice was too narrow to include parenting. And it was obvious that the texts and tradition didn't offer any overt teachings, suggestions, or encouragement. Diapering a baby, chasing after a toddler, and dealing with two-year-old temper tantrums are not addressed in the sutras and shastras.

The Buddha found it necessary literally to leave home to devote himself utterly to his quest for enlightenment. In the myth of Buddha's life there is the famous scene where he takes leave of his wife and creeps into his son's bedroom in the middle of the night to kiss the sleeping boy goodbye. He had named his son Rahula, which means "fetter," because he experienced the birth of his son as an attachment, an obstacle on the road to spiritual awakening. His way of overcoming that obstacle was to leave it behind.

If myths are stories that are archetypal and personally relevant to each one of us, then the myth of Buddha's home-leaving is one that all of us must wrestle with. For those who pursue the path of monks and recluses, this myth may express and confirm their deep desire to live a simple life uncluttered by sexual relationships and families. For those of us who are householders, we have the choice either to understand the myth symbolically as a stage in our meditation practice or to concede that we have chosen a nontraditional way of walking the path of enlightenment. The latter does not invalidate any of the Buddha's teachings, but does place upon us the responsibility of creating ways to honor and practice these teachings in our more complex family lives. We also must have great confidence in our path because of the lack of validation from our tradition, a tradition which asks us to transcend rather than to embody our individual lives.

The people who brought Buddhist practice to this country were monastics,[1] and so our early role models have been those people who chose the literal form of home-leaving as their path. This, combined with our cultural bias against including children, led to an early assumption that children and practice don't mix. Although several residential Buddhist communities experimented with including children as residents, their parents were often chastised for choosing family needs over the meditation hall. The natural sounds of children's play—their calls of pleasure or cries of distress—were experienced as annoying rather than as natural as the sounds of birds or a mountain stream. In these residential communities there was no talk of women's practices, spiritual childrearing, let alone concrete suggestions on how to balance the needs of the family, meditation hall, and community. This led to parents feeling disenfranchised, unaccepted, and misunderstood. People who were sincere practioners of Dharma felt invalidated and invisible. Many left confused and dispirited.

For me, the Zen concept that "practice is your everyday life" held up only until my everyday life no longer allowed me to participate in the daily schedule that my sangha followed. Because I couldn't participate in retreats and daily meditation I felt invisible. In fact, as a mother, often my spiritual practice *is* invisible. What I found most painful in my community were subtle—and not so subtle—judgments that mothering is not "really practicing." Now I believe that becoming a mother was a natural movement from a praxis of transcendence to one of embodiment. It was a shift from the realm where one goes out of or beyond daily life into the realm of the absolute, to entering the absolute through immersion in ordinary daily life. In this realm we cook and clean, work and play, give love and are hurt. This very world becomes our Buddhafield, even as we stumble over pink stuffed bunnies, fight with our spouses, struggle to create a few hours of quiet family time. Within this whirlwind of confusion and distraction we find opportunity for awakening.

For those of us interested in nurturing and nourishing a child's spirit as well as her body, there is no guidance in primary Buddhist texts. What we need to do, and what is now being done, is to become steeped in Buddhist understanding and then create family practices ourselves. We can find ways to remember that being present with a child brings us back to our true self, moment after moment. The work we are doing as parents is often on the scale of picking up toys or cleaning scraped knees, yet it is joyous and vitally important. Our children will shape the world to come, and especially at this precarious time on earth, what is more vital than raising sane children who are compassionate and have an inkling about the world's interconnectedness!

Parenting truly is an astounding opportunity for understanding Buddha's teachings. For example, the Buddhist teaching of impermanence becomes vividly alive as you watch your child grow and change day to day. One moment your child is a baby, and seemingly the next she is going off to school. Through our children we can feel the tidal wave of change carrying us into each unknown moment—there can be a visceral experience that there is not even a microsecond to hold onto. We also can't escape the paradox that a child is both self and other—came from you and yet is not you. This is especially true for mothers. From the moment of birth, mothering is a process of loving and letting go. A mother may both weep and rejoice when her child stops nursing, begins walking, or goes to school. And tremendous suffering comes if she tries to hold on, tries to keep her children tied to her when they are ready to step out into the world.

In parenting there are also abundant opportunities to practice mindfulness. When we let ourselves *just be* as we hold a new baby, we come back to our true selves. Or we may enter a toddler's universe. If we allow the child to be entranced by a butterfly and enter her enchantment, rather than pulling her on to the next item on our agenda, we create a pause in our lives to breathe and be present. Allowing a child to scream or throw a temper tantrum, we can see our own aversion to suffering. I have tried these things and found that my own world and breath became more alive even as my child and I had fewer power struggles. At one point I offered to kiss a bruised knee of my two year old and she said, "Don't take my hurt away." This was for me a direct teaching of compassion— I had to stay present for both her pain and my own. When emotions or difficulties come up, don't say a mantra, retreat and count beads, but enter and be present. Breathing in, I feel angry, breathing out, I am aware I still feel anger. Do this and it changes of itself.

Children respond to awakeness in our lives, indeed they rejoice in it. My Zen teacher and I were once tending our young children and trying to squeeze koan work in whenever they were occupied. I noticed that when we were just chatting they drifted off to their own activities. As soon as he and I entered koan work, they would stop their activity, come over and ask delightedly, "What are you doing? Can we play, too?" I had the feeling that they were delighted to see adults present, playful, and willing to make fools of themselves. And I felt all of us were engaged in a wonderful integration of formal practice and our everyday lives. I am reminded of a story: In Korea there was a woman Zen master whose grandson died. As she was weeping and wailing, the townspeople looked on in amazement. Finally someone approached her and said, "Why are you weeping and wailing? You are a great Zen teacher." The woman replied through her tears, "I am also a grandmother."

Meditation groups need to respond to the needs of family practitioners. During long retreats childcare could be offered and children incorporated into the schedule so that parents, especially single mothers, can attend. Our sangha does this by having childcare as one of the work assignments and offering a modified schedule for participating parents. Groups could also have children's services and Buddhist stories while the parents participate in daily meditation. By including children in our spiritual life and by setting up Buddhist preschools, schools, and orphanages, we would simultaneously assure that Buddhism will root deeply in this culture and support family life as fertile ground for awakening.

Thich Nhat Hanh is doing a marvelous job of interpreting Buddhism for householders without diluting it. He gives householders specific ways to practice as a family, such as using the mindfulness bell, walking meditation, tea meditation, songs, and gathas for parents and children. People are now coming together for "family days of mindfulness" to practice in this way as well as for support and ideas to use in their daily lives.

Because we are not yet a Buddhist culture, each Buddhist family has an opportunity to create little rituals throughout their day. My three-year-old daughter and I created an altar in her room. She chose a rainbow candle and a small gold Jizo for it. Now when she finds a leaf or a stone that moves her, she says happily, "This is for my altar." We bring it home, place it on her altar, light a candle, and then sit and admire it together for a few precious moments. At mealtime we sing a "thank you" verse to the food, and then talk humorously about where the food came from and how it got to us.

(This often becomes a game, with me asking if the carrots grew on an airplane and my daughter gleefully answering, "No, silly mommy.") She loves to chant and often demands that I join her in endless rounds of *Enmei Jikku Kanno Gyo* on long car rides. These refreshing and happy moments together help me to be more present and flexible during temper tantrums and sleepless nights.

Perhaps what is radical in our culture is to create a home rather than to leave one, to draw people back to heart and hearth, letting the lovingkindness of the home fire radiate peace and happiness to the rest of the world. The word "focus" comes from the Latin word meaning "hearth," and to rekindle the hearth as the focus of spirituality is a worthy undertaking. Parents can take pride in their spiritual practice as householders and confirm the importance of their offering to the world. They are helping to create a Buddhism appropriate for America, where their houses are their meditation halls, their children their sangha.

Notes

[1] Editor's note: This does not reflect all American experience—the Japanese, for example, brought a family-oriented Buddhist practice to this country in the nineteenth century.

Eliot Fintushel

❀

Zazen *en Famille*

To sit is not necessarily to meditate. Not to reveal the body in the three worlds, that is meditation. Not to rise up from concentration in which the inner functions are extinguished and yet to conduct oneself worthily, that is meditation. Not to abandon the way of the teaching and yet to go about one's business in the world, that is meditation. Not to give one's spirit abode within or without, that is meditation.... Not to cut off disturbances and yet to enter Nirvana, that is meditation. Anyone who sits thus in meditation receives the seal of the Buddha.

Vimalakirti Sutra

Before the sun has risen, settling everything in this world into its particular place, when nobody knows whose bottom's on my zafu, or if it's a bottom at all—Mu!—my four-year-old comes knocking.

"Papa!"

I, or someone, has been sitting. My head turns. I smile and nod. Nothing at all has moved. Thumb in her mouth (—*Whose mouth?*), blankie trailing, she runs to me. She melts into my lap, her head against my heart. My hands move away to the knees, or they cradle her; *she* has become my mudra.

Or maybe it's...

"Papa, help me get dressed."

"Just a minute," I say. No one has spoken. They are not thoughts now that fill the space between silences or sounds of passing cars. Rather, the kinesthetic sensations of uncrossing legs, of someone's hands slapping the cushion back to round, the slight blur of intentional movement, rising, as everything settles into its particular place.

(Maybe there's a regret here: "Better to have kept on sitting!" *Tic-tok! Tic-tok!* Maybe not. It passes, like some twinge, or a chill, an odor, a hum, a dry spot on the tongue, an itch, an inkling, *annutara samyak sambodhi.* It goes by. If not, it's trouble; the body has revealed itself in the three worlds, and decay sets in quickly.)

I don't know if I'm sitting zazen or pulling pissy underwear down my daughter's legs. We laugh. Sometimes we fight. The sun is rising. There begins to be two of us in this world, each with a name and a set of particular characteristics. The tyke wants to wear a dress every single day!

My wife joins us. No one has moved.

Of course, if you believe—in your heart of hearts—in *clocktime,* then the world seems quite otherwise. The sun is always out somewhere; everything has its exact limits, including you, including me. Papa, Mama, and Baby are on a constant collision course, pushing to the periphery anything like zazen, because zazen, sunlit, will exist only and exactly in this particular hour, that space, this body, that mind, and nowhere else. Things can't stop moving. Children and spouse are an imposition. Everybody talks at once, and there's not enough time for Big Z, no, not enough time for big Z, and now you're too sleepy for anything but a little little Z at last. Surely, sleeping couldn't be zazen?

Nobody's reading this. What's to look at? Your child calls. Your spouse needs a hand. The clock hand isn't moving, but nothing is still. A car passes in the street. Is there a tush against that cushion or is it a heavy thought? One's breath is a sink full of dishes. The straightness of the spine is a child moping for your company. There is no sunlight anywhere except my belly shining where the palms rest, and I don't know whose or when.

Don't ever get up from zazen, that's the surest thing. And never imagine you've done so.

Mobi Warren

❀

Partners in the Practice

Does Buddhism offer fresh insight into children? I believe it does and that such insight can help us create happy forms of family practice in North America. Buddhism encourages parents and children to be partners in the practice, mutually to respect and assist each other.

What I take to be the Buddhist way of looking at things is filtered through all the diverse influences in my life—the examples of my Methodist mother and agnostic father, my friendships with Native American storytellers, the years I spent living with the Chinese-Vietnamese family of my first husband. As Thich Nhat Hanh has said, "Buddhism is made up of all non-Buddhist elements." Nonetheless, since I was in my late teens, Buddhist meditation and mindfulness practice have been the essential inspiration and form of my spiritual life. Breathing, observing my thoughts and feelings, mindful sitting and walking, reading stories of the Buddha and his early disciples, making an effort to study and observe the precepts I have taken—my practice is not that of a scholar. It is a simple practice, carried on day by day.

I understand Buddhism as a lifelong commitment to remaining open to receiving the viewpoints of others (human and non-human alike) in order to respond to and transform suffering. This deep listening gradually makes it possible to let go of a false sense of self as we come to recognize others as mirrors to our own being. The parent is in the child and the child is in the parent. "This is because that is. This is not because that is not," said the Buddha.

53

The parent-child relationship is a very rich, very basic ground from which to discover and develop Buddhist insight. I am a North American and I am a parent. It is only natural that my particular development of a Buddhist life cannot be seen separately from my experiences as a mother or from the circumstances and contacts of life in contemporary North America.

Though there do not seem to be many written records in the history of Buddhism that describe Buddhist practice within family settings, my own experience tells me that countless families, living in different times and places, have indeed contributed to the longevity and flexibility of Buddhism. Family style practice, like much of women's practice, has been largely hidden from view, de-emphasized or ignored. Part of our task is to bring family practice out into the open, to celebrate its richness and diversity, its gentleness and practicality.

Moments after my marriage to my non-Christian, Asian husband was blessed in the Catholic church, I was asked to sign a statement that I would raise my children in the Catholic faith. My love for the church I had converted to at age twenty was deep. Up to that moment, I had been sure that I wanted to share it with my children. Of course, I knew that we would also be sharing Buddhist practice with them. The years I spent living and working with the community of Thich Nhat Hanh prior to my marriage had woven Buddhist practice into my daily life. In fact, I had been drawn simultaneously to Buddhism and Catholicism as a young adult. Catholicism satisfied my hunger for the mystery and ritual I'd missed in my Protestant upbringing. Buddhism appealed to me for its focus on meditative discipline and its openmindedness. At that time, my husband was not much interested in "spiritual concerns" and was happy to leave childrearing decisions about churchgoing to me.

The signed statement required by my church challenged my assumptions. I began reflecting on what raising a child in the church would be, compared to raising a child in a Buddhist home. Several years of reflection and experimentation followed, during which my husband renewed an interest in his own Buddhist roots. I found it increasingly unnatural to base my spirituality in a monotheistic, God-centered belief. To me, "God" is the dynamic totality of all that is, best expressed in the Buddhist language of interdependence. I wanted my children to be free to evolve their own consciousness concerning God. It became clear that I wanted to raise my children in a Buddhist home.

Thich Nhat Hanh encourages his students to return to their own roots and find the Buddhism inherent there. Rather than seeing this important process of discovery in terms of returning to Christianity, I have been looking more deeply at family and ancestral patterns. My parents are openminded and tolerant people who encouraged a spirit of inquiry in their children. I did not feel rigid expectations from them, but rather an innate trust that I could, by being true to myself, live a fulfilling life and find ways to be of service to others. When I recently gave a talk to a class of high school students about Buddhism, one student wanted to know how my parents felt about my choosing to follow a different spiritual tradition. I answered, "Actually, I consider my parents to be two of the best Buddhist teachers I've had!"

Some of my ancestors came to North America to seek religious freedom. Their willingness to risk the unfamiliar in order to listen to and act on their own experience of spirituality is something that has been transmitted to me. These ancestors are part of my Buddhist lineage. I always considered it particularly appropriate for my children, half-Asian, to be raised as Buddhists. I now see that their European ancestors are as much a part of their Buddhist heritage as their Asian ancestors. Seeds of Buddhism have been planted by both sides.

The Third Precept of the Order of Interbeing
Do not force others, including children, by any means whatsoever, to adopt your views, whether by authority, threat, money, propaganda, or even education. However, through compassionate dialogue, help others renounce fanaticism and narrowness.[1]

✿

> *The Buddha said, "There once were a couple of acrobats. The teacher was a poor widower and the student was a small girl named Meda. The two of them performed in the streets to earn enough to eat. They used a tall bamboo pole which the teacher balanced on the top of his head while the little girl slowly climbed to the top. There she remained while the teacher continued to walk along the ground.*
>
> *"Both of them had to devote all their attention to maintain perfect balance and to prevent any accident from occurring. One day the teacher instructed the pupil, 'Listen, Meda, I will watch you and you watch me, so that we can help each other maintain concentration and balance, and prevent an accident. Then we'll be sure to earn enough to eat.' But the little girl was wise and answered, 'Dear Master, I think it would be better for each of us to watch ourself. To look after oneself means to look after both of us. That way I am sure we will avoid any accidents and will earn enough to eat.'"*
>
> *The Buddha said, "The child spoke correctly."*[1]

These texts illustrate how Buddhism views children as spiritual equals—beings who hold the same millenniums of human and nonhuman experience, the same capacity for wisdom, as any adult. They are not vessels to be filled or lumps of clay to mold. Meda's story reminds us that children are capable of deep wisdom and sudden insight. Children often see with fresh-eyes-wisdom, as my Native American friend Paula Underwood calls it.

When children are viewed as spiritual equals, there is much less emphasis on teaching them those things we adults hold to be true and more emphasis on enabling them to get in touch with their own understanding, both innate and unfolding. There is less desire to shape a child's thoughts and behavior, and more desire to discover and support who the child is. The Buddhist practitioner strives to be freed from dogma and ideology. Parents with such an orientation can allow their children the freedom to participate or not participate in aspects of the practice, according to their own needs and interest.

In my own family, this has meant little time spent in teaching any sort of Buddhist catechism. Instead, we share breathing and smiling, drinking tea and walking slowly. The children are introduced to mindfulness practices (breathing at the sound of the telephone, for example), which they are free to use or not use according to their own needs. It seems to me that the chief thing the Buddha required of his disciples was that they ask their own questions and discover their own deepest yearnings. The children enjoy hearing stories about the life of the Buddha and other Buddhist tales. On full moon days we read the precepts together, followed by tea and cookies. We have discovered how valuable it is to attend retreats where we can practice together with other families.

At times I wonder if my children have found the mindfulness practices at all applicable to their own lives. I wonder if I have deprived them of something important by not exposing them to a more formal religious education. The children answer these concerns, unsolicited, by sharing unexpected gems of insight and compassion. For example, a few weeks ago my teenage daughter and I were in the car when an ambulance sped by. My daughter turned to me and said, "Whenever I hear an ambulance, I stop and return to my breathing. It helps calm me when I hear the siren, but I also do it in order to be in touch with the person who is hurt and suffering."

✿

I have encountered two different approaches from Buddhist teachers regarding children's involvement in the practice. Both approaches seem to me to respect children as whole beings while also acknowledging they have special needs. The first view, expressed by a friend who was a Japanese Zen monk, is that children are whole and complete, naturally spiritual just as they are, and so have no need for things like formal prayer or meditation. The second approach is the one I find in Thich Nhat Hanh's practice, in which children fully participate in the same practices as adults—sitting and walking meditation, precepts recitation, and dharma talks. Adults and children practice right alongside each other. The child in the adult and the adult in the child are equally honored. The only thing that differs is an understanding of the special energy needs of children, and so children are encouraged to leave the meditation hall when they tire or are in need of active play.

As an educator, my experience is that children learn most effectively in situations where they have a real voice in designing their own learning. An optimal learning environment is one in which children learn *how* to learn rather than simply acquire skills that may have little relation to their actual life experience. Buddhism encourages us to view spiritual practice in the same way. In Buddhist ritual we are reminded that in bowing to the buddhas and bodhisattvas we bow to ourselves. Ritual and practice must answer our own needs, must spring from our own experience.

Children respond to ritual that is meaningful to them. In our family, our monthly precepts recitation is one of our few regular, formal practices. My ten-year-old son tells me that reciting precepts is his favorite family practice because "the precepts are a way of life that is not harmful. They show you can live without violence."

I think that children often have a natural affinity for the "no path, no attainment" way proclaimed by the *Heart Sutra,* and do not desire to be encumbered with too many rituals. On the other hand, my children have created powerful and moving rituals on their own for meaningful moments in their lives. Years ago, when my first husband and I announced to our two children that we had decided to divorce, my seven-year-old son left the room and returned with two little boxes which he gave us. Each box contained half of a favorite but broken watch of his. He joined our hands and told us he loved us. I stared at that broken piece of watch, like some quizzical koan. My husband said, "The children understand more than we do." I kept that broken half of watch as a son-given symbol of the continuing yet changed bond that my former husband and I share as parents of the same children.

What rituals can match the rituals that children create? On shorter legs, they seem more in touch with earth's rhythms. Last summer, my son and stepson created a ceremony to honor the animals buried over the years in our backyard. They asked if they could have some sticks of incense. Later I looked out the back window to see them walking solemnly, lighting incense, and offering small bits of food at the graves of cats, guinea pig, hamster, bird, and even ant.

The presence of family ritual, simple as it is, provides a common context to explore the big and little questions of life and to travel life's many dimensions. Buddhist practice offers ritual without dogma, so that each family member is free to experience spirituality in his or her own way. Our differences open us up to new possibilities. We empty our little self and experience the big self that is connected to all others.

Buddhism teaches that children are continuations of our lives just as we are continuations of the lives of our parents and grandparents. We know that our children inherit all our ancestral seeds, and that like us, they have the capacity to bring seeds of love and understanding to fruition, and to heal seeds of anger and sorrow. Practicing as a family creates a supportive environment in which family members can learn to recognize family seeds and patterns. We can then support one another in transforming harmful tendencies and in nurturing those qualities that bring healing and liberation.

I used to laugh about how my grandmother couldn't bear to see an uneven stack of papers. She couldn't pass a coffee table without straightening the magazines. As an adult I discovered myself doing the same thing. My daughter does it, too! This is an amusing ancestral seed (and practice soon dries up without humor) that I have converted into a mindfulness practice. When I catch myself straightening papers, I stop and breathe. I greet my deceased grandmother, "Hello, grandmother, I know you are here." Compulsion to be neat transforms into a lovely encounter. Evening up the magazine pile while mindfully breathing becomes Buddhist practice.

Perhaps one day a grandchild of my own will discover a way to encounter me in her breath. And perhaps by her generation there will be sutras about family practice, sutras that sing of the Awakening that is nurtured when parents and children are partners in the practice.

Notes

[1] Thich Nhat Hanh, *Interbeing: Fourteen Guidelines for Engaged Buddhism,* Revised Edition, (Berkeley, CA: Parallax Press, 1993), p. 17.

[2] Thich Nhat Hanh, *The Miracle of Mindfulness,* Revised Edition, (Boston, MA: Beacon Press, 1987), pp. 63–64.

Christina Feldman

❧

The Yogi and the Householder

Ten years ago I led the first family retreat at the Insight Meditation Society in Barre, Massachusetts. It was a great experiment—prior to this I had taught only silent meditation retreats for adults, and the center had hosted only silent, intensive retreats. None of us knew what would happen as we opened the doors to a group of families with small children. My own daughter, three months old, was the youngest participant. Since then, this retreat has taken place every summer and is regularly attended by fifty children and a hundred adults.

Originally the family retreat was intended to provide an opportunity for adults to meditate without having to separate themselves from their children. There appeared to be few centers that offered any facilities for children, and parents always had to "go away" to develop their spiritual lives. Is was clear that in the West, the "spiritual life" was considered to be an adult activity. Over the years, our emphasis has changed considerably. The children are now included in as much of the retreat as possible. They take part in meditations, discussion groups, rituals, chanting, and periods of loving kindness meditation.

In the West there is a strongly held notion that to pursue the spiritual life a person needs to be single, unencumbered by the world, and free from intimate relationships. Anything other than this is considered to be somewhat inferior. This idea is the legacy of revering the monastic tradition over the life of the householder. Meditators with families and relationships frequently come to believe that because of the choices they have made, liberation is no longer possible for them. Instead, meditation is seen as a vehicle that will provide greater calmness, equanimity, and balance—but not the freedom that is seen to be the territory of those who are able to separate themselves from the "world."

Hopefully, family retreats will challenge these artificial separations that are made between the "spiritual" and the "worldly," the "yogi" and the "householder." We do not become spiritual through creating separations between ourselves and the world; we are spiritual when our path of exploration and understanding embraces the whole of our lives.

It is equally clear that spiritual aspiration is not the exclusive territory of adults. Children too, wish to live a life that is free from pain and fear, where there is a fullness of peace and joy. They hold a great potential for wisdom and compassion. We adults must ask ourselves, What opportunities for nurturing this wisdom do we offer our children? What opportunities do our traditions offer our children?

Many adults engaged in a meditative path no longer belong to a particular religious tradition. Our schools rarely offer to children an exposure to the spiritual life, and our culture increasingly worships the trinity of "having," "achieving," and "possessing." Bombarded by these values, children begin to believe that this is what life is all about. It is of vital importance that our children equally have access and exposure to spiritual values and symbols that emphasize ethics, compassion, and wisdom. This requires more than simply attending a church, synagogue, or retreat. As adults we are called upon to translate the values we cherish into the grist of our lives.

Superficially it seems that the life of the yogi and the householder are polarized. It is easy to define the yogi's life as "spiritual" and the householder's life as "worldly." The yogi's life possesses all the forms and symbols we regard as spiritual—silence, dedication to formal meditation practice, renunciation. The householder's daily life is often devoid of these forms and symbols—they are replaced with noise, busyness, interaction, and relationship. The presence or absence of these forms do not in themselves make either lifestyle wise and meaningful. If you were to invite a monk or nun into your family and ask them to raise your children and provide for them, to manage your household and relate intimately with another person and the world, and to do this with great care and love—what qualities would they need? To undertake this with impeccability they would need boundless patience and equanimity, acceptance and discipline. They would require great renunciation, faith, and calmness.

If you were to put yourself into a monastery and undertake an intensely contemplative life, what qualities would you need to do this well, with care and impeccability? You would also need patience and equanimity, acceptance and discipline, the willingness for renunciation and the capacity for calmness and faith.

The contemplative life and the householder's life both challenge us. From the outer world and the inner world, we meet the challenges of our expectations and reactions, our desires and resistances. We are faced with impatience, anger, resistance, and avoidance. In a retreat we are encouraged to look upon these challenges as opportunities to discover greatness of heart, deep acceptance, and patience. We are asked to look upon them as teachers and teachings that help us to practice and apply equanimity and mindfulness and to let go.

Outside of the context of a retreat, it seems much more difficult to greet these challenges with the same benevolence or to look upon them as spiritual opportunities. Instead, we tend to see these challenges as personal failures and limitations. Their appearance tells us it is time to go sit on another retreat so that we can get rid of our "demons" or avoid them. People living in the world are often sadly lacking in the support which enables us to see our imperfections in the context of spiritual growth. Family retreats—integrating children and families into the sangha—provides this vital support and enables us to embrace the difficulties in our lives as being rich in possibility.

It is the sense of possibility that gives spiritual richness to our lives, and this sense of possibility is not dependent upon any form.

Openness to learning, willingness to grow through challenge is what brings wisdom to any life. Without these even the most idyllic retreat situation simply becomes a spiritual desert. We need to know deeply and unshakably that wisdom and compassion are not the territory of any special group of people or any form. Our lives are an invitation to deepen these qualities, to be awake, and to touch the world around us with love and understanding. In being connected with this sense of meaning and possibility we are able to transform our world.

The retreats—now going on around the world—that embrace yogis of all ages are radical in their emphasis. Their message is that wisdom and compassion are possible for each one of us and that our lives are the vehicle for their deepening. The family retreat at Insight Meditation Society has become a special time of year for everyone involved. The center echoes with noise and laughter, and an underlying sense of commitment to understanding and sensitivity.

Lee Klinger-Lesser

❀

Karma, Dharma, and Diapers

The vivid image of a two-year-old boy, sitting quietly at a table with his shoulders hunched up to his ears, remains with me after more than ten years. This was a posture I had frequently seen his mother assume when she was nervous or tense. Her son was simply adopting it through observation. Alice Miller wrote: "Whatever we put into a child's soul we naturally will find there, but if we become conscious of what we are doing, we then have the chance to free ourselves from the constrictions of our past."[1] Children learn from everything we do and don't do, from everything we say and don't say.

Each month, when I see the full moon in the sky, I find the words from the Full Moon Ceremony returning to me: "All my ancient, twisted karma, from beginningless greed, hate, and delusion, borne through body, speech, and mind, I now fully avow." Now, instead of being in the zendo, I am in the midst of my home, realizing that my own karma is constantly informing the lives of my children, as theirs does mine. The more conscious I can be, the less I will interfere with the unfolding of my children in accordance with their own natures, and we will be able to meet true nature to true nature, as I vowed to do with my husband when we married each other.

It is distressing to me how deeply we ignore and undervalue the quality of family life in general in our society, and that we have continued this neglect in the cultivation of our spiritual practice. I can think of no other area in which the impact of our own mindfulness is as profound as it is in the raising of children.

After practicing Zen from 1978 to 1983 in the formal, monastic setting of Green Gulch Farm and Tassajara, I find that my family is now my Practice Center. One of the challenges of family as Practice Center is the lack of established forms. I have to be responsible for how I practice in a way that is distinctly different from strict schedules and shared formal practices.

In my home, our most basic practice is breathing together. Becoming quiet and aware of breathing is possible for each of us at any moment. We work with this in different ways. During a recent retreat for young people with Thich Nhat Hanh, we learned a song that is linked to breathing with each line accompany an inhalation or exhalation: "In, Out, Deep, Slow, Calm, Ease, Smile, Release, Present moment, Wonderful moment."[2] The tune itself is soft and calming. When I am aware of being agitated or irritated, I can sing this song as a form of meditation that brings me back to myself in the midst of any activity.

One evening, as I was preparing dinner, my twenty-month-old daughter was being her familiar inquisitive self. She went from discovering a glass of water and emptying it onto the floor, to exploring the contents of the compost bucket, to pulling the dog's tail. At the same time my six-year-old son was pleading with me to help him make some paper airplanes and complaining about being hungry. I began to notice the distinct signs of irritability rising in me, my shoulders tensing, my stomach tight, breathing shallow, movements sharper, a desire to yell. It seemed like an opportune time to stop and sing. After singing "In, Out..." five or six times, I found I was smiling. And I was content and grateful to be where I was. Jason watched with quiet curiosity, as he saw me transform my state of mind. Several weeks later I overheard Jason trying to help Carol quiet down and perhaps go to sleep in her room. He was singing, "In, Out...."

I taught this song to two mothers with whom I participate in a mother's group. Neither of them practices Zen or Buddhist meditation. They told me that the song has become a part of their lives. One who has a four-year-old daughter told me that her daughter asks her to sing the songs when she is out of control, crying, or deeply upset. One night when her mother wouldn't let her have a snack five minutes before their dinner, she began to cry. Her crying built out of control. Still sobbing at the table, she pleaded, "Mommy, sing the song!" Her mother did, and gradually she became calm. This had become a tool that helped them both to seek comfort, even in the midst of conflict with each other, so that emotional distress moved to conscious breathing, to calm, and even to connection with each other.

My other friend's family has adopted the song to calm their six-month-old baby. Her four-year-old daughter and her husband both sing the song to the baby and the baby stops crying. Singing this song does not guarantee that the baby will stop crying, but provides us with the opportunity to maintain our own calmness no matter what happens.

Another tool we use in our family is a "Bell of Mindfulness." It lives on the altar in Jason's room, where anyone can get it at any time and bring it to sound anywhere in the house. Whenever the bell is sounded, we all stop whatever we are doing and breathe three times. Then we continue mindfully with what we were doing. Our bell has been sounded to greet new guests, on the way to the bathroom, in the midst of bustling dinner preparations, during meals, in the heat of arguments, and directly after angry outbursts.

Once, when I was afraid that Jason and my then infant daughter might have whooping cough (we were waiting for test results), Jason and I were working together in the kitchen and he did something I had asked him not to do. I roared at him with the full force of my preoccupation. A few minutes later I heard the sound of the bell. As I breathed with the tears that instantly arose in me, I heard a clear, little voice say, "Mommy, I rang the bell so you wouldn't be so angry."

I find there is so much for me to learn and practice with in relation to the anger and frustration that arises in me with my children and immediate family members during even the most trivial of interactions. During one of his talks at the young people's retreat,

Thich Nhat Hanh spoke of anger, saying it needs a friend and the friend is mindfulness. Families provide wonderful opportunities to practice the cultivation of this friendship. It is important to me that Jason knows that sometimes I am mindful and sometimes I'm not, that I can come back to my true self, and that he can help me. I think he understands this about himself, too. Having the bell, a tangible practice we share, is empowering for Jason, especially in the face of what can be overpowering adult emotions and judgments.

I know that as Jason gets older our rituals will change, and this too is part of our practice. Most likely the altars we have all around our home will stay. In each of our bedrooms, in our bathrooms, and in our kitchen, they are invitations to be aware. For the past year and a half, at night before bed, Jason and I have offered incense on his altar. Jason's altar is a place where he puts things that are special to him. He has two Jizo figures standing side by side on top of a purple silk sandbag that I made for him after I made one for a friend of mine who was dying; a clay face that a friend made as a portrait of Jason; a big conch shell; some favorite rocks; a photograph of a lion that Jason took at the zoo; photographs of Jason with his grandfather in a frame with a special letter from his grandpa; a scarf that belonged to my mother, whom Jason never knew; a piece of shed snake skin; and a variety of ever changing items.

Jason lights the match and gives it to me to light the candles. He doesn't feel comfortable enough yet with the fire in his hand to do it himself, so he goes instead to turn off the lights. He offers a stick of incense. Then he sounds the Bell of Mindfulness, sits down on my lap, and we sit and breathe together for three breaths in front of his candlelight altar. Sometimes we sit there for ten or fifteen breaths. When Jason is ready he snuffs out the candles. We turn on the lights, get into bed, and read a story.

The other day in the car, as my husband Marc and I were talking about a Day of Mindfulness, Jason blurted out, "I hate meditation!" After a slight pause I said, "But we sit meditation every night in front of your altar and you seem to like that." With tolerance for my ignorance he replied, "No, I don't mean that. I like that. I mean real meditation like they do at Green Gulch for forty minutes."

I trust that someday Jason will know that sitting in front of his altar breathing quietly three times is also real meditation. And I trust that the experience of happily sitting together will remain with him. We are trying to give our children practices, rituals, and experiences that they can own, incorporating our values into our lives and letting our children grow up tasting them. At Zen Center, my husband and I saw little offered to children that they could own. We both come from Jewish heritage, but not Jewish practice. It has been a rich process for us to use our experiences practicing Zen to become more open to the wealth of Jewish family ritual and tradition.

Each week, we observe the Sabbath; it is our weekly Family Day of Mindfulness, beginning with a service at sunset on Friday night and ending with a service when the first three stars appear on Saturday night. Adding new rituals to our family life is a slow process. We spent one year just lighting the candles on Friday nights and eating a nice meal together before we were ready to give up shopping, television, working, or going places on Saturday. Our intention is to do what nourishes us as a family. Celebrating the Sabbath has become a gift for us. It is an opportunity to go beyond the pressures of constant juggling and being squeezed by time, to be together in the spaciousness and simplicity. It is like bringing a touch of monastic life into our family each week, a rich and fertile blend.

It is also a time shared with other generations. Every Friday night we sit down at the table: Carol, twenty months old; Jason, six years old; Marc, thirty-seven years old; myself, thirty-eight years old; and my father, eighty years old. The table is set with my mother's wedding silverware, a lace tablecloth made by her mother, gold-rimmed holiday glasses from my father's mother. As we start to light the candles, Carol knows what is coming and begins to sing with soft, bird-like sounds, her own blessing of our being together.

I remember a rabbi once describing the lighting of the candles of Friday nights as a marking of the ending of one moment and the beginning of another. In Buddhist practice we speak of impermanence, interdependence and nonattachment. In our family we are borrowing from the wisdom, history, and traditions of both Judaism and Buddhism, seeing how they come alive through our daily lives of innumerable beginnings, endings, and present moments. How does the reality of impermanence affect how I live?

As part of my own bedtime ritual I have begun to do three full bows in front of the altars of each of my children. I see them sleeping and quiet. I breathe with them. With the detachment of not needing to interact with them, our connection is refreshed for me. I see them with more quiet eyes. Perhaps I see them more clearly. Sometimes as I watch them sleep I allow the question to arise in me, "If my children were to die, what would I regret the most. . .?" Continuing to breathe, I open to what arises in me and work to give it room to influence my actions.

Our children are with us so briefly. They change so quickly. What we do now helps to mold them and their future families, and *their* future families. To be mindful in what we do requires intention and effort. To give our own true mind to the intricacies of family relationships is a Buddha field to practice in. If we can be happy and peaceful within our families, it can't help but impact our wider world. If we neglect the opportunities to practice with our families, that too can't help but impact our wider world.

Notes

[1] Alice Miller, *Thou Shalt Not Be Aware: Society's Betrayal of The Child* (New York: New American Library, 1986) p. 154.

[2] The tune is basically the same as "Twinkle, Twinkle, Little Star."

Terri Muir-Small

❧

Two Suns

I like to write stories so I have decided to write one to explain . . . well, that part will come later.

It was a beautiful day when the woman and her daughter took this particular walk. It was warm and sunny with enough breeze to keep the air fresh and sweet smelling. The sun was behind them and cast long thin shadows before their toes. All at once, the daughter espied something and ran ahead, going so quickly the woman couldn't catch up, running as fast as she could. Soon the daughter was out of sight and the woman stopped to catch her breath and decide what to do. Just then the young girl came running back, saying, "Look! I've found another sun to light the sky!"

And lo and behold, there it was! Another large, round, warm, and bright sun coming from the east to travel across the sky with the first sun. Laughing delightedly, the daughter pointed down to where the woman, like everything else, now had two shadows. The woman found she was very uncomfortable with this phenomenon. She spent a lot of time moving around trying to get the two shadows to merge and become one shadow again. When this failed, she retreated beneath a large tree under whom she had no shadow. There she rested and thought on her predicament.

Finally, finally, she realized that while she now had two shadows, there was still only one of her and that she, herself, was all she needed to worry about, come to terms with, take care of. Suddenly, she was free to join the daughter in joyfully exploring the new wonder of a world with two suns. It felt good to have made peace with this strange phenomenon, though sometimes she suspected, when the suns were in a certain position, that her shadows talked together about her behind her back.

Well, that's the story. And it's not just "a" story, it's my story. I am a Roman Catholic and, along with my husband, have been planning to raise my children in that faith. Our daughter, Adrienne, has found that her faith journey is, at least partly, a Buddhist one. My relatively liberal views would not allow me to take an "either/or" tack, but where would our Catholic faith fit in for her?

At first I sought ways the two paths were the same and how I could make them One, for I found there was much in common between Buddhism and many of my own beliefs. It was soon obvious that was the wrong way to go—it took away from the value in each. They were not just shadow versions of each other representing some vague outer "reality"; rather, each had the potential to illuminate the Truth within. Even the seemingly insurmountable difference between belief in reincarnation and belief in resurrection became surmountable for me within the context of that illumination.

Catholicism, as I have grown up with it, tends to be exclusive. Buddhism offers a path to follow in addition to other religious paths, honoring the diversity of all without forcing a choice. I am taking it up on its offer, its invitation, as I explore with Adrienne the wonder of a world illuminated so brightly by so much.

Ryo Imamura

❀

The Buddha Loves You as You Are

We Buddhists of Asian descent must grow up in America as both religious and racial minorities. It is especially difficult for the children, who are constantly reminded that they are different and therefore unacceptable. Being physically small in stature and relatively quiet in demeanor, our children are often excluded from or not chosen to participate in popular youth activities. They often do not match the cultural ideals of the majority regarding maleness and femaleness, and therefore have difficulties in establishing and accepting their identities in positive ways. And there is still a lot of ignorance about and prejudice against Buddhism, which leads to some embarrassment and shame about being Buddhist. Growing up in America can be very difficult for Asian Buddhist children.

It is not our cultural practice to openly discuss and analyze our difficulties in a direct or therapeutic sense. Instead it is more comfortable to address issues indirectly through parables and stories told within the framework of a nurturing and unconditionally supportive community. Let me share with you one such story that helps our youngsters accept painful experiences of rejection.

Long ago in a tiny house deep in the mountains of Japan, all the bugs and their friends gathered together for a party. There were snails, spiders, bees, flies, bugs, caterpillars, inch worms, beetles, butterflies, grasshoppers—every kind of insect you can imagine.

Hopping, crawling, and flying, they made their way through the gate into the entrance hall, where they stopped to remove their little straw sandals before entering the house. Oh, what a grand party it was going to be!

A long table heaped high with good things to eat stood in the main room. Laughing and talking, everyone helped themselves to the rice cakes and sweet dumplings while the ladybugs filled each cup with a drop of tea. Suddenly, amidst all the festivities a baby ant who had eaten far too many dumplings began to cry out in pain. With tears rolling down her tiny cheeks, she sobbed, "Oh, my stomach hurts!"

All the bugs began talking at once. "We must get the doctor immediately!" "But who shall we send to fetch him?" "We cannot send the snail because he is much too slow." "The worm cannot see, so she would surely get lost."

The beetle, listening to all the commotion, stood up asking for silence. "Because the centipede has one hundred legs, he would be the best choice to send," she said. Turning to the centipede, the beetle continued, "Mr. Centipede, since you have more legs than anyone else here, you should be able to walk the fastest. Please go fetch the doctor."

"Oh, yes," cried the other bugs in agreement, "Please, please go."

The centipede, feeling very flattered, answered, "Of course, you are right. I am the most logical one to go." He then rushed quickly out of the room.

In the meantime, the mother bugs took turns holding the baby ant, trying their best to help her forget her upset stomach ... but the doctor did not come. They waited and waited, but still there was no sign of the doctor or the centipede. The bugs began to worry. "What could have happened?" "Did he lose his way?" "We had better go and find out." Two ants went running out of the room to find the centipede.

When they reached the entrance hall, they found the centipede there. "What happened?" they asked. "You are so late! Where is the doctor?"

The centipede, looking a little perturbed with them, shouted, "This is no joke! Just look at all the sandals I have to put on. It will be some time before I can go for the doctor."

The ants looked down in surprise, and sure enough, on half of his hundred feet were carefully tied fifty straw sandals! Of course, another messenger was sent to get the doctor. He came at once, gave the baby ant some medicine, and the party continued on happily into the night. But the bugs learned a very important lesson — he who has the most legs is not always the fastest.

*Nicolee Miller, Tyson Sean Miller,
Dana Sorrenne Miller*

❀

A Mother, a Son, and a Daughter

Nicolee Miller

❀

Balancing

Meditating in between my first child's naps was the beginning of a challenging and wonderful journey of integrating spiritual practice with family life. It was not easy. It has been one of the most demanding koans I have ever had to chew up and digest.

I have been married since 1967 and have two grown children. In 1969, I was drawn to Transcendental Meditation, but after two years I let go of mantra practice and began to sit thirty to forty-five minutes in the morning and evening. Contrary to what is generally recommended for practice, I did not make a special place to meditate. At night, after the children were in bed and the "good nights" completed, I would alternate each night meditating in one of the children's rooms. They liked this quiet presence so well that they would argue about whose room I was supposed to meditate in well into their teens. Finding ways to integrate practice into our family life in an unspecial way seemed to help them not feel shut out and allowed us to join in a natural way.

By 1980, it became evident to me that I needed to work with a teacher. I was teaching T'ai Chi Ch'uan at the time, and one of my students guided me to the Zen Center of Los Angeles, directed by Taizan Maezumi Roshi. Zen practice and studying one-on-one with a teacher was what I was looking for. My commitment to practice increased substantially—I began sitting seven-day sesshins six or seven times a year, including two month-long retreats. I traveled four hours round trip once a week for dokusan. What was driving me was an intent deep within the marrow of my bones to clarify the Buddha Way. At the same time there was an inner demand not to make my husband and children orphans to spiritual practice. I didn't know how to do both. This tug of war finally resolved itself when I realized that these two aspects of my life were not in competition with each other: my practice is to give fully to whatever is at hand. When I'm with family, I'm with family. When in sesshin, I give fully to sesshin. To further the breakup of the family versus spiritual practice koan, I had to suspend my ideas of timing and work as well as I could with my circumstances. I found the Soto Zen precepts, especially the precepts of not killing, not elevating oneself to put others down, and not speaking ill of the Three Treasures, helped me realize that I am already living Buddha's life and whomever I am living with is also Buddha living Buddha's life. Practicing in this way reminded me not to elevate my spiritual practice as being better than my family, because then I am subtly negating the life of those with whom I live. In time, the practical means of how to integrate family life and Zen practice began to unfold.

As I am self-employed as a Marriage, Family, Child Counselor, I organized my work on a ten-month schedule, including weekly half-day round trips to Los Angeles. My husband, who does not sit zazen nor is formally involved with Zen, works full time. Though it was very stressful to have me gone so much, with the help of my mother, his mother, and the cooperation of our children, we managed, after much trial and error, to smooth things out. Each family's circumstances are unique, and for our particular family, my leaving and rejoining the family was especially trying for all of us. I felt guilty and selfish yet determined to go to sesshin. Working with the precepts reminded me not to kill my family's reactions by judging them or making them wrong. For me, this has been a very challenging part of family as spiritual practice. My family's reactions so clearly mirror my own fixed ideas of how I think things should be. Learning how to open my heart to them, let go of judgments, and not separate myself from their desires and pain has deepened my understanding of the Buddha Dharma. In time, certain practical measures helped to ease the transition of leaving and rejoining the family. I have found the following particularly useful:

- Having another family member replace me while I was gone. In our family, my mother and mother-in-law were available until the children were in their teens and able to drive.
- Leaving a card for my husband expressing caring and appreciation for his efforts and the space he gives me.
- Calling daily if possible.
- Packing my clothes while everyone is gone so that there is time together before leaving.
- Making meals they love and freezing them to be eaten while I was gone.
- Having their favorite snacks in the house: the family appreciated this kind of nurturing when I wasn't there.
- Bringing presents if possible.
- Praying daily for the family while I was gone so that their well-being was present in my heart.
- For our family, it worked best for me not to talk about my sesshin experience upon returning; instead, I would play and cuddle with my husband and children and hear all about their week. This way we would join in an arena of shared experience, and if they asked me about my week, I would share that with them. It was important to the family that I come back into family life as quickly as possible.

In 1991, I was ordained as a Soto Zen priest. Part of the ordination included having my head shaved. This part of the ceremony was very trying for several members of the family, and again, the precepts of not reviling the Three Treasures, not elevating myself, and not killing their reactions helped me to better accept and give space for their pain. They and I passed through the discomfort and fear, and we all adjusted to the changes that were occurring.

My husband's patience, honesty, support, and caring have always been beneath his confusion and resistance to what was and is happening to his wife. He has a wonderful saying that is very grounding: "We are all plumbers with a different set of tools." He has helped me see the "nothing special" quality of Zen practice.

Relationship is a very precise mirror of how I and others think life should be versus the way it is. I might have wanted to do zazen, but when a family member had been hurt, I got up from zazen and took care of what was needed. Nothing extra. Family is a very rich and fertile aspect of practice.

Tyson Sean Miller

※

My Mother's "Other World"

I use the words, "other world" because that was how I viewed my mother's spiritual practices when I was a young boy. I never experienced any feelings of animosity or anxiety regarding what she did. In fact, I thoroughly enjoyed and benefited from what my mother learned and applied from the Buddha's teachings. She was always subtle in her ways, never pressuring me to conform to or even acknowledge the Buddhist way of life. She would meditate in my room, which brought a balanced energy into the room. Her way of interpreting life taught me that things are always changing. So in elementary school it was easier for me to accept when my team lost because I enjoyed the game itself and was not attached to the idea of only winning.

At an early age my mother encouraged me to learn the ways of Aikido. This art is Zen in motion to me and has had a significant impact on the way in which I experience life. Just as balance is one of the most important aspects of Aikido, it seemed that balance was what enabled my mother to have a normal family and also continue with her Zen practices. It was when my mother was out of balance that the family was affected. Month-long sesshins were difficult for me to accept and definitely added a sense of confusion. Not understanding what a sesshin really was, I could not grasp how or why my mother would leave for a month to sit still.

Recently I have discovered some of the answers to my questions, for I myself have begun to meditate. My mother taught me at a young age the basic principles of meditative practice, and in doing so once said, "Training is like sharpening a sword—it takes focus and discipline, and doesn't start out as a gleaming, razor-sharp piece of artwork." She has not sharpened the sword, but has had much to do with the molding of the metal.

Dana Sorrenne Miller

❀

Challenge and Inspiration

I feel extremely lucky to be my mother's daughter, not only for the unconditional love and acceptance she has provided me, but more fundamentally, for the unique perspective she has guided me to attain. Throughout my childhood, my mother met the challenge of child rearing with an indefatigable source of sensitivity and a genuine sense of fairness. Out of her experience with Zen Buddhism, my mother developed a very deep understanding of the Universe and its oneness. One of the values she impressed on me the most is the need to respect nature, all nature, from the snails to the stars.

Whenever I came to her with a problem I was having, she would help me to look into the source of my pain, which always ended up being a fear of something. Her remedy was to extend love to whatever I am fearing, a philosophy derived from her understanding of Buddha. When I was very young, my mom taught me how to "center" when I felt a loss of control over my own life, and from this ability, I was able to learn how to trust myself from within. Despite the hardships of life, there is always a sacred source of energy within us, which has the power to soothe one's pain and create a sense of groundedness where chaos once existed. I first became aware of this soothing energy during the times my mother would meditate in my room, which is something she did quite frequently. Once I experienced this healing energy, I was able to find it within myself.

Along with the positive influence my mom's Zen practice brought into my life, I also went through times of hurt, confusion, and anger related to the very same source. Zen Buddhism was not a norm in the community I grew up in. During my pre-adolescent years especially, I felt I needed to conceal my mom's interest in Zen, so as not to appear different or weird. This meant never having my friends over when she meditated and shoving her zafus in the closet whenever possible. Fortunately, as I grew older, I recognized the uniqueness of my mom's interest in Zen, and my friends did as well. Another aspect of her practice that was difficult to overcome was the time factor. I felt, and still feel, that month-long sesshins pose a tremendous threat to the well-being of the family unit. In my family's case, these problems were alleviated when my mom divided the amount of time she spent sitting sesshin into smaller blocks of time.

Probably one of the hardest times I have ever experienced was the months following my mom's ordination ceremony. Part of the ritual included the shaving of her head, which had a somewhat negative effect on various family members, including myself. I felt that the implementation of this ancient tradition contradicted the innovative direction of Zen to adapt to the changing world. If my mom was to strike a balance, and maintain her position within society and within our family unit while fulfilling her need for spirituality, why was it necessary for her to complete this act which was clearly iconoclastic to her world on a broad scale? I found this ritual to be almost disrespectful and certainly antagonistic to the nonspiritual side of Nicolee Miller. However, I do admire my mom for the strength, sensitivity and intuitiveness with which she overcame the difficulties posed upon her family life.

I feel that Zen practice has permeated every aspect of my mom's being to a certain extent, leaving her and those close to her with the immeasurable gift of understanding and caring. I am very proud of my mother—she has claimed her independence and pursued it with diligence. She continues to be a wonderful role model for me. Her actions have led me to believe that being a woman does not mean I have to give up personal goals. More recently, she has given me faith in the institution of marriage, as she has been able to maintain a healthy marriage with my father while remaining true to her own spirituality.

Grace Karr

❀

Growing Up in Zen

Looking back on what it was like growing up in a Zen center, I think first of my rebellion. In junior high and high school, when every insecurity is painfully magnified, I was embarrassed about growing up so differently from my peers. It was hard to be surrounded by the very world I was rejecting.

As you can imagine, it's hard to carry on a social life when you are trying to hide such an important part of your family life. Bringing friends home posed a major problem. I remember bringing home one of my first boyfriends, when I was in junior high school. As we walked up the stairs, my mind quickly ran over all the possible ways to conceal my parents' strangeness. Unfortunately, this was quite difficult, since evidence of Zen practice was everywhere.

The zendo library happened to be in our own living room, where a huge Buddha sat on a table. Zen pictures were all over the walls, and Zen books in every corner. As fate would have it, on this day Abbot Mel Weitsman, looking very bald and wearing his black priest's robes, was having a practice talk in the library with another Zen Center member. They sat on zafus, solemnly facing each other. Luckily, I got in early enough to shut the door before Gavin could see. Over time, I developed the habit of quickly rushing my friends up the stairs and into the security of my room.

Then there was the chanting. To me, the sound was actually soothing, mixed with the smell of sweet incense in the air. But I was afraid that to an outsider it would sound like the mutterings of a frenzied cult. (Remember, I was an adolescent.) Timing was all important—I needed to coordinate when my friends arrived and left so as to avoid the sounds of chanting. Nothing could muffle this sound, even if I closed my window, put a towel over the window crack and blasted my music.

Many things were hard to accept, like bald women—even worse than bald men. But I have fond memories of the zendo as well. Three things stand out as positive symbols of my childhood: cats, plums, and recorders.

Cats were all over: meowing, playing, sleeping, fighting, mating, eating, peeing, scratching, purring. I had three of my own, but there were many more. Their grace and easygoing nature made them ultimate Zen masters.

Much of my childhood was spent sitting in plum trees, preferably with my friend Miriam, who was my neighbor at the Dwight Way Zendo. Plum trees were our private clubhouse, kitchen, and observation post. We were always ready when it came time to harvest the greenest, tartest plums we could find. I was glad there were still plum trees when we moved to Russell Street, though they weren't the same without Miriam. Mels' wife Liz would use the plums for delicious plum ice cream and strong plum wine. The zendo's new name, Old Plum Mountain, seems very appropriate to me.

Mel is a wonderful recorder player, and the sound of its sweet notes is a part of my childhood. He used to give me recorder lessons, which were at first frustrating and later, when I got better, inspiring. Playing the recorder was my own type of Zen practice.

Looking back, I think it's unfortunate that I was so set on rejecting the Zen Center for all those years. The community could have been a wonderful support group if I had let it. But in any case, it was a place that provided a lot of quiet, peaceful time for me. Most people don't realize how much the Zen community has influenced my life. So don't be surprised if you see me walk into the zendo one day, holding my own zafu.

Sam Hamill

Natural History

Late afternoon, autumn equinox,
and my daughter and I
are at the table, silently eating
fried eggs and muffins
sharp cheese and yesterday's rice
warmed over.

We put our paper plates in the woodstove and go outside:
sunlight fills the alders with
the geometries of long blonde hair,
and twin ravens ride rollercoasters
of warm September air
out, toward Protection Island.

Together we enter the roughed-in room
beside our cabin and begin our chores together:
she, cutting and stapling insulation
while I cut and nail tight rows of cedar.

We work in a silence broken only
by occasional banter. I wipe the cobwebs
from nooks and sills, working on my knees
as if this prayer of labor could save me,
as though the itch of fiberglass and sawdust
were an answer to some old incessant question
I never dare remember.

When evening comes at last,
cooling arms and faces, we stop
and stand back to assess our work together.
And I remember the face of my father
as he climbed down a long wooden ladder
thirty years before. He was a tall strong sapling
smelling of tar and leather, his pate bald
and burnt to umber by a sun
blistering the desert.

He strode those rows of coops
with a red cocker spaniel and tousled boy-child
at his heel. I turn to look
at my daughter: her mop of blonde curls
catches the last trembling light of day.
Weary, her lean body sways.

Try as I might, I cannot remember
the wisdom of fourteen years, those pleasures
of discovery. Eron smiles. We wash up
at the woodstove as the sun dies into
a candle-flame. A light breeze rustles the first yellow leaves
of autumn as boughs slowly darken.
A squirrel, enraged, castigates the dog
for some inscrutable intrusion,
and Eron climbs the ladder to her loft.

Suddenly, I am utterly alone,
a child gazing up at his father, a father
smiling down on his daughter.
A strange shudder comes over me
like a chill. Is this what there is
to remember: long days roofing coops,
the building of rooms on a cabin, the in-
significant meal?

Shadows of moments mean everything
and nothing, the dying landscapes
of remembered human faces frozen
in a moment. My room
was in the basement, was knotty pine,
back there in diamondback country.

The night swings out over the cold Pacific.
I pour a cup of coffee, heavy in my bones.
Soon, this fine young woman
will stare into the eyes of her own son or daughter,
years blown suddenly behind her.

Will she remember only this ache,
the immense satisfaction of this longing?
May she be happy, filled with the essential,
working in twilight, on her knees,
with her children, at autumn equinox,
gathering the stories of silence together,
preparing to greet the winter.

Dharmacharini Sarvabhadri

❀

Family Life, Spiritual Life

As women practitioners of the Dharma we naturally look to the Buddhist scriptures for records of women whose lives inspire us and whose example we can follow. The Buddha had women disciples, both monastic and lay. The *Therigatha* tells the moving stories of women who dedicated their lives to the Dharma as bhikkunis or nuns. However, there are few accounts of the lives of women who practiced in the family context. Family life is usually seen as being disadvantageous to leading a spiritual life. Yet those of us who have children have to use our situation as a working basis for our practice. We have to work out for ourselves how Going for Refuge — that act which makes us a Buddhist — can be expressed in our own situation. In the Western Buddhist Order we have an Ordination that is neither lay nor monastic, but rather stresses the centrality of Going for Refuge giving all women, whatever their circumstances, an opportunity of expressing their commitment to the Three Jewels.

I first came in contact with the Dharma when I came across the Friends of the Western Buddhist Order in the summer of 1976. After a few months I acknowledged to myself and others that I had found what I was looking for: a framework in which to live and grow. I asked to become a Mitra. At that time I had two daughters, aged seven and eighteen months. My whole experience of being a Buddhist, therefore, is as a mother, and I can say that I have felt very little conflict between the two. I cannot imagine my life without the children, nor can I imagine it without the Dharma. They are both precious to me and each feeds into the other.

Fifteen years on I have three children and two grandchildren. I was ordained into the Western Buddhist Order seven years ago while teaching full time and looking after my three children. (I live on my own with my children, but get support from their father.) I have learnt that family responsibilities are both demanding and rewarding, and that they require long-term commitment. Taking responsibility for my family has helped me develop the strength and maturity necessary for Going Forth in the spiritual sense. To Go Forth when living in a family situation means working against the tendencies which are so common in nuclear families to be restrictive, falsely protective, and closed to outside influences. It means, in the words of Kahlil Gibran, thinking that "your children are not your children." I had this quotation pinned to the wall when the children were young. It means extending the love and nurture that you feel for your own children further and further into the world, your ideal being no less than the Bodhisattva Ideal, which seeks to embody love and empathy for all sentient beings. Through having children I have experienced how strong and powerful mother-love can be. Through meditation and the Buddha's teaching I have learnt how to broaden this love, how to use it to begin to break down the barriers between myself and others.

One of the delights of being a mother is to see a human being unfold, and being able to assist this process by providing the right environment. In meditation we set up the conditions for positive mental states to arise within ourselves. In the same way we can try to provide the right conditions for our children's growth. But we have to bear in mind that our children bring a unique blend of their own past conditioning into this life. We can have no expectations of what our children will become. I have learnt to let go of expectations through the experience of seeing my own children grow up. They have their own particular path through life. I can only trust that the foundations I have helped to lay were the best I could offer at the time.

These foundations are based on Buddhist ethics, in particular the Five Precepts. It is such a relief to have a reference point for all the moral dilemmas that arise. The Buddhist viewpoint helps in answering those questions which all children put to their parents. Buddhism has an imaginative, expansive view of the universe that appeals to young people. Sangharakshita once answered in two words the question that many a young person asks—"What is the meaning of life?" The answer—To grow. Dhardo Rinpoche, one of Sangharakshita's Tibetan teachers who ran a school for Tibetan refugee children, said once that from their education he hoped his pupils would at least learn that actions have consequences. These simple but profound teachings have helped me in bringing up my family.

Although one cannot bring children up as Buddhists (since to follow the Buddha's path has to be the free choice of the individual) one can surround them by positive influences—and what can be better for a child that to have around her- or himself adults who are fulfilled, growing as individuals, and trying to lead an ethical life?

As well as benefits for children, a family life in the context of practicing the Dharma also brings benefits to the mother. Through bringing up my children I have learned patience, understanding, an ability to put myself in another's place. But I think the biggest lesson for a mother is in the meaning of impermanence. The process of separation starts from the moment a child is born. You are faced with the experience of attachment and the need for letting go in a very tangible way. Children grow and change so fast that every day brings with it a lesson in impermanence.

As well as these benefits, there are, of course, difficulties in leading a spiritual life in a family context. For a mother, trying to lead a spiritual life—finding a balance between the demands of a family and her own spiritual practice—is not easy. Everyone who practices the Dharma, parent or otherwise, has to work with the opposing tendencies of "self" and "other," but this dichotomy is highlighted when you have children, as their demands cannot be ignored. I realized when my children were still quite young that I was better able to give to them when my own needs were being met. If I was able to meditate for a short time and go on short retreats regularly, I was a much better mother and it worked to everyone's advantage. I learnt that it is important to keep a clear perspective on one's direction. Time to oneself is essential to avoid getting bogged down in mundane difficulties.

As children grow up the demands change. More is needed for their emotional support, but one is given more time and space. Sometimes I have experienced frustration at not being able to do as much as I would like to do. For instance, I have not yet been on a retreat lasting more than two weeks. I am not able to meet up with my sister Order members as often as I would like. And I can't help remembering that there are many, many people waiting to hear the Dharma—and my time and energy are limited. I try to live in the moment, but I trust the time will come when I will be freer of family responsibilities. I hope that the time I have spent practicing in the family context will stand me in good stead. One formulation of the Buddhist Path is the Threefold Way of Morality, Meditation, and Wisdom. These three stages are not discrete, but progressive, each arising out of the one before. My years of practice whilst bringing up my family have been based on Morality with comparatively small amounts of Meditation. When I finally do have time to meditate more consistently, I trust that the seeds I have planted over the years will bear fruit.

Our Movement tries to provide women (and men) with the facilities they need in order to grow spiritually. There are our residential Communities and our team-based Right Livelihood businesses. There is Taraloka, the FWBO's Retreat Centre for Women in Shropshire, England. There are plans to establish a women's Meditation Community at some point in the future. There is the "Going for Refuge" retreat center project, which will cater to women who have asked for Ordination. It would be good to bear in mind the possibility of creating supportive situations for people with children. Perhaps eventually we could have a Buddhist village where childcare is shared; where children are taught by Buddhists; where there would be Buddhist cultural and artistic activities. We need to develop an alternative to the nuclear family—a sharing, supportive envi-

ronment for people with children that helps them to grow spiritually; an environment in which life is shared, not isolated; where
there are real friendships, not exclusive couples or lonely single
parent families. Some pioneering has been done with mixed results,
but I feel confident that in another fifteen years we may have come
a long way towards realizing at least some of these ideas.

Part Three

The Children's Sangha

Thich Nhat Hanh

❀

Family Mindfulness

Two years ago, I presented to the community at Plum Village a very special vase of flowers. It took me about fifteen minutes to arrange these flowers in front of the community. The whole community was breathing and smiling while I arranged these flowers. But that pot of flowers was quite different from any other pot of flowers I have arranged, because that evening, the flowers that I arranged were children. I invited about ten of them up and then I arranged them into a very beautiful combination of flowers. Flowers are always smiling. One flower was sitting, one flower was kneeling, another was lying down.

Each child is a flower. Adults should remember that children are flowers to be taken care of, in order for joy and happiness to last. A flower does not need to become another flower to be happy. A flower can be happy by being herself. The only thing she has to do is to be alive, to be in touch.

To be in touch is the source of love and understanding. We do not have to look for something else. We have to be entirely ourselves. It's like the river. The river doesn't have to go to the sea in order to be happy. She can be very happy being a river here and now. You don't have to become something other than yourself. A rose can only be happy being a rose. If happiness is not there, it is because communication is not there, and real contact with life is not there. In us, we find the seeds of everything, the seeds of understanding, of awareness, of love.

Watering the seeds of Buddhahood, you water yourself. You water the seeds in yourself, and you water them in your environment. Where do I water the seeds of American Buddhism? I water them in my heart, I water them in my body, I water them in my family. All these seeds are there. I go back to Christianity and I water the seeds of Buddhism there. You find the seeds of Buddhism in Christianity. You find the seeds of Buddhism in Judaism. You find the seeds of Buddhism in the Native American culture. You don't have to go to another country to bring the seeds of Buddhism over.

If you want to build American Buddhism, you have all the ingredients, all the elements, within your own culture, within yourself, your family structure, and your religious institutions.

It's very hard to draw a line between Buddhism and non-Buddhism. Sometimes we have to be careful in talking about Buddhism. The way we talk can construct a barrier that will destroy Buddhism, because Buddhism does not recognize frontiers. Everything that has the capacity of bringing us to awareness, everything that can generate understanding, mutual acceptance, and love, can be called the seeds of Buddhism, even if Buddhist terms are not there.

I believe that the family is a very important center of practice. Buddhism in North America, at least in the immediate future, will be lay, not monastic Buddhism. This is why the practice of Buddhism in families should be given priority. In the last few years I have led many retreats with the theme of the family as a practice center. How to practice Buddhism, to practice mindful living, living with joy and awareness in family life? These are our questions.

A gentleman in Rochester told me he had practiced for ten years but his daughter did not know what he was doing. I said, "That's not the correct way of practicing. If you practice correctly, then your daughter would know what you are doing and she would be able to participate. Otherwise, your practice will not bring happiness and peace."

It is possible for children to participate in mindful living, the kind of life we want to live. It is possible to invite our children as co-practitioners, as Dharma brothers and sisters. We have demonstrated this again and again in the children's retreats and in retreats with adults and children together.

If you engage your children as you go, little by little, with the sangha of the family, if you include children in practice it will become a cornerstone of their lives. When we include children, we make our own practice better and more joyful.

Opportunities for practice are all around us. How to organize dinner in the evening? That is our practice. Eating our dinner in such a way that awareness, mindfulness, peace and joy can be found during dinner—that is our practice.

If in the family there is one person who practices mindfulness and is able to enjoy mindful living, then that person can help the whole family to practice. She knows that it will be wonderful if everyone in the family has a chance to practice breathing and smiling. That is why she suggests that a "breathing room" be arranged in the house. We might not like to call it a "meditation room," but simply a "breathing room," where we can be alone and to practice just breathing and smiling, at least in difficult moments.

That little room should be regarded as an embassy of the Buddha. It should not be violated by anger or shouting, but should be respected. When a child is about to be shouted at, he or she can take refuge in that room. Neither the father nor the mother can shout at him or her anymore. He or she is safe on the grounds of the Buddha. Mommy also needs that. Sometimes she wants to take refuge in that room, sitting down, breathing, smiling, and restoring herself. Daddy also. Therefore, it is for the benefit of everyone in the family.

If you set up such a room in your house, you don't need a lot of furniture, just a few cushions and perhaps a small table with a flower. It would be helpful to have a bell in your breathing room. You don't even need to have a statue of the Buddha. In fact, it's better not to have a Buddha statue if the statue does not represent serenity, happiness, and a smile. When artists make statues, they have to practice smiling and breathing. Otherwise, when children look at the statue, they may be scared. In that instance, it's better to have one flower on the table. During the first few hundred years after the Buddha passed away, Buddhists did not make any statues of the Buddha. They only carved the bodhi tree with an empty seat. But I think a few hundred years after that, people began to miss him, and they began to make statues. That was from the image within; they conceived the Buddha and made it real. So when we bow to the Buddha statue, we really bow to the image of the Buddha inside.

Each time that we feel a little bit shaky, nervous, or worried, we know that the best thing to do is not to do anything, just to go toward that room, slowly, and open the door. Close the door in mindfulness, making a bow. Sit down, begin to breathe. The bell would be very helpful. It helps not only the person in the breathing room, but it helps the person outside also.

Suppose your husband is irritated. Since he has learned the practice of breathing, he knows the best thing is to go into that room, sit down and practice. You don't know he is doing this as you are cutting carrots in the kitchen. You suffer also, because you and he have just had some kind of altercation. You are cutting the carrots a bit strongly, because the energy of the anger is translated into your movement.

Suddenly you hear the bell. You stop cutting and breathe in and out three times. You feel better, and you may feel proud to have a husband who knows what to do when he gets angry. He is now sitting in the breathing room, breathing and smiling. Suddenly a feeling of tenderness arises. After three breaths, you begin to cut the carrots again, but this time quite differently.

Your child, who was witnessing the scene, knew that a kind of tempest was going to break. She was expecting that tempest, which is why she withdrew to her room, closed the door, and silently waited. Suddenly she heard the bell. She knows what it means. She feels that her daddy is wonderful, and she wants to show him how she feels. She goes slowly to the breathing room, opens the door, and sits down very silently beside him, to show her support. That helps the husband very much. He already feels ready to go out, because he is able to smile now. But since the daughter is sitting there he wants to invite another sound of the bell for his daughter to breathe. So he invites the bell a second time.

In the kitchen, you hear the second bell and know that maybe cutting carrots is not the best thing to do now. Maybe you should go and sit with him, to show your own peace now. So you put down your knife and go to the breathing room. Your husband is aware that the door opens and his wife is coming in. Now he is feeling fine, and smiling. Since you have come, he stays on and invites the bell for you to breathe. That is the most beautiful scene of the family. It is the practice of peace and reconciliation.

Happiness is made of mindfulness. The most meaningful Dharma talk is to live your family life in happiness. With mindfulness, everything becomes different and you live your daily life in a much deeper way.

Mobi Warren

❀

Storytelling Dharma

My mother was a storyteller. At night before we children slept, she made up stories to tell us. I remember the delicious feeling of sitting on a bed cuddled against my brothers and sister in a shadowy room, listening to the gentle richness of my mother's voice. The stories were wondrous, but even more wondrous was our mother's loving presence and our knowing how completely she was with us during those moments of storytelling.

To me, storytelling and mothering are inseparable. Storytelling evokes the feeling of being encircled by love and feeling connected to all else. Now as a mother myself, and as a Buddhist woman called upon to share the dharma in my immediate family and in the larger sangha, I find it quite natural to use storytelling as a dharma vehicle. I like to remember the Buddha's words: "Just as a mother uses her own body to protect her only child, every person must open their heart to love and protect every living being." It is with that spirit of love that I would like to share storytelling as dharma.

Storytelling is ancient and universal. Buddha and other great teachers often used stories to teach their disciples, recognizing how stories can plant the seeds of understanding through their power of sound and imagery.

While I have often read that it is the ability to recount stories that sets the human species apart from all others, I have a hard time subscribing to that view. I agree that we are the only species engaged in writing down words into books or committing them to computer disks, but when I hear how humpback whales form a circle and sing together, or when I lay awake at night listening to a mock-ingbird trill an endless variety of notes for the pure joy of making sound, I am struck by the oral traditions of other species. Their joys and sorrows, the experience of the present moment, and the passing on of memories—whether by instinct or conscious teach-ing—bind many species together.

We know that observing one's breath mindfully is both a method and fruit of practice. If we can truly be present to one breath, with that breath we are a Buddha. Similarly, storytelling is both a vehi-cle and fruit of dharma and sangha. It helps us to share and illu-minate dharma and yet is also the very essence of a healing and lov-ing sangha. When people sit in a circle to listen to a story there is an experience of shared community that binds and strengthens all present. Together we become Buddhas and Bodhisattvas. Story-telling can be a delightful and powerful way to give a dharma talk. It speaks across ages, enabling children and adults to share a com-mon learning experience and to explore the many faces of the dharma together.

My children and I like to remind each other of Thich Nhat Hanh's invitation to "live simply and sanely." Storytelling can be both. Re-quiring no props, it is as portable as the human voice. It is adapt-able to any conditions—stories can be short or long, and selected according to the needs of the time, place, and audience.

Storytelling as dharma requires both mindfulness and letting go of self. When I tell a story (unlike when I read a book), the eyes of my listeners keep me fully anchored in the present moment. Once a friend of mine was nervous as she prepared to tell a story to a group of schoolchildren and asked if I could offer any suggestions about how to tell a story well. I told her, "Put yourself aside and let the story tell itself. Let the the audience draw the story out according to their needs. If you are truly present to those before you, you will find just which words to use. The story will flow with-out your needing to memorize it."

Long neglected in our culture, storytelling is experiencing a renaissance. Often when I perform stories, one or two people will approach me afterwards to say that they have been feeling a great interest in telling stories themselves. This is certainly true in the American Buddhist community. We have wonderful models, such as Rafe Martin, who performs and has committed to writing his versions of many Jataka tales. These are traditional tales of the past animal lives of the Buddha, which provide a wonderful resource for persons interested in using storytelling dharma in their own families, lay sangha groups and Buddhist centers. Thich Nhat Hanh's version of the life of the Buddha, *Old Path White Clouds,* is another rich resource of dharma tales.

I had a special experience once retelling one of the episodes in *Old Path White Clouds* at a retreat in Colorado. The story I read concerned an untouchable boy named Svasti who was befriended by Siddhatta and invited to share his rice. The rice had been brought to the Buddha by a girl named Sujata, the daughter of a wealthy family. Both children are confused and amazed when the Buddha offers Svasti the first drink, and tells them that people are not born with caste. But, says Sujata, everyone else believes differently.

Siddhatta tells the children, "The truth is the truth whether anyone believes it or not. Though a million people may believe a falsehood, it is still a falsehood. You must have great courage to live according to the truth."

Later that day a woman who had heard the story approached me, her short silver hair framing her smiling face. She explained that hearing the story had been very powerful for her, carrying her back to an experience she had had at the age of three. She had been taken to visit her grandfather and upon entering his home had spontaneously hugged the housekeeper, who was black. She had been reprimanded severely by her grandfather on the spot and told that she was never again to hug a black person. She felt horrible humiliation for herself and for the housekeeper, and in her three-year-old heart knew that her grandfather was wrong. For all her years growing up she never wavered from her belief that the segregation espoused by all around her was deeply wrong. "Though a million people may believe a falsehood, it is still a falsehood."

Hearing the story that morning had been a healing experience for a childhood wound. Her words to me were a storytelling gift, strengthening my understanding of how stories can be precious experience of dharma.

Many legends and folk tales contain the seeds of the dharma. I like finding ones that speak in a special way to me in order to share them later with others. Living with my children has provided me with a rich treasure of true-life tales to tell.

Some weeks after attending the children's retreat with Thich Nhat Hanh, my six-year-old son Bruce was home from school with a bad cold. I was in the front room doing some translation work when Bruce entered. He looked sad and said, "Mama, yesterday when Emily was giving Hero (our dog) a bath I saw fleas jump off him. I could tell they were trying to jump to safety because they wanted to live, but they just landed in the water and drowned."

I agreed it was a sad thing. Then he asked me, "Can I make an altar for the fleas?"

On his own he set up a little altar. He placed a tiny stub of incense in a doll's cup. He was especially happy to remember he had a tiny Buddha no bigger than a thumbnail to put on the altar because "It's just the right size for the fleas. They won't be afraid."

After lighting the incense he rang our bell of mindfulness and sat in meditation for several minutes, after which he rang the bell again and did a beautiful walking meditation around his tiny altar.

For me it was a lovely and unexpected glimpse of the seeds of the dharma ripening in my son after his experience at the children's retreat. And it was certainly a story I enjoy sharing with others.

Mary Beth Oshima-Nakade

❀

The Poem

Every night my three-year-old daughter Amy sleeps cuddled up next to me. Every morning she wakes up, flings her little arms around my neck, kisses me and says, "I love you, Mommy. It's time to rise and shine!"

One morning a few months ago when Amy was still two-and-a-half, she sat up in bed, rubbed her eyes, and came over to whisper something into my ear. I yawned, wondering what secret my little girl had for me this time. Then her words came, as soft and gentle as a lullaby. This is what I heard.

"Breathing in, I calm body and mind. Breathing out, I smile. Dwelling in the present moment, I know this is the only moment."

I blinked, wondering if I was dreaming. But there was Amy in her nightgown, grinning proudly.

"That was beautiful sweetheart," I said. "Please say it again."

Once more Amy put her mouth to my ear and whispered, "Breathing in, I calm body and mind. Breathing out, I smile. Dwelling in the present moment, I know this is the only moment."

Still amazed, I hugged my little girl and said, "Thank you for starting Mommy's day in such a nice way." She smiled and kissed me again.

It's amazing how naturally children learn. I had been using this poem by Thich Nhat Hanh to help my child calm down. Whenever she was angry, frightened, or frustrated, I held her close to me and whispered the poem into her ear. It calmed both of us. Amy memorized its soothing lines, in the same natural way she learned songs and nursery rhymes.

Today this poem is one of our favorites. Sometimes we recite it together. Sometimes we create our own melodies and sing it. Amy was able to connect breathing in and breathing out with feeling happy and peaceful. She especially likes the part that goes "I smile"—at this point we always smile at each other and hug!

Laura Wilson, age fourteen

❧

Everyday and Special

Life itself is a spiritual experience, isn't it? I can't tell you just how my beliefs interact with my everyday life, any more than I can tell you how my life will turn out. I can't describe it, they just do, and if I make it so, it is on an unconscious level.

But some days seem special and I can tell you about them. There are days when I just say, "Yes, Universe!" When I feel like hugging everybody I see, when I am joyful for no other reason than being joyful. Then there are the special days when it is a holiday or celebration of some kind. On these we celebrate according to what day it is, but we usually light candles and sing songs and be together.

Diane di Prima

Letter to Jeanne (at Tassajara)

dry heat of the Tassajara canyon
moist warmth of San Francisco summer
bright fog reflecting sunrise as you
step out of September zendo
heart of your warmth, my girl, as you step out
into your vajra pathway, glinting
like your eyes turned sideways at us
your high knowing 13-year-old
wench-smile, flicking your thin
ankles you trot toward Adventure
all sizes & shapes, O may it be various
for you as for me it was, sparkle
like dustmotes at dawn in the back
of grey stores, like the shooting stars
over the Hudson, wind in the Berkshire pines

O you have landscapes dramatic like mine
never was, uncounted caves
to mate in, my scorpio, bright love
like fire light up your beauty years
on these new, jagged hills

Elizabeth Erin Luthy

❧

An American Zen Buddhist Education Program for Children

My husband and I had struggled along on our own spiritual paths before we had children. Then, the quest for a path that would work for my family helped me focus on my central values. I wanted a set of teachings that would help guides us through the difficult choices that must be made in life. I wanted a community of support from fellow seekers. I wanted each of us to have guidance, as needed, to live ever closer to God.

First we discovered what didn't work. One program expected preschoolers either to be separated from their parents for long periods of time or to stand through long rituals without squirming or squeaking. Another emphasized coffee and doughnuts over spiritual growth. My son soon hated religion as foreign to his needs and child's nature. By the time he was a preteen, he didn't want a new peer group or the teachings—"authority figures"—of a religion. For a while we gave up on finding something for our whole family, and concentrated on an adult Zen meditation group. After our two daughters were born, I resumed my search.

Meanwhile the priests at our Zen Center were trying their own experiments with family education. Sensei Gyokuko Carlson tried reading chapters of *Journey from the West,* translated by Arthur Waley, but found the readings too tedious. She tried an active program of work and discussion between children and adults but found this too long and involved. Trying these programs with my three-year-old daughter, I agreed on their shortcomings. Then Sensei

Gyokuko encouraged me to create a new program with her, from scratch.

We knew that we wanted the kids to have fun and develop their spirituality. Beyond that we had only wisps of ideas floating about between us. We decided some research was in order and began in the public library, with ages and stages of moral development.

The preschooler learns from a mix of stories, fact, and imagination. My preschooler wonders, "If God is in my heart, doesn't he get blood on himself?" and, "Is Buddha Jesus' daddy?" The line is still fuzzy between what is imagined and what is real. All things are possible. Working through their ideas and fantasies is best done at the child's level. Playing, pretending, drawing, and creating are the child's way of processing difficult concepts, including death, sex, divorce, and violence, as well as religious teachings. They need a supportive atmosphere and some tools to make sense of it all.

The school-age child, from six to twelve years old, clearly knows the difference between fantasy and reality. She has a better developed conception of the world and her place in it, but reality tends to be limited to what she can see and verify for herself. Most eight-year-olds do not look under their bed for alligators. A pitfall of this new-found realism is that, unless the family makes a point of respectful awareness of other people's beliefs and customs, school-age children can be caught in the idea that their family's religion is the only right way. Jean Fitzpatrick suggests presenting religious teachings in terms of personal experiences:

> If she asks about God's creation of the world, for example, we need not stammer endless explanations about the way the Genesis accounts relate to evolution. Instead, we can ask our child to remember a time when she made something very special, such as an art project. How did she feel about it? Does she keep it in a safe place and take care of it?[1]

As our children move into their teen years, they become increasingly capable of abstract thought. This enables them to question and see beyond the literal stories and teachings of their religion.

There is a testing of new ideals against new experiences. In Zen we say the ideal meets the actual. This experience creates fertile ground for growing faith. It is important to remember that the teen years are a time of trying things out. Your teen may reject religion altogether, embrace its literal teachings, or ponder its ambiguities. It's a fluid time of life. They are doing their best, as we all are, to sort out a confusing world. They need our support—when they choose to accept it!

Sensei Gyokuko and I visited several religious education programs, including the Oregon Buddhist Church (Jodo Shinshu) and the Franciscan Montessori Earth School. As Buddhists are a minority in America, finding materials specific to Buddhism and children was a challenge. The Oregon Buddhist Church generously loaned or gave us many of their materials, including Buddhist coloring books, plays, songs, and curriculum.

The Franciscan Montessori school gave us many ideas for a hands-on program. Their program includes emphasis on small versions of religious articles for the children to manipulate, parables acted out by the teachers and retold by the children, timelines on a scroll to help older kids get a sense of their relative place in time, and an enclosed corner with a sheepskin rug for children who wish to pray or meditate.

We took the theories and program models and developed goals for our particular religious community. Naming goals clarifies what we are working toward, so that all the parents and teachers work in concert. Most important to us was the first precept, Do no harm. We didn't want to turn off kids to religion or harm their spiritual development. We wanted the kids to feel comfortable and accepted at the Zen Center. Beyond that we identified the following goals:

1. Learning appropriate behavior at the Zen Center.
2. Understanding basic Buddhist concepts.
3. Encouraging the development of each child's meditation practice.
4. Recognizing each child as an important sangha member.
5. Having developmentally appropriate lessons.

The teachers include a priest, a mother, and two non-parent sangha members. Choice of teachers is important: Are ideas presented kindly and thoughtfully with attention to how each child interprets them? Are the teachers a model of meditation in action? Are expectations developmentally appropriate? Recently we have encountered a problem that may be common: having too many female teachers and a lack of male role models. Preteen and teen boys were dropping out after several visits. One of our male sangha members graciously stepped forward to form a new group for young men.

To work, our program needed to consider not only the needs of the children but also the parents. The parents at our Dharma School are busy people who need their own time for spiritual reflection concurrent with Dharma School so that the needs of the whole family can be met at once. Twice per year all parents are invited to a curriculum planning meeting to discuss ideas or bring up issues. Most parents also choose to contribute special skills such as music, dance, or art. We have designated September and January as trial months when new families can come and try out the program. Once a new family decides it likes the program, we ask that attendance be regular to make planning easier. We vary our lessons somewhat from year to year, but find that the same lessons take on new meanings as the child grows. Here is a sample lesson plan following the Buddhist liturgical calendar:

September 13
> *Content:* Trial month. Rules, getting to know each other,and work for the Zendo (envelope stuffing or weeding.)
> *Goal:* Reflect on why the Zen Center is a special place. How do our actions reflect that? How does how you feel inside affect the mood of a place?

September 27
> *Content:* Build a birdhouse or a pine cone bird feeder.
> *Goal:* Learn to care for our world and others. Prepare for hard times such as winter for a bird. We may wish to use the Three Pigs story. Prepare for emotionally and spiritually hard times.

October 11

Content: The older kids pretend to be hungry ghosts for the little kids. That way it is less intimidating when a grownup does it at the next meeting, in full costume.

Goal: Reflect on how we all hunger for the truth, not just the hungry ghosts. Discuss the karma of greed. How can we present things to people so they can best understand it (e.g., bribing the hungry ghost).

October 25

Content: A grownup is the hungry ghost for the kids.

Goal: Discuss why civilizations make up traditions with ghosts and spooks. What are they symbols of?

November 8

Content: Make vegetable soup.

Goal: Teach mindful cooking, and why Buddhists are traditionally vegetarian.

November 22

Content: Make monks begging bowls from clay.

Goal: Discuss gratitude for what you receive in life.

December 13

Content: Have adults role-play Buddha and Jesus.

Goal: Discuss what it is like to be Buddhist in a Christian world. What do each believe? Who are Buddhists and how do they fit in our society? What are all those mangers doing in the mall? How does it feel to be a minority? Which other religious systems are minorities?

December 20

Content: Have a winter party.

Goal: Socialize and develop a feeling of community.

January 5

Content: Develop a New Year's resolution.

Goal: Discuss how sometimes controlling one's will and exercising discipline are necessary for meeting our goals.

January 19
   Content: Discuss the first three precepts.
   Goal: Apply the precepts to current problems in the children's lives. Have the younger children act out common problems using puppets and work out answers that are in keeping with the precepts.

February 7
   Content: Discuss the next three precepts and ask which of the older kids is ready to take a vow to keep the three pure precepts. Have the kids rehearse for the ceremony.
   Goal: Help the kids understand the precepts and why we use them to guide our lives. Discuss the nature of taking a vow and the benefits of being able to follow through on commitments.

February 16
   Content: Tell the story of Buddha's death, Nehan, and the handing down of his teachings.
   Goal: Allow for a discussion of death as well as how the Buddha's life was mythic.

March 1
   Content: Discuss precepts and rehearse for those taking their vow.
   Goal: Apply the precepts to current problems in the children's lives.

March 15
   Content: Have a Jukai celebration with cake for those taking vows.
   Goal: A public acknowledgment of the child's commitment to making spiritual progress.

April 12
   Content: Have an Easter egg hunt.
   Goal: Discuss greed.

April 19

> *Content:* Plant a vegetable garden.
> *Goal:* Discuss spring and spiritual rebirth.

May 3

> *Content:* Do a dance project choreographed around one of the songs we use or Sufi dancing.
> *Goal:* Experience the body/mind/spirit connection.

May 31

> *Content:* Celebrate Wesak, the Buddha's birthday.
> *Goal:* Discuss our gratitude for those in the world who nurture and teach us.

June 14

> *Content:* The end of term picnic in the park with the parents.
> *Goal:* Socialize and develop a feeling of community.

July 20

> *Content:* The Dharma school camp-out for all the families. Gather an altar made of forest things. Say our "thank yous" for the natural world. Put on a skit. Go swimming, make a campfire, and roast marshmallows. Have the adults take turns hiking and talking together.
> *Goal:* Learn to live, work, share, and play together as a community.

The Dharma School year begins in the fall. Sunday mornings work best because they do not conflict with sports schedules. During the morning we balance social activities, music, ritual, and eating. We mix quiet and active times.

As families arrive, they usually hurry in the door. (It is difficult to get everyone up and organized on the weekend.) The children remove their shoes and join the circle in the tea room. The peaceful ambiance of the Zen Center slowly seeps in on parents and children alike.

We greet each other and learn about any significant happenings in each other's lives. The Zen Center has a transfer of merit board where small cards are posted if someone needs the Sangha's prayers and support. The children use it to bring up any difficulty in their lives. The group can then support the individual in the death of a pet, illness of a friend or grandparent, or grief associated with divorce.

Another source of support is Sanzen, a private meeting with a priest. When a pet died, my four-year-old received great comfort in talking to Sensei Gyokuko about her fears of her own death. Personal insecurities or indecision about taking Jukai vows are other topics that have been dealt with privately.

During our initial gathering we sing several songs—sometimes with older kids playing musical instruments—as parents depart for the adult Dharma talk. Then we split into groups: the three- to five-year-olds, the five- to seven-year-olds, and the seven- to twelve-year-olds. Groups are determined by the number of teacher volunteers and the dynamics of the kids.

The younger kids join in a circle before a bare altar. The teacher reminds them that this is a quiet time. A cabinet holds a statue of the Buddha with children in his lap, a precentor gong, a bell, a candle, and incense. Children who are still and ready are asked to take out an object and place it on the altar. We light the candle, and a child offers the incense. We look for opportunities to praise the children's attention and stillness.

We talk about each of the objects: the statue reminds us of the Buddha spirit in all living things and of the good person Gautama Buddha, who gave us his teaching; the precentor gong and the bell call us to meditation; the candle reminds us of the light in our heart; the incense is our gift to Buddha.

At each meeting different children sound the gong. We sit for about three minutes to listen to the stillness of our hearts. We have also tried several variations on walking meditation. We may walk for a minute and then freeze and ask the children what they were thinking or feeling.

After meditation the children take the objects off the altar one at a time. We ask them what time it is now, and they invariable scream, "Noisy Time!" Activity time for the little ones may be dancing to a kid's exercise tape, tossing bean bags, dancing with scarves, blowing bubbles, pretending to be a bubble, being a horse or rabbit or frog, or generally burning off some energy.

Meanwhile, the older kids continue to meditate in a Zendo upstairs. They do their meditation in a more formal way. Each child offers incense and bows to a zafu and sits. Silence, stillness, and posture are encouraged.

When the younger children finish their active time and the older kids finish meditating, we either merge the groups or do separate lessons, depending on the topic. For example, celebrations are all done together, but precepts study is for older kids only. We close with snack time at about 12:30.

I am grateful that I now have a religion and community that work for myself and my family. I know many people who are still searching. My children's understanding has grown in a way that I could not have created on my own. They are learning from others' experiences and perspectives. They benefit from having adults and older kids as role models.

Explaining Buddhism to children has greatly enhanced my own understanding and appreciation for the practice. I am continually breaking my explanations down to their simplest forms. By the time I do that, even I can understand it!

For eight years I have studied the liturgical calendar and the seasons of our lives with children. Some of the children are almost grown now. Each year brings new wonder as I observe not only the changes in them, but also the softening in myself.

Notes

[1]Jean Grasso Fitzpatrick, *Something More—Nurturing your Child's Spiritual Growth* (New York: Penguin Group Publishers, 1991) p. 127.

Elena Rivera, Jaymz Asher,
Sarah Nancy Cutts Weintraub, Dhyana Cabarga

❀

Four Children

Elena Rivera

❀

Arrival

Tassajara was a crevice, a cracked rock; sulfur poured out of its robes, a hot spring for visitors; water flowed to smooth the bumps while all the while creating new ones. We arrived, my brother, sister and I, on an orange afternoon. The hills were dry and the dust rose beneath the wheels of the jeep. I was fifteen. We stood at the entrance, up above the zendo, after our adventurous ride over rocks on the winding door which had opened at Jamesburg. Tommy came out to greet us with shiny head smiling and something cool to drink.

In my dream I was a monk in India. I was very happy to be there, except that there is a period where everybody should be silent; I don't understand why. I pay admission to the museum; it's a huge mountain with holes. I am silent, everything is silent. I walk.

We looked down from the high spot where we stood and saw that our mother was there; we had felt her immediately among the faceless black robes. She looked surprised, a doe's glance that has smelled change. She had been a Tassajara for a year—she, the deity who came forward. "Mommy!"

We had come from Los Angeles and it was the beginning of summer. We had lived with our father in a house off Santa Monica Boule-

120

vard. We had lived in the screened heat of a town making itself into a tragic land, tap dancing classes, two new brothers for the year, and Wonder Woman and Spiderman.

Our mother came up towards us. The Zen students watched, watched silently as she held and touched her children, a laugh echoing in our skin. They watched us, beheld the mother in her black robe and her children, full of her smell and eager to see her. We felt them, these black robes like tall trees. (This was not the first time. We were used to differences. We had lived with Sensei Deshimaru in France, our hair had been touched and cut by Kalu Rinpoche.) A syllable to be spoken, a meal to be made, a chant to be repeated—"Innumerable labors have brought us this. . ."—that was the adventure, and the mountains and hills became a familiarity to dive from, where we put on concerts (which wasn't very Zen), wrote newspapers (which survived the first fire but not the second), and cut gallons of lettuce, onions, and grated carrots.

Jaymz Asher

❀

A Fireside Chuckle

So I got to thinking about ol' Green Gulch Farm and being reared there an' all, and I was reflecting on the notion that my memories and ideas are continually being restructured in retrospect as time flails away. Sounds obvious an' all but, By Gum, it just occurred to me that for several years after moving from Green Gulch I was quite embarrassed about having lived in a Zen monastery. Then in high school it became a small source of pride; it was "cool" and "alternative" when the sixties-seventies revamp was becoming popular. In England I hesitate to mention it because reactions have been particularly snide. However, I'd like to believe that the spirit of children has some sort of universal consonance, and I still remain imbued with fond sentiment for my childhood at Green Gulch, though at the time my feelings were more ambiguous.

For instance, I can chuckle now over certain anguished moments which tormented me as a child. The whole idea of living on a Zen farm with a bunch of mysterious bald people was always embarrassing at school, and having my father show up to my soccer games, bald head a'shining, cheering wildly from the sidelines still wearing half his zazen wear (if not robes), became a constant fear after the first time it happened.

The usual social hierarchy amongst children growing up together was especially prevalent at Green Gulch, as I remember. The harassment was passed down the line. As a "little kid" I received endless torment from the "big kids" and doled out my share of it in turn. Excluding the omnipresence of a hoard of parental figures, there were essentially three types of people at Green Gulch for us kids: there were the babies, like my sister, who were too small to torture (at first); there were the little kids—that was me for the longest time; then the big kids, which usually included one or two stray Muir Beach hooligans. Every morning during the school year all of the kids would gather at the base of a hill where cows and horses grazed. We would wait for all the kids to assemble before climbing over the fence and trudging up the hill to the highway where the school bus stopped. I recall one morning as a young'n when the bigger kids waiting with me were particularly friendly; they had given me a chocolate chip cookie to bring to school. It was a giant one, the kind you get out of a big glass jar at a delicatessen and I was advised not to open my lunch box till I got to school or some hoods on the bus might take it from me. Oh boy, did I covet that cookie!—and it surely was huge as it clunked about in my Incredible Hulk lunch box. But I kept to their advice and happily scampered up the hill to catch the bus to school, beaming with joy. That kind of thing just makes a kid's day; the world is a happy place, the big kids are suddenly your best friends, school becomes fun, dogs no longer appear to be waiting to bite you, the school bus isn't doomed to drive off a cliff after all, why heck, even brussel sprouts could be edible! Well, maybe not brussel sprouts but certainly asparagus.... Squash? Eggplant?

When you're a little kid and you have a giant chocolate chip cookie in your lunch pail you're invincible, the Incredible Hulk. Nothing can bring you down when you're the owner of an ENORMOUS CHOCOLATE CHIP COOKIE! And so, when I eagerly joined my comrades, the lunch box brigade, out on the benches for recess, I was glowing like a sweepstakes winner, a newlywed, (a taker of saunas?). With an irrepressible smile I tore open my lunch box like a Christmas gift and revealed the biggest, most gigantic dried cowpie in the ENTIRE UNIVERSE, crumbling and flaking onto my carrot sticks, scattered over my peanut butter sandwich, contaminating my whole lunch! I heaved the lunch pail to the ground in horror. The sky went black with thunderclouds, the braying of a million rabid dogs filled the schoolyard, somewhere a school bus careened off a cliff, Lucy the cook was steaming up a heaping pot of brussel sprouts for dinner. And eggplant ice cream for dessert.

The big kids got me that day, but perhaps it was just some kind of karma for days to come when I ruled the farm with my tyrannical cohorts, dishing out constant ridicule and harassment to those younger than I, playing my part in the timeless ritual.

No doubt the details of our memories are different, individual, but would it be fair to say that the spirit of children remains the same? Regardless of the environment we were raised in, regardless even of the political climate of that environment? I'd like to believe so. Iraq, Russia, South Africa, California, England, China, Croatia, etc.... You know, nothing heavy; just the spirit of children ... you know?

Sarah Nancy Cutts Weintraub

❀

Zen Parents

My parents say some unusual things. For example, a few days ago I pushed my little brother and pretended nothing happened. My mom, instead of saying, "Don't push your brother," or something like that, said, "Think about your state of mind when you push your brother."!

Another incident happened this morning: I was about to eat my cornmeal and molasses when I noticed two brown dots on the edge near the side of the bowl. "Daddy," I said, "What are these things?" "They are the pre-voice of the ten thousand molasses," answered my dad. "What's pre-voice?" asked my brother Dave. So my dad explained: ". . . There are ten thousand Sarahs and ten thousand Daveys." "If I'm ten thousand I don't have to ask to be excused from the table!" cried Dave. He jumped off his stool and put his head through the arm of my dad's vest, then he began dancing around the room.

To remember to write this I wrote "Zen Center Story" on my hand. My brother Dave told me to write "Davey is ten thousand," on his hand. So much for a Zen teaching.

Dhyana Cabarga

❀

"Not" Chanting

During the meal chant before dinner at Zen Center, sometimes Audrey and I would say the chant adding "not":

Innumerable labors did *not* bring us this food,

We should *not* know how it comes to us.

Receiving this offering, we should *not* consider whether our virtue and practice deserve it.

Not desiring the natural order of mind, we should *not* be free from greed, hate, and delusion.

This food is *not* for the Three Treasures, it is *not* for our teachers, family, and all beings.

The first portion is *not* for the Precepts . . .

Saying the chant this way was fun, and no one knew we were doing it. And we didn't know if our virtue and practice deserved it anyway.

Maggie Gluek

❀

Work and Play at Gorrick's Run

How to make our children feel a part of our sangha? How to include them in a sesshin? When a work sesshin at Gorrick's Run in Australia was proposed for a long weekend in October, it seemed a good occasion to take up the challenge. The normal sesshin schedule was to be modified in any case to maximize work time. There was much work to be done on building the dojo, as well as urgently needed repairs to fences and creek-crossings. So why not extend the experiment to accommodate a "children's camp"? Pip Atkins agreed to act as children's coordinator. She drew up a children's schedule, organized material for kids' activities, and rostered willing adults for periods of childcare duty.

When the time came, we were seventeen adults and six children ranging in age from six to ten. The children, most of whom had never met, were quick to become acquainted and soon comprised their own energetic community within the larger group. This sense of community was encouraged by their having their own space, a large tent situated far enough from the dojo that "noise" was not an issue. While they slept in their family tents at night, this kids' tent was the focus for their daytime gatherings and meals. At all times there was one roster person (aptly renamed foster parent by one of the children) in attendance. The sesshin planners had envisioned various meditative-style activities for the children such as yoga, imaging exercises, and listening to tales of the Buddha. There were naturally some quiet periods and a couple of particularly interesting writing sessions, but given the fine weather and wide, flat surrounding spaces, the order of the day was exuberant physical activity, such as bush walking, swimming in the creek, and ball games.

The kids came together with the larger group at work time each morning, contributing their energy where they could. They helped mainly with bridge building, finding logs and stones, and making sandbags for reinforcement. Traveling to and from the crossing sites, the work crew delighted in bumpy rides in the trailer. Then twice during the day they joined us in the dojo, once for a zazen period and again for sutras before bedtime. They were encouraged to change into dark clothes before coming in; some made offerings of natural objects—stones, bushflowers, leaves, or a lyrebird feather found earlier in the day.

Most of those who took the zazen option settled on their cushions with extreme gravity and then escaped after a few minutes. Chanting drew a fuller attendance, affording a real sense of participation in the practice. Sutras in the just-fallen darkness were a unique experience for us all.

From a personal point of view, this sesshin was important and successful. I had not been without misgivings about the enterprise. I worried, as parents will. Will the kids get along? If not, will their discord disturb the sesshin? Will one of them tread on a snake? Will I be able to sustain my practice without being constantly distracted?

Of course, these anxieties resolved themselves. The children showed maturity in working out problems. Bumboots were worn in the bush and not one snake was seen. Sitting was distracted initially. I felt that half of me was in the dojo and half of me was being pulled out the window. Will Phoebe know where to find her toothbrush? Will Hugh help her? As someone said, one had to let go of having to be there oneself. A lesson in relinquishing control and allowing space. In any case, the children were very much enjoying spending time with other sangha members who were not their parents.

I am grateful to all the foster parents who shared responsibility for childcare. In my mind it was this sharing that made the sesshin really work. It meant not only that everyone could participate equally but that our sangha could truly develop and function as a family.

Children practiced self-reliance and cooperation, being "adult." Adults were challenged to find the playful child in themselves. Come join in the game! Jump in the swimming hole! Working and playing in the same spirit.

Jacqueline Kramer

❦

Mountains and Flowers

When I sent a check to secure our reservations for a family retreat I envisioned sharing lots of quality time with my daughter. I pictured us sitting together, eating together, healing together. I was so happy to have a chance to share the precious jewel of Buddhism with my only child. My daughter, Nicole, age eleven, had been hurting terribly for the past few years. I wanted to put a balm on her wounds and provide her with the tools she would need that would enable her to rebuild her self-esteem in a world that could be confusing and hurtful. We arrived in Le Casa de Maria at night and settled into our dormitory room — its sole occupants. We awoke to a foggy morning and a smattering of early retreatants eating pancakes at the dining room. After breakfast, Nicole and I walked back to the dorm to get ourselves organized. Nicole was lying on the bed when I approached to invite her for a walk. She was crying. "Nobody likes me here. I want to go home." I was stunned at this sudden unhappiness and made the mistake of trying to talk her out of it. I got so frustrated I knew I needed to go out for a walk to clear my heart. While walking out my frustration, I met up with a girl Nicole's age and invited her to come meet Nicole. The two girls went off together for a walk in the orange grove.

As the retreat commenced, Nicole was less and less in my presence. She wasn't interested in coming to the meditations or the walking or the talks. She didn't want to eat with me or spend free time with me. She was pouring her energy into making new friends and doing God knows what when her new friends were participating with the rest of the community and she was by herself.

I watched mothers sitting with their children, I watched the children up close to Thich Nhat Hanh drinking in his words, I watched the adults being like mountains and the children being like flowers on the mountains. I longed to share this with my daughter. I knew that forcing her to participate would only create more rebellion, so I just watched the longing, the anger, and the wanting. I wanted her to hear what Thây was saying about enfolding anger with loving arms; I wanted her to hear what the gentle sister was saying about sexuality and its place in a loving context. All the hurts Nicole was feeling were being addressed, but she was too withdrawn to drink this medicine.

I let go. I let go of trying to direct Nicole's healing. I felt the support of a community of loving, mindful people. They were there for us if we needed them. We were safe. I could finally relax and let go of my daughter, knowing that if she fell, there was a whole community of people to help her get back on her feet again. I was beginning to trust that Nicole was taking care of her own healing even if it looked to me as if she was drifting and lost.

The last day of the retreat was sunny and flowerful as Thây and the community walked to a field to celebrate Buddha's birthday. We gathered around a statue of the baby Buddha on the fresh green grass and sang songs of simplicity and awareness. After three breaths, I looked up and there was Nicole standing next to Thây. His arm was around her, and she was singing with the rest of the community.

Later that day, we were in our hotel room preparing for dinner. I walked into the bathroom and there in the tub was my sweet Buddha child singing, "I vow to develop understanding in order to protect the lives of people, animals, and plants." My eyes filled with tears to witness the healing I longed and prayed for, which had come about in its own mysterious way without effort on my part. I had simply become a mountain amongst mountains—solid and present, unmoving in my commitment to love. The precious tulip child drank in the air, sun, and water. She had become fresh and new again.

Wendy Johnson

❀

The Flowering of Buddha's Birthday

Every spring at Green Gulch Farm Zen Center in northern California, just as the wildflowers of the coastal mountains begin to unfurl, we celebrate the birthday of Shakyamuni Buddha. In Japan, Buddha's birthday coincides with the flower festival Hana Matsuri and we follow this tradition. Our celebration fairly bursts with flowers, balloons, a flying dragon, picnic food, masks, music, and song, and—most important of all—many, many children from all over the San Francisco Bay Area.

The young people of our sangha have grown up hearing the story of the life, awakening, and teaching of the Buddha. This story has always been powerful for our children because it is a story of transformation and truth. The Buddha appeared in the world more than six hundred years before Christ, born in what is now Nepal, the son of King Suddhodhana and Queen Maha Maya. He was raised as a prince and was married to Princess Yasodhara at the age of sixteen years. They had one child, a son named Rahula.

In his twenty-ninth year the Buddha left his royal life upon seeing Four Great Signs: an old man, a sick man, a dead man, and a recluse monk. He spent six years in the Indian forest practicing many forms of self-mortification until he discovered the Middle Way between abandoning the world and indulging the senses. Through following the Middle Way and practicing deep meditation, he gained enlightenment as the Buddha. After he became the Buddha at the age of thirty-five, he taught gods and men, women and children, day and night, for forty-five years. At the full age of eighty years he passed away, leaving an active sangha to continue and to develop his teaching.

The life of the Buddha is a life of great resolve and determination, for the Buddha did not turn away from difficulty and challenge but sought instead to look deeply into the nature of existence, vowing to include all beings in his search for truth and liberation. Children see that baby Buddha is a human child, not a god, and in this birth they see that everyone has the possibility of awakening and understanding and loving. Our celebration and enjoyment of the birth of the baby Buddha, dedicated to our children and to the open human nature and flower nature, has been a vital source of nourishment and inspiration in the Zen Center sangha.

Because we connect the birth of the baby Buddha with the emergence of spring wildflowers, our celebration begins a day early, walking in the spring mountains above our coastal valley and gathering a single blossom of each of a profusion of wildflowers. The name of each flower is woven into a special list which we chant during our ceremony on the following day. From our gardens we collect armfuls of cultivated flowers and with them we festoon a small, pagoda-like house for the baby Buddha. The children particularly love this part of the preparation. The next day, dawn of the birthday morning, we carry the flower pagoda out to the main meadow which is in the center of our community. Nearby we set up a beautiful ceremonial altar with all the wildflowers arranged as an offering. In the flower pagoda we place a small statue of the baby Buddha, one finger raised to the sky, a secret smile on his baby face.

Our day of pageantry begins with the children gathering in the meadow to decorate a small elephant cart. The elephant of this cart represents the mythical, six-tusked white elephant that visited Queen Maha Maya to announce that she would bear a son. The children fill this cart with flowers and decorate it with balloons and streamers. Then they gather on the grass for a reading of the story of the birth of the baby Buddha. They listen actively, calling out a running commentary eagerly, with curiosity and enthusiasm.

Following the reading, the young people assemble and the ceremony begins. The oldest children lead a long, serpentine procession of all the children quietly into the meadow, where the adults, often more than 200 strong, are waiting in a big circle surrounding the flower altar and Baby Buddha Pagoda. The oldest children herald the festivity by carrying ten-foot bamboo poles with bright paper parasols on top and yards and yards of ribbon streaming out from the parasols in the spring wind. The leaders are surrounded by the tiniest children, each one scattering flower petals on the face of the meadow, welcoming the holiday. Behind them come all the other children carrying the elephant cart. Together they slowly circumambulate the altars. When the procession and circumambulation of the children is complete, a procession of priests enters and makes the traditional offering of food, light, incense, chanting, and spring flowers to the Buddha, with everyone gathered joining in the chanting. This is done in grand Soto Zen style, with drums and gongs, fly whisks, full ceremonial robes, and deep prostrations by the officiating priest.

In the flower pagoda the baby Buddha stands in a bowl of sweet tea. Taking turns, all of the children come forward and bathe the baby Buddha with ladles of sweet tea, welcoming him, refreshing him, and bringing him into the present moment with their attention and awareness. After this offering the formal part of the celebration ends. The children fall back into the great circle and a magical pageant of the birth of the Buddha commences.

A few years ago Norman Fischer, a resident Zen priest who is head of practice at Green Gulch Farm, a poet, husband of Kathie, and father of twin sons, took the traditional story of the birth of Buddha as told by the Indian Buddhist poet Ashvaghosa, and adapted it into a playful epic poem and pageant.

For five seasons, this pageant has been performed in delight and homage. With each performance, new petals of creativity spontaneously unfold. The pageant takes the form of a pantomime that employs music and dance. Each stanza of the poem is read dramatically by a narrator sitting high up in an oak tree overlooking the meadow. At the end of each stanza a gong is struck and every-one joins in with the refrain, "Homage to the World Honored One." And then the action described in the stanza is performed in grand style. All of the players wear powerful, ornate masks crafted by Annie Hallet, a brilliant mask-maker and theater performer who is a local practitioner at Green Gulch. The young people participate fully in the pageant: they play all the roles, from wild animals to ghoulish goblins to attendants of the Buddha.

From the moment the pageant begins, the real world fades away. With the momentous entrance of the giant, six-tusked elephant (played by four mysterious adults), trumpeting wildly in elephan-tine joy, triumphantly dancing with the beautiful Queen Mother, magic dominates the meadow. And magic and mystery herald the entrance of the Lord Buddha, rising up behind veils to stand revealed in glory, his vast golden mask smiling benevolently at the astounded crowd, his right hand raised in the universal mudra of peace and acceptance. Around the baby Buddha the storm and passion of human life is enacted: the Buddha stands still in the center, burned into the imagination of the assembly, teaching with silence and presence. It becomes difficult to see where the cloth of the imagi-nary and the real is stitched together: the pageant renders it all one seamless piece. One year, at the close of this epic performance, the children from the audience rushed forward, offering flowers, candy, balloons, and fruit to the monolithic Buddha to whom they burst into song, "Happy Birthday to You!" at top volume. But finally the pageant does end and we gather for a big picnic lunch on the meadow, above which we fly our ten-foot-long dragon kite, lifted into the spring sky by billowing balloons.

When I consider the holiday of Buddha's Birthday, celebrated for more than twenty years at Zen Center, I find a dynamic expres-sion of the present vitality of Buddha's teaching in our modern soci-ety. Because the birthday party is dedicated to all children and flow-ers, to dragon kites and the magnificence of a six-tusked white elephant, I feel encouraged: perhaps we can be lighthearted in our Way-seeking and unafraid to reveal this playfulness to all beings.

We encourage all of you who may find yourselves near Green Gulch Farm around April 8th to join us for Buddha's birthday. But wherever you are, you can celebrate with your children. You don't need any special effects at all: just your love for one another. In this way we lift up and transform our life, revealing the simple treasure of awakening in every moment, with every breath. This is the true flowering of Buddha's birthday.

Norman Fischer (after Ashvaghosa)

The Birth of Buddha

1. Listen to the story of the birth of the Buddha,
    a story that is always told
    whenever beings gather together
    to work or to play
    and even when they fight or shout.
    The story of the birth of the Buddha is told
    on every breath, in and out.

CHORUS: Homage to the World Honored One.

2. There was a king of the mighty Shakya tribe.
    Suddhodhana by name,
    Whose purity and grace of manner
    caused him to be loved by his people
    as pens love paper, flowers love the spring.

CHORUS: Homage to the World Honored One.

3. His queen was Maha Maya
    whose splendor bounced from the clouds to the earth
    And she was like the earth in her abundant solidity
    In her beauty like a great blue heron or like
    a mass of willow trees at dawn seen from a distance from a
        truck.

CHORUS: Homage to the World Honored One.

4. This great king and splendid queen in dallying
    spread open happiness like a picnic basket in May
    And without any ants or spilled wine extruded
    the vine-like fruit of a gestating babe,
    as concentration and mindfulness together
    gently produce the winds of the wisdom gone beyond.

CHORUS: Homage to the World Honored One.

5. Queen Maya before conceiving saw in her sleep
    a great white lord of an elephant emerge from a cave and
    come close to her
    envelop her
    incorporate her
    into his all-embracing comprehension
    like a nation state
    a political movement,
    a trance, or a soothing bath.

CHORUS: Homage to the World Honored One.

6. This Lord of Elephants With Queen
    dissolved into a pure melody and so she sought
    In all purity, piety, and joy, without illusion,
    a place in the sin-free forest
    A valley among trees by the sea, a place
    suitably arrayed for the practice of meditation and birth,
    called Lumbini.

CHORUS: Homage to the World Honored One.

7. Here the Queen, aware of the stirrings of beginnings and
        endings,
    Amid the welcome of thousands of waiting women
    On her couch covered over with awnings and leaves
    gave birth without pain from out of her side to a son
    born for the weal of the world from out of her vows.

CHORUS: Homage to the World Honored One.

8.   Forth he came yet not from earth or cloud or spirit
     but as if from out of the empty sky,
     Pure of being as the breath itself, long or short,
     without beginning or end, fully aware,
     And like a brilliant sun in the summer sky
     his beautiful gaze held all eyes
     like a full moon in autumn.

CHORUS: Homage to the World Honored One.

9.   For like the sun he awakened all the life on earth
     the trees and the children, deer and little fish,
     He woke up stars in the night that whispered to one another,
     He woke up seas and breezes, the tall mountains that nail the
     universe shut, and the streams in the mountains that flow
     to the rivers like tongues.

CHORUS: Homage to the World Honored One.

10. And standing straight like a mountain attending above and
        below,
     He took seven silver steps his feet lifted up unwavering
     and straight the strides spanning earth and heaven
     ONE   TWO   THREE   FOUR   FIVE   SIX   SEVEN

CHORUS: Homage to the World Honored One.

11. And like a lion in charge of the forest
     Like an elephant ruling the grounds,
     Proclaimed the truth and sang: "I am born for
     Enlightenment,
     for the good of all beings!"

CHORUS: Homage to the World Honored One.

12. Hot and cold running water like jewels from the sky poured
     forth for his refreshment,
     The softest couch appeared

bedecked with pears and apples flowers potatoes lettuce
   and peas.
The invisible dwellers in the heaven shielded him
with their giant umbrellas.

CHORUS: Homage to the World Honored One.

13. And the dragons of the earth and air
   flew and blew the air for him.
   And the dragons of the seas
   tipped the purple waves with points of silver,
   And the dragons of the houses
   flapped the houses like nightgowns, bedsheets
   or banners.

CHORUS: Homage to the World Honored One.

14. And animals stopped eating one another
   to take a look,
   And people stopped killing one another
   to take a look,
   And noxious creatures and ghosts stopped haunting one
      another
   to take a look—
   they all looked and wept with unconsidered joy.

CHORUS: Homage to the World Honored One.

15. For he will give up his kingdom to be a light removing
   darkness from all beings,
   And he will be a boat to carry the beings up from
   the ocean of suffering overspread with
   the foam of disease
   and the waves of old age and the flood of death,
   And the world will drink of the stream of his Law
   to slake the ageless thirst born of affliction.

CHORUS: Homage to the World Honored One.

16. People are lost in the desert
    baked and blistered—
    he will show them a trail out.
    People are sweltering in the humidity of desire—
    he will rain the cool rain of Dharma down.
    People are locked up in themselves—
    he will offer the key of awakening to open up the doors.

CHORUS: Homage to the World Honored One.

17. He will cool us with the tractors of concentration,
    He will make us solid with precepts like pine trees,
    He will cause us to dance with the joy
    of the ducks of deepest vows.

CHORUS: Homage to the World Honored One.

18. And so in this world and in the world beyond,
    in time and space and out of time and space,
    The baby's steps and the song ended struggles
    that had no end
    And all beings were permanently
    disordered with delight.

CHORUS: Homage to the World Honored One.

Sandy Eastoak

❦

The Wheel of the Year

In our eclectic household, the most accessible means for sharing spiritual celebration is marking the cycle of the seasons. Although we come from Buddhist, Moslem, and Roman Catholic traditions, our holidays are borrowed from ancient European pagans.

The old cycle of the year was marked by two solstices, two equinoxes, and four midpoints between each of these pairs. In our household, four adults and five children aged two to seven, we observe these holidays in order to bring our awareness to the cycles of nature, attune our lives to these natural cycles, harmonize our divergent religious practices and family heritages, and provide meaning and fun for the children. We hope to deepen each individual's private journey and to find, strengthen, and rejoice in shared experiences.

I first began celebrating winter solstice in 1969 when Christmas no longer held my religious beliefs. Even then I could foresee a need to celebrate the other points of the year, but it took years gradually to formalize these. This past year was the first in which we celebrated all eight fully. I noticed with some emotion that this year I have not once felt that embarrassing sensation, "Oh, my, where did summer go?" or "Is it almost winter already?" I have been in tune with the passage of time and the change of seasons.

I am not sure how to give my children Buddhism. However, in the cycle of the year, we can become aware of the mighty movements of nature and all its echoes in the largest and smallest cycles of our lives. If Buddha is not here, where?

Winter Solstice—December 21

This is the time of greatest darkness—and also the time when the light returns. It is the longest night of the year; from now on the days grow longer. Nature is in quiescence. Plants have died back, lost their leaves, and become dormant. Animals have hidden themselves away, gone south, or turned to our feeding stations. It is a time for us to slow down also, to go within, confront loss and failure, and pare down to the kernel that will seed the growth of the next cycle.

Our celebration of winter solstice is very Christmas-like—in fact, *all* the elements of Christmas were found in pre-Christian pagan yule festivals, right down to the virgin mother of a divine child, originally a parable for the return of light to the winter dark world

The central symbols are the tree and lights. The ancient custom of cutting a tree and bringing it inside as a symbol of the rebirth of spring promised by the returning sun was appropriate in the thick-forested land of its origin. Today, when deforestation is a global threat, rebirth can only be symbolized by a live tree, which will soon be planted as *our* promise to nurture return of abundant life.

We hold a ceremony of light, which has changed and evolved as we learn and grow. We may have each person stand at a light switch (candles may be used if children are old enough) and turn them off one by one, remembering privately or aloud a loss of the year past. After a time of meditation in the darkness, a procession of children carrying lights proclaims the return of the sun. Each person then turns his or her light back on. Then we gather around a bowl of scented water that has been sprinkled with glitter. The water is sprinkled on each person's head to bless her or him with the returning light.

Another ceremony for the Winter Solstice is a peace ceremony. Ours usually includes peace chants and songs and, depending on the energy of the children present, a meditation and visualization on world peace. On this occasion we join PEACE THE 21ST ceremonies that take place around the world on the Sunday before the solstices and equinoxes.

Finally, we have a traditional feast and exchange gifts. We enjoy the fruits of the preparations that have kept the children excited throughout the month: decorating the tree, learning carols, baking cookies (especially the kinds that can be stored before eating), reading seasonal stories and poems, and shopping for, making, and wrapping gifts. We sing songs, welcome friends, drink wassail, and share love and good wishes. In a few days or weeks, depending on the weather, we plant our tree.

Candlemas or Imbolg—February 2

This is also a festival of light, with a different emphasis. Now we are halfway between winter and spring. The light has been returning slowly to us. We have passed the nadir or turning of the year. As the life hidden in seeds and buds is invisibly stirring, so in us the plans and promises of a new year's endeavors are taking shape.

Now we use candles to symbolize the careful nurturing of new beginnings and to celebrate gentle, exact attention to the special needs of delicate new growth. Outdoor work is just beginning—planning the garden, tending the compost, repairing the disorder wrought by winter weather. We find in ourselves the stirring toward new projects.

We may celebrate this time by standing around a table, each with a candle to light in honor of a wish or plan for the coming year. We visualize our best intentions bearing fruit. We read a story or poem that expresses the meaning we seek. We watch the sky, the birds.

Spring Equinox—March 21

The ancient name for the Spring Equinox was Oestre. In Iran, where my husband grew up, this is the biggest holiday of the year—Nourooz or New Year's. We set up a special table used in Persian tradition which is covered with a special patterned cloth. On it we place sprouted grain, a bowl of goldfish, flowers, colored eggs, a mirror, and seven items beginning with "s" (in Persian): apples, two kinds of spice, coins, greens, vinegar, garlic.

We also have an Easter egg hunt. The Easter egg custom originated in ancient Persia and was common all over pagan Europe as a means of celebrating the new fertility of spring. We dress in new clothes, welcome our friends, feast, and chant for peace. We play music together and enjoy Persian delicacies.

In ourselves we enjoy the warm happiness (and a little uncertainty) that comes with the bursting forth of spring in all its rich promise. As in our garden, we will learn by harvest time which promises are to be fulfilled and which are not. Planting the garden, we are confident that all will flourish and we picture the lush order. Later the gophers and slugs and late frosts will set us straight, reminding us how "with the ideal comes the actual."

Beltane—May 1

This is the holiday of flowers celebrating the fertility of the earth. (Between Nourooz and Beltane, my family makes an annual pilgrimage to the nearest Zen center for the flower celebration of Buddha's birthday.) We usually begin this day by gathering flowers with the children from whatever our field and garden may provide this early. We thank the garden for the richness it is beginning to offer, and we await the arrival of friends, with whom we will romp, play, laugh, and indulge youth and silliness.

In ancient times, quite lascivious means were used to enjoy this day. We express our wantonness by setting up a day of children's games. While all the children enjoy themselves, we adults draw a fresh breath of air deep into our often forgotten child-selves, reveling in outdoing one another in making fools of ourselves. For some reason, the game "duck, duck, goose" seems to work especially well for this purpose.

Inwardly, it's a time to use the fertility of life, imagination, and communal energies to nurture our work and set us firmly in the right direction. In the garden we are finishing planting and beginning the right practice of weeding, watering, and maintenance. The excitement of putting in seed and seedlings and imagining the pleasures of the distant harvest is giving way to the day-to-day, repetitive responsibility of nurturing. It is a fully outward time, as we go into the world to care actively for what we wish to grow and harvest. This is a time of involvement and interaction.

Summer Solstice — June 21

Although this is the time of the return of darkness, this is not explicitly celebrated. Rather we mark the fullness — the longest day, the greatest light. As the *I Ching* says, "Be not sad, be like the sun at midday." We have climbed up the year and there is nowhere to go now but down. When the circle is full, emptying begins. But it is not a time to celebrate emptiness; rather, we enjoy fullness.

The garden is lush, days are hot, and nights are warm. We are in the heat of our plans and projects. The world around and within us teems with life. This we celebrate. We pause in the work, the movement, to feel the fullness, to express gratitude, and to strengthen awareness of the gifts that are ours and the natural flow of abundance.

Inwardly we evaluate and choose our means toward completion and harvest. We share summer food with friends. We chant for peace. We make music together. We dance. We sit on the back porch into the summer night.

Lammas — August 2

The tradition of this feast day is that the first bread shall be baked from this year's grain. We don't grow wheat, so sometimes we bake bread symbolically, or sometimes we create food emphasizing the sacredness of our backyard harvest. This past year we served a food mandala: black, red kidney, and pale garbanzo beans, carrots, zucchini, cucumbers, peppers, beets, and tomatoes arranged beautifully on a big platter.

We also had a corn ceremony. We sat in a circle, marked out by sprinkled cornmeal, and passed an ear of unhusked corn, each person taking time to look, touch, and contemplate how each kernel was filled after a pollen grain traveled the length of a silk. We passed a tray of fruits, each feeding our neighbor.

Then we had a play day for the children, with friends once again joining us for games on the lawn. The feeling is slightly different from the May celebration—a little less revelry, a bit more friendship.

It always touches me how in August—even in the heat of summer—I can begin to smell winter decay. The colors and smells change subtly. We begin to feel at this time how quickly indeed life passes away. So while we play together, we also reach out hands and hearts to comfort each other toward the end we can see foreshadowed in this peak of giving. The corn fills out the ear, and the stalks ready themselves for death. Purposes are playing themselves out. Ends are appearing logically. We turn our attention to the completion of projects, of tying ends together during the next weeks, toward the slowing and inner focusing of the year's end.

Autumn Equinox—September 21

This for me is the real time of Thanksgiving, fitting naturally into the wheel of the year and not tacked politically into the last Thursday of November. The harvest is being completed, both in the garden and in our own work. There remain pumpkins and chard, turnips, a few tomatoes, but the richness, the sure overflow of ripe activity, is past. Weather grows uncertain, the stragglers may or may not grow to fruition. We naturally meditate on the passing of things and begin to lay up food for a long, lean time.

We make a feast of appreciation of the abundant time, that will soon be gone. We deepen our awareness that the peak is past and celebrate our hope that what we have harvested will sustain us through the dead time. We feast with friends, chant for peace, and tell stories. We pass the time in gentleness and kindness.

Halloween or Samhain — October 31

In the old lunar calendar, Samhain was the extra day (thirteen 28-day months equals 364 days, hence the expression "a year and a day") between the old year and the new. It was believed that the veil between the world of the living and the world of the dead lifted and communication between the two — for good or ill — was easily made.

Despite the provocative implications, we mainly make this a children's holiday, partly in response to their excited anticipation. They love this one. (Is it because they crossed between the two worlds not so long ago?)

We use construction paper to make black cats, jack-o-lanterns, and paper chains. We have a party with just the right combination of scary and safe activities for the ages of our kids — including songs, stories, games, and a puppet show. We take the biggest pumpkin from our frost-damaged garden and make the scariest jack-o-lantern we can, letting its candle burn deep into the night to keep bad spirits away.

We take time out from the revelry to name those who have died during the last year, ringing our meditation bell after each name, being with each other in a solemn, thick quiet. In our hearts we make connections with the world of the dead, with lost loved ones, with our ancestors, and with the awesome mystery of birth and death. We look to nature, to the garden for clues: the disappearance of abundance, the paling, storing of life, the gathering into hiding places of the life forces that will, after the long dark rest, burst forth again.

Rafe Martin

❀

The Wise Quail

Once, the Buddha was a wise quail, the leader of a flock. One day, a hunter came into the forest. Imitating the quails' own calls, he began to trap unwary birds.

The wise quail noticed that something was amiss. Calling his flock together, he announced, "My fellow quail, I am afraid that there is a hunter in our forest. Many of our brothers and sisters are missing. We must stay alert. Danger is all around us. Still, if we work together we can stay free. Please listen to my plan. If you should hear a whistling call—*twe whee! twe whee! twe whee!*—as if a brother or sister were calling, be very watchful! If you follow that call, you may find darkness descending upon you. Your wings may be pinned so that you cannot fly, and the fear of death may grip your heart. If these things happen, just understand that you have been trapped by the hunter's net and *do not give up!* Remember, if you work together you can be free.

"Now, this is my plan. You must stick your heads out through webs of the net and, then, you must all flap your wings together. As a group, though you are still bound in the net, you will rise up into the air. Fly to a bush. Let the net drape on the branches of the bush so you can each drop to the ground, and fly away from under the net, this way and that, to freedom. Do you understand? Can you do this?"

"We do understand," answered all the quail as one, "and we will do it! We will work together and be free."

Hearing this, the wise quail was content.

The very next day a group of quail were pecking on the ground when they heard a long whistling call. *Twe whee! twe whee! twe whee!* It was the cry of a quail in distress! Off they rushed.

Suddenly darkness descended on them and their wings were pinned. They had indeed been trapped by the hunter's net. But, remembering the wise quail's words, they did not panic. Sticking their heads out through the webs of the net they flapped their wings together, harder and harder and slowly, slowly, with the net still draped upon them, they rose, as a group, through the air. They flew to a bush. They dropped down through the bush, leaving the net hung on the outer branches, then flew away, each in their own direction, this way and that, to freedom. The plan had worked! They were safe! They had escaped from the jaws of death. And, oh, they were happy!

But the hunter was not happy. He could not understand how the quail had escaped him. And this happened not just once, but many times. At last, the hunter realized the truth. "Why," he said, amazed, "those quail are cooperating! They are working together! But it can't last. They are only birds, featherbrains, after all. Sooner or later they will argue. And when they do, I shall have them." And so, he was patient.

Now, the wise quail had had the same thought. Sooner or later the birds of his flock would begin to argue, and when that happened they would be lost. So he decided to take them deeper into the forest, far from their present danger.

That very day something happened to confirm the wise quail's thought.

A quail was pecking on the ground for seeds when another bird of the flock, descending rapidly, accidentally struck it with its wingtip. "Hey! Watch it, stupid!" called the first quail, in anger.

"Stupid is it?" responded the newly-landed quail, flustered because he had been careless. "Why are you so high and mighty? You were too dumb to move out of my way! Yes, you were too dumb—you dumb cluck!"

"Dumb cluck is it?" cried the first quail, "Dumb cluck? Why, talking of dumb, it's clear that you can't even land without slapping someone in the face! If that isn't 'dumb,' I don't know what is! Who taught you to fly anyway—the naked-winged bats?"

"Bats is it?" yelled the second quail, enraged, "Bats? Why, I'll give you a bat, you feathered ninny!" And with a loud chirruping whistle he hurled himself straight at the other quail.

Chasing furiously after one another, loudly hurling insults and threats back and forth, they flew, twisting and turning, between the great, silent trees of the grove. An argument had started and, as is the way of arguments, no end was in sight.

The wise quail was nearby and he heard it all. At once he knew that danger was again upon them. If they could not work together the hunter was sure to have them.

So again he called his flock together and said, "My dear brother and sister quail. The hunter is here. Let us go elsewhere, deeper into the forest and there, in seclusion, discipline ourselves, practicing our skills in working together. In this way we shall become truly free from the danger."

Many of the birds said, "Though we love our present home, we shall go with you, Wise Quail. The danger is great and we wish to find safety."

But others said, "Why go from this pleasant spot? You yourself, Wise Quail, have taught us all we need to know in order to be free. We know what to do. We just have to stick our heads out, flap our wings together, and fly away. Any dumb cluck can do it! We're going to stay."

So some of the birds flew off with the wise quail, while the others stayed.

A few days later, while some of those who stayed were scratching around for their dinner, they heard a whistling call. *Twe whee! twe whee! twe whee!* They ran to answer the call when suddenly, darkness descended upon them. Fear gripped their hearts. They were trapped in the hunter's net! But, remembering the wise quail's teaching, they stuck their heads through the net, and one bird said, "On the count of three we all flap. Ready? One, two, thr—"

"Hey!" called another bird, "Who made you boss? Who said you could give the orders?"

"I'm the hardest worker and the strongest," said the first bird. "When I flap my wings, the dust rises from the earth and whirls up in the clouds. Without me you'd never get this net off the ground. So I give the orders, see?"

"No, I don't see!" shouted another bird. "What you've just described is nothing. Why, when I flap my wings, all the leaves move on the trees, the branches bend and even the trunks sway. That's how strong I am. So if anyone should be giving orders around here it's me!"

"No, me!" shouted a third bird.

"Me!" yelled a fourth.

"No! No! Listen to me!" screamed the first bird again above the rising din. "Flap! Flap! Flap! I tell you. Flap your wings all together when I say 'three!'"

But no one flapped. They just argued and argued. And as they argued, the hunter came along and found them and their fate, alas, was not a happy one.

But the quail who had gone off deeper into the safety of the great forest learned, under the wise quail's guidance, how really to cooperate. They practiced constantly, until they were, indeed, able to work together without anger or argument.

Though the hunter tried many times to catch them he never could.

And if he never caught them, why, they're still free today.

Part Four

❧

Simple Teachings

Sahel Eastoak-Siletz, age five

※

My Little Tiny Buddha

my little tiny Buddha
is a very treat
I can hold it in my hand
and feel better
my big Buddha
in the medicine wheel
that's my whole family's
when I'm sad
I go to her
and/or him
and I be nice to it
if it's a she
or a he
I don't know which
one it is
I never knew
I like to sit here
with Buddha
sometimes I go inside
and do some
meditating
and that's all
and that's all

Thich Nhat Hanh

※

Buddha and the Banana

I would like to tell you a story of a monk named Hu, who was my student. In 1964, he became the director of the School of Youth for Social Service in Vietnam. He trained young people, young monks and young nuns, to go out into the countryside and help people to rebuild their villages, which had been bombed by airplanes. But when he was young, about six or seven years young, he asked his father and mother to let him go to the temple to become a monk. I'll tell you why.

He used to go to the Buddhist temple every fortnight, on the first new day of the month and on the fifteenth day of the month. The new moon and the full moon days, he went to the temple to offer flowers and bananas and mangoes. He noticed that every time he went to the temple, he was treated very nicely. But when he went home or to school and elsewhere, people were not as nice as at the temple. Do you know why? Because when people come to the temple, they practice smiling, breathing, so they are nicer than elsewhere.

Each time he came, the head monk would give him a mango or tangerine, and so he loved going to the temple. One day he said, "Mommy, I want to become a monk and live in a temple."

I think he wanted to become a Buddhist because he liked to eat bananas; I don't blame him. Finally, his father and mother let him go to the temple as a novice. When he was fourteen, he came to study with me and he told me this story.

He believed that the Buddha loved bananas, mangoes, and tangerines, because every time people went to the temple, they brought bananas, mangoes, and tangerines to offer to the Buddha. It must mean that the Buddha loved these things very much. So he was interested to see how a Buddha would eat a banana. One day, he waited until the people all went home and he stood outside of the Buddha hall. He peered into the Buddha hall to see how a Buddha would pick up a banana and eat it, because the statue of the Buddha was as big as a human being.

He imagined that the Buddha would take a look to make sure that everyone had gone home and then the Buddha would reach out for a banana. The young boy waited and waited and waited for hours and did not see the Buddha picking up a banana. He could not understand why the Buddha did not eat the bananas that the people kept bringing to the temple.

The young boy did not dare to ask the head monk, because he was afraid that the monk would say that he was crazy or silly. Actually, young people often feel like that. We have something in us and we don't want to say it, because we risk being called silly. So the same thing was true for that young monk. He didn't dare to ask, so he suffered. He suffered, but nobody knew. He suffered because he could not understand. But Hu did not go to anyone. He had to fight alone.

One day, he got enlightened. He realized a very important thing: that the Buddha statue is not the Buddha. What an achievement! He was so glad. And then he said, "If the Buddha is not in the Buddha hall, where should we find him or her?" The question made him suffer a lot, because everyone came to the temple and bowed to the statue of the Buddha. And now he had found out that the Buddha statue is not the Buddha.

When he met me at the age of fourteen, I was able to tell him that the Buddha is in here, the Buddha is our capacity of loving and understanding. I taught him like this: "A doctor is a doctor because he has something different from other people. That something is the capacity to understand diseases and to help heal people. So without that kind of knowledge and capacity, people cannot be called doctors, right? A Buddha is different from other people because he or she has this capacity of awakening, loving, and understanding, you see?"

Anywhere you see understanding and loving, you see the Buddha, and as you practice, you see that in yourself there is the capacity of loving and understanding. You know that the Buddha is within yourself. Therefore, when we bow, the Buddha begins to become real in you. Looking for the Buddha, we have to look in ourselves.

Ken Tanaka

❀

Jodo Shin Teachings
for Young People

The Dharma school had a profound impact on my own early Buddhist education. The dedicated group of volunteer teachers planted in me a seed of curiosity that became one of the primary reasons for choosing Buddhist scholarship and ministry as my career. As Buddhists of varying traditions explore the subject of religious education in this country, I believe the Jodo Shinshu experience can serve as a valuable resource.

The Buddhist Churches of America has represented the Jodo Shinshu tradition in America since 1899. Urgently concerned with youth education, it established Sunday school in 1913. By 1930, these schools were operating in fifty-six temples with a total of approximately 7,000 students.

With the rapid increase in the number of young children in the 1920s, the missionary priests from Japan and their wives could no longer conduct these classes by themselves. Efforts were made to recruit and train lay instructors, particularly among the members of the Young Buddhist Association. English instructional materials came to be in increasing demand since the students and the growing number of lay instructors were American-born. These instructional materials produced before World War II served as model for much of the subsequent materials created after the war.

In 1960, Reverend Ensei Nekoda, the new director of the Sunday School Department at the San Francisco headquarters, began promoting a multiresource approach including audio-visual media and curricula based on thematic presentation of Buddhist lessons. A few years later the department came under the jurisdiction of the Bureau of Buddhist Education, which coordinated various programs for youth religious training: the Youth Department, Sales Department (books), Audio-Visual Department, Boy Scout Committee, and public programs.

During the 1980s, a major project was undertaken to update and systematize the textbooks from kindergarten through high school. This prodigious project has now been completed, thanks in great measure to the efforts of the late Mrs. Etsuko Steimetz. Today, the Buddhist Education Department is under the leadership of another educator, Reverend Carol Himaka.

Following is a condensed section from a pamphlet I wrote and the department recently published.[1] The pamphlet addresses my ardent desire to make the Dharma accessible to young readers by directly addressing their immediate concerns. Buddhist teachings need not be esoteric, exotic, and mystical. I believe the essential teachings of the Buddha can be fully appreciated by thoughtful young Americans when presented directly, honestly, and innovatively.

A Three Step Process of Everyday Reflections and Action for Young People

Don't you think the Buddhist teaching is too difficult to understand?
You may be right, if you mean its philosophical doctrines. But you will find the basic teachings surprisingly down to earth.

Can I apply it to my everyday concerns and problems?
Yes. The Buddha's spiritual journey began with his desire to solve the problems that deeply bothered him. What personal concerns are bothering you?

Well, I can think of several, but the one I am struggling with now is how to cope with my recent breakup with my former girlfriend. Also, I very much feel the loss of my grandmother, who passed away last year. Another "monkey on my back" is difficulty getting along with some of my peers.

You are not alone in being concerned with such problems. In fact, the Buddha mentioned them specifically. However, before talking about them in detail, I would like to present the basic teaching in a somewhat "provocative" manner.

How is that?

I propose "a three-step process of everyday reflection and action." This is simply one among many approaches in helping interested seekers apply the Jodo-Shinshu Buddhist teaching to their lives. You may adopt it whole or in part, to meet your unique personal needs.

What are the three steps?

1. "Think BIIG!" 2. "Wake up!" and 3. "Give back!"

Please explain what you mean by "think BIIG."

The BIIG stands for the four basic truths about life which are taught in virtually all schools of Buddhism.

1. Life is a *B*umpy road (in Sanskrit, Duhkha)
2. Life is *I*mpermanent (Anitya).
3. Life is *I*nterdependent (Anatman, "non-self").
4. Life can be *G*reat (Nirvana).

Please explain a little more.

"Life is a Bumpy road" means that we all experience disappointments, anxiety, and sadness at some points in our lives. These bumps are built into our road of life. Some experience more bumps than others, but no one can avoid them. The bumps are not abnormal but are a natural part of our human existence. So, we shouldn't turn away from them, but turn them into lessons for personal growth.

"Life is Impermanent" means that nothing remains the same from one moment to the next. This is true for the atoms that make up our physical world, the movements in the distant galaxies, our relationship with our friends, and the feelings and thoughts that cross our minds. So, from a Buddhist perspective, every encounter is unique and precious. And if things are going badly now, one can find hope in knowing that things will surely get better.

"Life is Interdependent" means that I am a product of myriad causes and conditions that create who I am and how I feel. Like a wave in the ocean, I am essentially not separate from the universe. Just hold your breath for thirty seconds if you are not convinced. As this truth sinks in more, we cannot help being overwhelmed by the feeling of appreciation and belonging.

"Life can be Great" means that with the right view, I can find much joy and meaning in my life. At times, life seems pitch dark, but I can make an effort to bring some light through the teaching of the situation. Buddha admonished, "With our minds, we make the world." Life is very much what you choose to make it.

"Thinking BIIG" sounds clear enough, except for the first truth. Life should be happy. Why do you say that "life is a Bumpy road"?

Because it is! Buddhism asks us to see life squarely ("as it really is") and *not* ego-centrically ("how I want it to be"). Life can certainly be great (as the fourth truth states). But we must first see life as it really is. When we do, wouldn't you agree that life is a bumpy, rather than a smooth road?

The Buddha spoke about those bumps in explaining the first of the Four Noble Truths. These bumps, according to the Buddha are 1. illness, 2. aging, 3. death, 4. birth, 5. not getting what one desires, 6. being separated from loved ones, 7. having to associate with persons you do not get along with, and 8. being attached to the five components (of senses and thoughts) that we call "I" or "self."

All of us will experience these bumps some time or another. In fact, all three of your personal concerns are mentioned—the breakup with your girlfriend is #6, the death of your grandmother is #3, and difficulty with your peers is #7.

Unfortunately, our society tends to shove them under the rug. We are made to feel guilty talking about them since these bumps are often seen as failures and even punishments. But they are just as real as our happy experiences.

How does "thinking BIIG" help me?

It gives one a "bigger picture" of things. Have you noticed that when you are down or depressed, more often than not you are carrying your heavy "ego" on you shoulders? You're only "thinking small," saying to yourself, "Why can't things go my way?" or "People don't appreciate what I do for them," or "Why can't the world understand me better?" When you're thinking small, you're not getting a full and clear picture of life.

But when you "think BIIG," you are more in tune with the rhythm of life and the universe. You are able to see yourself more clearly and get a better understanding of others and the world. Like good medicine, "thinking BIIG" may be difficult to swallow, but will help you feel better mentally and be uplifted spiritually.

"Thinking BIIG" offers a general way of looking at life, but please suggest concrete guidelines for action.

Perhaps the well-known Six Paramitas can fulfill your needs. Please realize that we modern lay persons with school, work, and family obligations will not be fully able to live up to these high ideals. Nevertheless, the Paramitas point us in the right direction and clarify our ideals.

1. Being open to other views and giving of yourself (Other-centered sharing—Dana)
2. Being responsible to oneself and others in one's action (Conduct—Shila)
3. Making an earnest, sincere effort to resolve problems (Effort—Viriya)
4. Being patient, so as not to expect immediate solutions (Patience—Kshanti)
5. Being mindful of one's mind so as to be honest with one's feelings, to cultivate the mind of equanimity with regard to others and not to insist always on one's views and expectations (Mindfulness—Samadhi)
6. Being aware of the truths of BIIG (Wisdom—Prajna)

Of these, Wisdom is the most important and basic, since it determines how the other five Paramitas are practiced. Your deeper personal appreciation of the truth of BIIG is vital!

How about the second step, "Wake up!"?

By "thinking BIIG" you are helped in "waking up" to the two dimensions of yourself: the small self and the Big Self. This second step points to the heart of Jodo-Shinshu teaching. "Waking up" has to do with a deeper spiritual level and a more mature awareness of oneself and the world.

What do you mean by "small self"?

The small self is the imperfect, limited dimension of yourself. As you "think BIIG" with regard to events in your life, you will inevitably come to gain a more realistic picture of your self. It becomes difficult to live up *fully* to "thinking BIIG."

For example, you find some comfort in knowing that all relationships undergo changes, often ending in separation. You are not alone. And you try to accept the outcome. But ... the heart has a difficult time keeping up with the head. You still miss her terribly and wonder, "Why is this happening to me?" In moments of weakness, you resist and don't want to hear that "Life is impermanent" because you are hurting so badly.

In "losing" someone, we often realize how dependent we actually are on others. We would like to think of ourselves as rugged, self-reliant individuals. But we are emotionally devastated when we lose that someone special. Gradually, we wake up to our real condition, one which is dependent and in need of someone special to depend on and to share life experiences with. Thus, when we hear that "Life is interdependent," it hits home as a deeply personal truth.

Shinran Shonin[2] probed even deeper into our human nature and concluded that our motives and even our very existence were essentially self-centered. For example, without taking the life of some living beings for food, we cannot survive for long!

Then what do you mean by "Big Self"?

This is the collection of innumerable factors that sustain and nurture one's small self. The Big Self includes the water that quenches our thirst, the myriad foods that nourish our body, and the warm sunlight that gives life to all living things. The Big Self also includes the sources that uplift our spirit: the beauty of nature in its myriad expressions of wonder, the inspiration derived from great works of art and musical performance, and the thrill of unbelievable athletic accomplishments. The Big Self is further represented by the absolute love and care of our family, the teacher's encouragement and sharing of knowledge that give us greater confidence in ourselves, and our friends' concern for us when we are down.

This Big Self is, thus, none other than the Universe. Its cosmic compassion is revealed to us as everyday compassion. Shinran Shonin deeply experienced the peaceful joy of being embraced by this "Other Power":

> Oh, how happy I am! I have experienced the Tathagata's[3] compassion deeply, and I sincerely cherish the kindness of my teacher.[4] Happiness abounds and reverence grows deeper. . . .

How are the small self and the Big Self related to each other?

They are two dimensions of the same life. The small self is like the wave, which is minuscule in size and duration compared to the ocean. The Big Self is the ocean. The wave, in reality, is not separate from the ocean, but is one with it. In fact, the wave has *always* been connected to the ocean, but it is mistakenly perceived as separate. So long as the self is perceived only as the wave, one is bound to disappointments and feelings of abandonment. However, when a person wakes up to the fact that the self is the wave *as well as* the ocean, he cannot help but experience an abiding sense of Oneness. This is accompanied by feelings of being embraced and assured that "all is fundamentally well," for even when the wave is exhausted, it simply returns to the immense ocean which awaits with open arms.

What do you mean by the third step, "Give back!"?

As we come to lead a more Buddhistic life, we feel a spontaneous desire to acknowledge the enormous indebtedness and gratitude that we feel toward the rest of the world. This would be felt with our heart, with our total being, not merely with our head. This is expressed in the "Shinshu Creed":

> I shall respect and help my fellow beings, and work for the good of my community.

And when we recite the "Golden Chain" we promise:

> I shall keep my link bright and strong. I shall be kind and gentle to every living thing and protect those who are weaker than myself.

Isn't helping others easier said than done?

Yes, I believe you are expressing a Jodo-Shinshu understanding of human nature. Due to our own needs and obligations, we fall far short of our expectations to help others as much as we wish to. And when we are able to give back to the world, we should not be motivated by a desire to "be a good person" or "feel righteous." What we give back pales in comparison to what we have actually received. We will never be able to return fully our debt to the world.

Does that mean we shouldn't give back?

No, it's not a moral question of someone else telling you whether you should or shouldn't help. A person who sincerely tries to walk the Jodo-Shinshu path will do their share to give back to the world. Such persons will do this out of heartfelt joy, appreciation, and concern for others. The amount and kind of sharing will differ, according to their respective live circumstances.

What are some concrete ways that I can give back?

The best way has always been to share the Dharma (teaching) with others. The Dharma brings about the greatest genuine happiness, more so than wealth, status, or popularity. You can teach Dharma school, speak to your friends about Buddhism, and support the Sangha in its educational programs. Of course, becoming a minister yourself will enable you to touch the lives of many more people.

I don't know enough about the Dharma to share with others, but I feel I can do other things "to work for the good of my community."

Don't give up learning more about the Dharma, for without a firm religious centering, anything you do for others will often become self-serving. While you continue to study and seek the Dharma, there are other ways you can give back. The Honpa Hongwanji Mission in Hawaii has suggested several:

1. Give blood/plasma to the Blood Bank.
2. Green our environment: plant trees.
3. Be mindful of fuel consumption: carpool, ride the bus, walk more; use less water, gas, electricity.
4. Show care and concern for those suffering illness, grief, homelessness; provide transportation for the aged/disabled.
5. Convey to everyone warm feelings at temple services and activities. Make everyone feel welcome.
6. Sing, write, create Buddhist music.
7. Dance in joy at Bon Dances.
8. Learn CPR, First Aid, Sign Language.
9. Understand other religions/denominations with an open, respectful mind.
10. Speak out/write about misconceptions of Buddhism.

What will be the outcome in my life when I try to live the teaching through the Three-Step Process?

Of course, the outcome will vary according to the individual. I am confident that if you apply the teaching with diligence and sincerity you will realize a greater degree of three vital aspects of Shinjin-awareness:

Appreciation—our fundamental outlook that life is a privilege, not a right.

Acceptance—our realization about our own imperfections and limitations and about the fact that we are unconditionally accepted and embraced by the limitless cosmic compassion we call "Amida."

Action—the energetic involvement with the concerns of other people, animals, plants and things because you cannot help but keep your link in the cosmic net of Interdependence bright and strong!

I wish you the best.

Notes

[1] Available from the Education Department, Buddhist Churches of America—see *Resources*.

[2] Shinran Shonin (1173–1262) was the founder of the Jodo Shinshu sect.

[3] In this case, "Tathagata" refers to Amida Buddha.

[4] Shinran Shonin's teacher was Honen (1133–1212).

Laurie Senauke

※

The Four Noble Truths
and Causation for Young People

The Four Noble Truths

Shakyamuni Buddha was a sensitive child. Although his parents did everything they could to shield him from suffering, his brief contacts with illness, aging, and death shocked him. He began a lifelong search to find an end to suffering—for himself and for all people.

As a young man he studied with all the wise teachers of his day. He found that they weren't able to get to the root of the problem. Finally, he sat down by himself under a tree, vowing to sit still until he had an answer. He sat in deep meditation for seven days, and his struggle with inner demons shook him to his core. On the morning of the seventh day he had a profound insight: "Wondrous! I now see that all beings everywhere have the wisdom and virtues of the enlightened ones, but because of misunderstandings and attachments they do not realize it." There's a story that illustrates this point:

A man visits a close friend, gets drunk, and falls asleep. His friend is called away on an important duty. Before he leaves he sews a priceless jewel inside his sleeping friend's coat as a gift. The sleeping man is unaware of this. After he wakes up, he travels to another country. He runs into trouble and becomes very poor. His friend happens to see him one day and says, "How did you get into such difficulties? Before I left you that night, I sewed a priceless jewel in your garment. Go now and trade it for what you need." Our Buddha nature is a priceless jewel inside each of us. We just need to discover it for ourselves.

The Buddha spent the rest of his life sharing his insight with others. He began by teaching a sermon called, "The Four Noble Truths." Here is a summary:

1. *Life, at least our usual way of life, is suffering.*
   People have great difficulty and suffering in their lives. Everything is always changing. Our bodies, hearts, minds, and the whole world are constantly changing. Because we don't look deeply at how things actually are, or take time to learn to live in harmony with the laws of the universe, we constantly struggle and suffer.

2. *Desire, or attachment, is the cause.*
   We want things to be exactly the way they aren't. We want permanent existence for ourselves and our loved ones. We're attached to the things we like, and we want to avoid the things we don't like. We want independence and control. At the same time we want everyone to love us. Since everything is constantly changing, there is no permanent existence, either for ourselves or for material things. Not only that, everything is connected to everything else. Everything is interwoven so completely that it's impossible to have the kind of independence and control that we want.

3. *There is a way out.*
   Once we know the cause, we can find a cure. We can learn to live in harmony with the true nature of reality, in harmony with all living things and with the laws of the universe.

4. *The Noble Eightfold Path is the way out:*
   Right Understanding
   Right Thought or Attitude
   Right Speech
   Right Action
   Right Livelihood
   Right Effort
   Right Mindfulness
   Right Concentration

The four noble truths are really a door into the whole world of Buddhist thought and practice. And it's a kind of circle. Through study and meditation, you can have a clear understanding and an attitude that works. As you become more aware of how you speak to others, you'll learn to speak with honesty and kindness. Your actions will be based on a sense of how everything is connected to everything else; this includes not hurting others, not stealing, not lying, not becoming intoxicated, not misusing sexuality. The way you earn your living will be in line with your beliefs—you won't profit from others' loss of life or others' suffering or addictions. Your efforts will be right on target. Your awareness and your ability to concentrate will increase and, like Buddha, you will have deep insight into the true nature of reality. This insight will help your life and benefit all beings.

Causation

One Zen Buddhist teacher said, "Our practice is the close study of cause and effect." In a way, there's only one truth—the truth of interdependence or interconnectedness. Earth, water, fire, air, animals, plants, and people are so intertwined that we can't really say where one thing ends and another begins. And everything's causing everything! Deep investigation of cause and effect will bring us to this truth. To undertake this study we need our most open mind—one that's calm, strong, unbiased, and flexible. The Buddha's suggestions, with the help of a trustworthy meditation teacher, can help you find this quality of open mind for yourself.

The Buddha does not ask us to accept this teaching on faith. Through still sitting and clear seeing you can experience it for yourself. Look closely, look deeply at your experience over a long period of time. You will experience for yourself the interconnectedness of all that exists. The more we investigate the causes of events and of our experience, going deeper and deeper, the more we will understand about how to act. And we will be able to act in harmony with all living beings.

The Buddha has a teaching about the chain of causation. First we have our senses—we see, hear, taste, smell, and touch. These are the building blocks of our experience. Then, we add feelings—we respond to the things we sense with like, dislike, or indifference. After feelings come cravings—we want the things we like, and we want to get rid of the things we don't like. So craving causes grasping—we attempt to control our world.

This grasping can be seen as our first active step away from harmony with the truth. It doesn't work because everything is in flux and not under our control. Even our desires are constantly changing. We don't like this, compared to that. We want what others have, but having it doesn't bring satisfaction. We're on to the next thing we want. Our desires are not fixed and dependable, but are dependent on changing conditions. They seem so real. We reach out to grasp, convinced that this thing we want will bring us happiness. But we don't create happiness this way. We only create ourselves again, running around looking for happiness.

To study cause and effect in your life, start with something simple, like a loaf of bread. Think of all the people—farmers, millers, truckdrivers, bakers—who had a hand in producing and delivering that loaf. Think of the knowledge going back centuries, the discovery of fire, the beginning of agriculture, the first accidental use of yeast. Think of the elements of nature—the soil, microbes, earthworms, wheat, sun, rain, and air. If you keep looking, you can find everything in the universe in that loaf of bread.

When I'm in difficulty, I take a moment to look at the causes, the many causes. Sometimes it's just enough to make me stop before I do something that will only make things worse. Sometimes I suddenly see a great solution to the problem.

It's very helpful to study cause and effect in this way. Even a glimpse of interconnectedness is a breath of fresh air in our lives. Meditation strengthens our ability to see interconnectedness. Our glimpses become more regular. Intense, steady contact with this liberating truth of cause and effect "brings forth the gold of the earth, and ripens the wine of the long river."

Ryo Imamura

❀

The Dukkha of Baseball

Do you like to watch major league baseball? Which is your favorite team? Having been raised in the San Francisco Bay Area, I still root for the San Francisco Giants and Oakland A's even though I now live in the state of Washington. Somehow I find it very difficult to get excited about the Seattle Mariners (true baseball fans will know what I mean).

Sometimes I feel foolish for getting so excited about some spoiled overpaid athletes, twenty years younger than me, who represent the Bay Area teams mainly because they are paid to. And it insults my big ego to think that some of them make more in one game than I do in a whole year and are still demanding more. Next year some of them might be playing for the Dodgers or Pirates or any other team depending on who offers them more money.

Even though I have those disturbing thoughts, I can't help but get excited watching them play. I have to marvel at their wonderful athletic skills. You see, I could never hit a curve ball, much less a split-fingered slider or knuckle ball.

The main difference between a major leaguer and minor leaguer is the major leaguer's ability to hit the curve ball. Almost everyone, with adequate practice, can hit a straight ball. But, to be a top

173

baseball player, you have to be able to hit the curve ball.

Did you know that, in the early days of baseball before the curve ball was invented, you could order your own straight pitch? You could dictate the speed and placement of the pitch. Most people are like the early batters. They want to dictate what life will bring them. They usually are thinking, "Do it my way or else."

For example, a child may think, "My parents won't let me do what I want, so I'll just act grumpy and fussy." A teenager might think, "I don't like the teacher, so I won't try very hard in her class." A parent may have the attitude, "I didn't get the pay raise I expected, so I'll threaten to quit or won't work as diligently." These individuals are unable to handle life's curve balls.

Unfortunately, life is full of curve balls such as illness, old age, bad grades, loss of job, income taxes, car breakdowns, death of a loved one, and disagreements. I'm sure you can think of many others. Some people will say, "Why did this happen to me? Poor me." Obviously they still expect straight balls down the middle of the plate.

Let us be reminded that the first of the Four Noble Truths states that life is dukkha, that is, full of curve balls. When we get thrown a curve ball, we Buddhists must say to ourselves, "Thank you for this valuable experience, for it has improved my self-awareness and appreciation." We Buddhists see life's curve balls to be challenges, opportunities for new beginnings, chances to become further enlightened, that is, to wake up to our true selves.

Let me give you a few examples. If a student receives a bad grade on an examination, he should accept with gratitude the reminder to study harder and be more diligent instead of blaming the teacher or looking for unfair questions. If a basketball player finds herself sitting on the bench a lot, she might be reminded that she needs to put more time into practice and conditioning instead of blaming the coach and the other players. If one is stuck behind a slow driver in the fast lane on the highway, it is much more fruitful to welcome the opportunity to practice the Paramita of Patience rather than curse the other driver and get high blood pressure. And when a loved one passes away, a Buddhist is reminded of the brevity of life and the need to practice wisdom and compassion with more conviction and energy.

Let's face it. Life is going to throw us a lot of curve balls when we least expect it. There's no running away from this reality. Just like the professional baseball player, we must train ourselves mentally and physically so that we can handle the curve balls. We had better be prepared or we are going to strike out.

Thich Nhat Hanh

❧

Meditation Practices for Children

Breathing

I would like to tell you something very important. Life is at this moment. We want to be right here when we eat, when we walk, when we drink juice or tea. If we are thinking about something else, then we miss what is right in front of us. There are many wonderful things in our life. We can get in touch with them if we know how to breathe.

"But," you may say, "I breathe all the time! What is so special about breathing?"

It is true that you breathe all the time. But very often we do not think about our breathing. It is just something we are doing.

But we can learn to pay attention to our breathing. Then we are able to pay attention to our life and the wonderful things around us. If we know how to breathe, we can get in touch with the the sunshine, the river, the clouds, our mother, our sister. This breathing is very simple to do, and very easy for children and adults to learn.

This is how we do it. "In" and "out" is the first lesson of breathing. When we breathe in and out, our breathing should be very gentle, very peaceful. Can you breathe in and out, gently and slowly, three times?

The more peaceful your breath is, the more peaceful you become. That is called conscious breathing or mindful breathing. Mindful simply means that we are paying attention to what we are doing, the way you must pay attention when you cross the street by looking very carefully.

When your breath becomes gentle and peaceful, you become gentle and peaceful. You are one with your breathing.

There is a wonderful gatha, or poem, about breathing. Can you learn this poem?

> In, out
> Deep, slow
> Calm, ease
> Smile, release
> Present moment, wonderful moment.

You can practice breathing mindfully by following this poem, saying it to yourself as you breathe in and breathe out. If you repeat the gatha three times, it will take you less than two minutes.

Your can also practice breathing mindfully in other ways. One way is counting the breath: you breathe in and you breathe out and you count "one." You breathe in and you breathe out and you count "two." Many people do that and they arrive at "ten" and begin again at "one." That is what we call breath counting.

There are also people who practice following their breath. They breathe in and they follow their in-breath with all their attention; they breathe out and follow their out-breath. That is called following the breath.

Mindful breathing can be applied in your daily life. You can make each day good by starting it with breathing and smiling. When you sit down with your family and you breathe together for two minutes, you start your day in a good way.

If during the day you see that you have two minutes, then you can practice whether you are lying down, walking or sitting, before your lunch break, after your lunch break, and so on. Once when I was a student, I had two exams in a row. Your know that if you take an exam you are exhausted, but what if fifteen minutes later, you have to take another exam? I found a place where there was grass. I lay down and looked at the blue sky, white clouds. I breathed in and out slowly for a few minutes and I renewed myself, and I did that second exam very well. All of you can do this during your day at school. If you find ways to practice breathing, you'll go home fresh and smiling. You will bring happiness to your family.

Everyone has to learn how to breathe. If you don't know how to breathe, you cannot cope with the difficulties in your life. Sometimes you are angry, sometimes you are in despair, sometimes you are sad, sometimes you are jealous.

When you breathe mindfully you can stop your thinking. Sometimes we suffer because we think too much. But if we pay attention to breathing in and breathing out, we become our breath. When we become our breath, we can cut through our thinking.

One day, the Buddha held a flower up in front of a community of 1,250 monks and nuns. Almost all of them were thinking very hard, "What is he doing? What is the real meaning behind it?" With all of that thinking, most of them did not get in touch with that flower. Only one person could do that—Mahakashyapa. He smiled, because he could get in touch with the flower. It was wonderful, and he smiled. The Buddha smiled back and said, "I have a treasure of wisdom, of enlightenment, and I have transmitted it to Mahakashyapa."

Mahakashyapa was breathing, and that is why he could get in touch with the flower. He penetrated deeply into the flower and the flower penetrated deeply into him. If someone presents you a flower and if you are not in the present moment, breathing mindfully, then you miss the flower.

Sitting Meditation

Once you know how to breathe slowly and peacefully, you can practice sitting meditation. If you are seven years or older, it may be quite easy for you to practice sitting meditation. If you are not yet seven, you may want to sit for only a short time before you get up. This is fine.

One way to practice sitting meditation is to gather ten pebbles or small rocks. Each person, young or less young, should have his or her own pebbles. To practice sitting meditation you simply follow the gatha and you breathe.

With your first breath you breathe in, saying to yourself, "in." Then you exhale, breathing "out." Your breaths should be real breaths. A real breath, a good breath, is a breath where you are concentrating. If, while breathing, you do not dwell completely on the in-and-out, and you think of something else, that breath is not perfect and therefore, you do it again. You do in-and-out until you are pleased with it, you have done it well.

Then you move to the second breath, "deep, slow." Breathing in, you say, "deep." Breathing out, you say, "slow." Make sure your breath is a good one. If it's not so good, then try it again. Deep, slow.

Now when you are pleased with the second breath, you move to the third one, which is "calm, ease." "Calm" means breathing in, I calm my body. "Ease" means I take it easy, I feel light, free, wonderful. Ease is one of the seven factors of enlightenment. Breathing out, I ease everything, all my muscles, all my tension. I ease everything.

Then you move to the fourth one. "Smile, release." Anytime we are angry or we are afraid, all the muscles on our face become very tense. Just look at someone who is angry, you can see the tension on his or her face. But if that person knows how to breathe in and out, smiling and releasing, the tension will be gone very quickly. Each person has a little bit of sorrow or suffering in his or her heart. Breathing out, we just let them go. That is release, liberation.

When you have finished the fourth line, you come to the wonderful conclusion of the gatha: "present moment, wonderful moment." Just sitting here and breathing and smiling like this— that is wonderful. When we go back to the present moment, we know that being able to sit, to breathe, and to smile like this is a wonderful thing. Many people do not have the opportunity to sit beautifully like this with friends and those they love. The present moment, if we know how to live it, becomes a wonderful moment.

After having completed the gatha, you pick one pebble and you put it on the other side. Then you begin again. "In, out, deep, slow, calm, ease, smile, release, present moment, wonderful moment." Make sure that each breath is successful. If it's not successful, you do it again. After the second gatha, pick up another pebble and put it on the other side. You do this until you have moved all your pebbles.

When you sit in meditation, you may choose any position—lotus position, half-lotus position, chrysanthemum position, or half-chrysanthemum position. Chrysanthemum position is whatever position you like. But look for a position you find most comfortable. The lotus position is when you put your left foot on your right thigh and your right foot on your left thigh. This is considered by humans to be the most beautiful and stable position. If I sit in lotus position, then my body is very stable. If you come and you push me, I will not fall over. When our body is stable, our mind will be stable too. In meditation, body and mind become one thing.

This practice will bring peace and happiness to us, especially when we have a problem. When we are suffering, it will bring us relief and calm. I tell you this out of my own experience. I suffered very much when bombs were being dropped in my village. There was a time when my brother was killed during the war and I suffered a lot. I had to practice this breathing in order to be calm, to release, to smile. That's why I was able to survive. Now I am sharing these wonderful methods with you.

If you feel wonderful and pleasant, your practice is successful. You don't need anybody to tell you whether it is successful or not—you know it.

What we realize in meditation is oneness of body and mind. Your breathing is the bridge between body and mind. Your breathing can unify body and mind.

Imagine a triangle: the line in the middle is the breath, and one line is the body and the other is the mind. The breathing brings body and mind together. When you sit in meditation and breathe with concentration, then your body, mind, and breath become one thing, and you have real concentration. You are truly yourself, there in that moment.

In our daily life, we're used to being distracted, our body in one place, our mind in another place. Sometimes some of our mind is in the past, and some of our mind wanders to the future, so we are not really whole, not really ourselves.

To be truly alive is to be able to get in touch with the wonderful things of life, like the sunrise, the sunshine, the beautiful sky, your beautiful young brother, your sweet mother, the good food you eat. But if you are possessed by worries, anxieties, anger, and hatred, you lose everything. Go back to the present moment. Breathe freely and get in touch with wonderful things, which I call true life. The practice of Buddhist meditation is the practice of going back to being alive and enjoying life.

The Bell of Mindfulness

Even if we try to practice breathing, we sometimes forget to be mindful. That is why we need something or someone to remind us. That is why the bell of mindfulness was invented.

When we hear the sound of the bell, we become mindful. We breathe in and out three times. Our breathing should be very gentle, very peaceful. The more peaceful it is, the more peaceful you become, because when you breathe like that, you breathe consciously.

You can get a bell for your own home. This is how to invite the bell. In my country, people do not say hitting the bell. They think that hitting something is not very nice. So instead we invite the bell to ring.

Every time we invite the bell, we have the intention of helping other people be mindful. Therefore, we should be mindful ourselves. If we are not mindful, how can we help other people be mindful? So when I am a bell-master, I have to prepare myself in order to be mindful before I invite the bell.

When I was sixteen years young, I was allowed to invite the bell for the first time. My teacher told me to bow to the bell, because the bell is a Bodhisattva, someone who is awake and trying to help other people to be awake. Therefore, I bowed to the bell like an awakened person. Breathing in, I knew that I was breathing in; breathing out, I knew that I was breathing out. I did that three times before inviting the bell. Later, I learned a very beautiful gatha:

Body and mind in perfect oneness.
I send my heart along with the sound of the bell.
May the hearers awaken from forgetfulness and transcend all
    anxiety and sorrows.

But you don't have to learn that by heart to be a bell-master. Holding the handle of the bell-inviter, I look deeply into it and I wake it up. That is what I call waking the bell, so that the bell will not be too surprised. You deal with the bell exactly as you deal with a baby, very gently. Then it will not be so big a surprise for the hearers, because if the sound of the bell is very strong, people will be too surprised.

Therefore, waking the bell up is very important. Mindfulness will be deeper. After waking up the bell, I invite it. As soon as I hear the bell, I begin to hold onto my breathing, breathing in and breathing out three times. "In, out, in, out, calming, smiling, calming, smiling, calming, smiling." After three breaths like that, I feel much better.

So, first I bow to the bell. Then I breathe three times. I hold the bell in my palm, holding it up beautifully at eye level.

I wake up the bell gently, then I invite the bell. I look at it deeply, smiling with it and breathing three times.
Then I put it down.

Practicing the bell, you feel peace in yourself and you help other people to feel peace in themselves. Our practice is the practice of peace and happiness.

182

Ari Gervon-Kessler

How I Meditate

The way I get into meditation is an easy and successful method.

First, I close my eyes, then while breathing in I say to myself "in" and when I breathe out I say "out." Then when I breathe in I say "deep." While I say these next words I pretend I am doing what I'm saying.

So when I say "deep" I take a deep breath in. Then I say "slow" and I breathe out slowly. The next one is "calm" which is for my breath in. Then "ease" is the exhale. Then I say "smile" while breathing in. Last of all I say "release" and I do just that. The whole time while inhaling and exhaling I do the feeling that the word is for.

To clear my mind of any thoughts I imagine that waves are going through my brain and knocking out any thoughts.

I am twelve years old and some of my hobbies are tennis, basketball, reading, and writing.

I enjoy meditating. It awakens my brain so I can think better and feel at peace with myself and others.

Deborah Hopkinson

❀

The Listening Place

A long long time ago, there was a girl named Myo who lived with her family in Japan. Their little cottage was on the side of a big mountain covered with meadows and pine trees. At the top of the mountain, there was the great temple of Bassui Zenji.

Each week, Myo went with her parents and other neighbors up to the top of the mountain to visit the temple. She liked to look at the smooth floors that shone like mirrors. She could even see herself in them. She liked to watch the long rows of monks chanting all together.

But most of all she liked the sounds of the bells. There were all kinds of temple bells. Some bells helped the monks to keep time while they chanted. Some bells announced that Bassui Zenji had arrived to give a talk. But the biggest and most beautiful bell of all was the great temple bell, which rang early every morning, calling all the people to come to the temple. That bell woke up the whole mountain!

After the monks chanted, Bassui Zenji would stand up and talk to all the parents and children, too. Myo liked Bassui Zenji. He was skinny and had a very bald head. His head was shiny just like the floors in the temple. And he always smiled at her and said hello as if he really was glad to see her. Sometimes Myo didn't listen very carefully because she was thinking about a story she had read, or about a tree in the meadow she wanted to climb. or a bird's nest she wanted to visit. And sometimes she listened very carefully but she could not understand all that the old man said because she was so little.

But one day, Bassui Zenji started to talk about birds. Myo liked birds more than just about anything, and so she lifted up her head and listened very very carefully.

Bassui Zenji was talking about how to listen to the birds sing. That's funny, thought Myo, everyone can listen to birds sing!

"You do not really hear the birds," said Bassui Zenji. "You must ask yourself the question, 'Who hears?' You must go to the place of *really listening* to the birds —and to all the other sounds — the wind in the trees, the temple bell in the morning, the woodcutter's axe in the forest."

Myo wondered about this. Where could she go to really hear the birds? Where was the listening place that Bassui Zenji was talking about?

She wanted to ask him, or to ask her mother or father, but she was too shy. Maybe I am the only one who doesn't know, she thought.

And so Myo decided that she would find the listening place all by herself. She loved to play in the fields and the pine forest near her cottage. After school, she would go and help her mother and father, and then she would be free to play and explore. She liked to look for flowers, hidden behind the stumps of old trees, and to watch the little mushrooms poke their heads out from under the moss.

Now, whenever Myo went to play, she tried to listen very hard to the birds. She listened to the birds while she sat at the top of a pine tree, where she could feel herself swaying gently every time the breeze blew.

She listened while she lay leaning against a warm rock on the hill, or when she was lying on the soft grass in the field looking up at the clouds rolling by.

Myo heard all kinds of birds. She heard the songs of the thrushes, the loud call of the bush warbler, and the soft voices of doves. But still, she could not find the listening place that Bassui had talked about.

"Maybe it is at the temple," she thought. So one day she walked by herself to the top of the hill and sat in the temple garden. It was a beautiful garden. It had a little stream and a bridge, and there was even a stone bench to sit on. Myo sat for awhile listening very hard. Then she noticed that the old teacher, Bassui Zenji, had come to sit beside her. He smiled.

"Hello, Myo. You are sitting here very quietly," he said.

"Yes," said Myo. "I am looking for the listening place that you told us about. I want to really hear the birds."

"Oh," he said. "Where have you been looking?"

"Well, I looked in the forest, and in the field, and in the top of a pine tree," said Myo.

"Those are good places to listen," said Bassui Zenji. "This is a good place, too. And whenever you come here, I will help you find the listening place. Do you hear the sparrow now?"

Myo sat on the bench with the old teacher for a little while. There were a lot of birds. She listened very hard. First there was a sparrow ... *chirp chirp chirp* ... and then everything was very quiet. And then a little thrush started calling to its mother to feed it— *chirrup chirrup chirrup*. After it flew away, Myo could hear a bush warbler crying out high in the trees—*toowee toowee toowee*.

One by one the birds sang and then it was quiet again. It felt good to sit and listen. She listened so hard she even forgot that she was trying to find the listening place.

"What do you hear?" asked the old teacher.

Just then a big crow called overhead.

"*Caw, caw*," said Myo. Then she laughed. Bassui Zenji laughed too.

All of a sudden the gong sounded for supper.

"It is time for all of us to eat," said Bassui Zenji. "Come back and sit with me in our listening place sometime soon. And remember, the listening place is always just where you are."

Myo laughed and ran all the way home, listening to the birds in the trees and to the sounds that her feet made in the pine needles.

"I can really listen all the time!" she said to herself. And she did.

Notes

This story is based on the famous koan used by the Japanese Zen Master Bassui: "Who is the master of that sound?"

Jerry Davis

❀

The Leather Purses

I am one of many people who live in a city on the East Coast of North America. My dear friend Richard lives here too. So do Richard's two young daughters, Eloise and Melinda.

One day, not too long ago, I was helping Richard learn how to make leather purses. Richard wanted to make two very special purses. He wanted to give them as very special presents to Eloise and Melinda, who are themselves very special. I was reading the instructions to Richard, and helping him understand them. I helped him do all the things he needed to do to the leather so it would become two very special purses.

All went well until the time came for me and Richard to dye the leather. Then something went wrong. The leather dyed all runny and pocky. It made a terrible mess.

I promised Richard I would take the leather back to the shop where we bought it. I would ask the people at the shop how to fix it.

So the next day I went off to the leather store. Now this store is in a large, dingy warehouse. It is not a pretty place to go at all. With a sigh, I walked into the store. I found the owner, Mr. Beans, and three others packing crates for shipping.

"I need some help to fix a problem with some leather I bought here," I said.

"I'll look at it," growled Mr. Beans, "but you'll have to stand over here by me while I work. We're busy."

Just then the phone rang. The clerk at the front called, "Mr. Beans, it's for you!"

Mr. Beans pushed past me and stomped all the way to the front of the store to answer the call. Poor me! I stood in that dark, somber place wishing I could just leave. I was a little frightened to be with such an unpleasant person. I dreaded having to depend on Mr. Beans for help. If it hadn't been for my promise to Richard, I would have just walked out.

But I had promised Richard, so I decided to make the best of it. I wondered, Can I change this situation by changing myself?

Then I recited the gatha, "I take refuge in the Buddha; the Buddha takes refuge in me. I take refuge in the Dharma, the Dharma takes refuge in me. I take refuge in the Sangha; the Sangha takes refuge in me." I began to feel a bit calmer. I repeated the gatha several times. Each time I felt more at ease. Finally I became completely peaceful.

Mr. Beans hung up the phone. He started back toward me, still scowling. As he came closer, his scowl slowly vanished. When he reached me he smiled, just slightly. Then, in a friendly voice, he said, "Come with me and I'll see what I can do."

At the back of the store Mr. Beans worked on Richard's leather for more than twenty minutes. He tried several different solutions. Finally he found a way to fix it. Then Mr. Beans handed me new dye and leather to replace the bad leather. Now Richard and I could make new purses for Eloise and Melinda. I reached for my wallet to pay him.

Mr. Beans shook his head and said warmly, "No, I'm giving this to you. I hope you have better luck next time."

I left the warehouse with my spirits soaring. Wow! By simply being there, doing nothing, I achieved my purpose!

Sukha Linda Murray

❀

Precepts for Children

All things are precious and to be respected—
I will learn ways to protect people, animals and plants
and try to care for them all in the way
I would like to be cared for myself.

I will not take the things that belong to others
and will try to share my own things as much as I can.

I will try to say things that are true and helpful
being honest to myself and a friend to others.

I will be loving and respectful of myself and others
in all our touching—keeping my own promises
and respecting those of others.

I will keep my body healthy and my mind calm and clear
and avoid things that will weaken and confuse me.

These precepts tell us how to prevent suffering for ourselves and others. They help keep us happy and out of trouble, and if we're happy and out of trouble, that is wonderful for us and for our friends and family around us.

How can we learn to keep these precepts more and more?

Repeating these precepts regularly will help us remember them.

Attention! attention! attention! The more we can see clearly what is happening to us each moment, the more we can see what to say and do or not say and not do to keep the precepts.

It also helps to discuss the precepts with others. Here are some questions to help your discussions:

1. Why, do you think, are all things precious and to be respected and cared for? Can you share ways you have been learning
   - to protect people
   - to protect animals
   - to protect plants?

   How do you like to be cared for?

2. What are some things that belong to everyone? What is stealing? What can be stolen? Who steals? Why? What is sharing? What can be shared? Who shares? Why?

3. What is it like when true and helpful things are said? What is it like when untrue and unhelpful things are said? What could we do?

4. What are some kinds of touching that feel good? That don't feel good? What do you know about sex? Do you know why people have sexual touching together?

5. How can we keep our bodies healthy? What things weaken and confuse our bodies? How can we keep our minds calm and clear? What things weaken and confuse our minds?

There are also activities we can do alone and with others to help us learn to keep the precepts. Here are some suggestions:

1. Do a role play for each of the precepts.
2. Letter a precept scroll and decorate it.
3. Recite the precepts together with other children once a month or more regularly if possible.
4. Recite the precepts before bed.
5. Think about one precept and try to understand it deeply — think about how you are doing with it over time.
6. Reflect on each precept in this way.

Sandy Eastoak

The Precepts for Young People

The Buddha taught us the Precepts as a guide to living so that we would not bring suffering to ourselves or others. The first precept of all is,

DO NO HARM.

The second is,

DO ONLY GOOD.

The third is,

DO GOOD FOR OTHERS.

These are called the Three Pure Precepts. They are the basis for all other moral teachings, and by themselves clearly tell us how to live a good life. But sometimes we need more specific advice, so beyond these come the Ten Great Precepts:

Not killing

All killing brings suffering. The ant and the dandelion love life, as we do. Well, maybe not as we do, but as an ant and dandelion do, which is something we cannot do, and so is completely precious. Not killing is about the absolute preciousness of every being, large or small. It is about physical lives, which most animals and some plants cannot help taking, just to stay alive. And it is about ways of being, which sometimes we kill by ridicule or neglect.

A blue jay once told me, God needs many eyes to see the world.

That's why it is better not to kill. Each eye sees the world differently, and all that seeing together makes the world as big and wonderful as it is.

Not stealing

This means not to take what isn't given. As we look around us, we see how much stealing is taken for granted in our world—and how much suffering it brings. Respecting others and practicing generosity are the cures for stealing.

What about picking an apple from a tree? Does the tree give, or do we steal? What about digging up a garden that was formerly a playground for mice and toads and grasshoppers? These are hard questions. Meanwhile, share your cassettes with your friends and don't snatch the comics from your brother.

Not saying what isn't true

Everything we say reflects some truth, even when our "no, I didn't" means "I'm afraid you'll yell at me if I tell you I spilled pudding on your sweater." One reason we practice being still inside is that telling the truth isn't easy. When we're little children we can be mixed up about what's really true and what is just our wish or our fear. When we're grown up, we can be mixed up about what's really true and what's just our wish or our fear. The stronger our wish or the more terrible our fear, the harder it is to stay clear about the truth.

When we don't tell the truth, we suffer, and all those around us suffer. Distrust and confusion come immediately, with fear and anger close behind. That all of us together can do the right thing in any situation, we rely on each other to be truthful.

Not misusing sex

This means we respect each other's bodies. We do not touch each other in ways that feel bad. We do not touch each other in ways that feel good for the moment but lead to feeling bad later. We are careful and loving and respectful of ourselves and others in all our touching. When people have promised to love each other, as in a marriage, we do not weaken their promise. We postpone sexual expression until we have developed our friendship and love for another so deeply that we make our own promise together.

It is easy to be confused, especially as we get older, by our desires for touching. To prevent suffering for ourselves and others, we make the effort to get clear about what is really healthy and respectful. We learn to be committed to that, and to avoid the rest.

Not using drugs

Every situation in life is at once very simple and very complicated, so it can be quite difficult to see clearly what causes suffering and what does not. If we use drugs, it becomes even more difficult to see clearly. All the things we practice to help us see clearly—meditation, patience, perseverance, compassion—slip away from us. By drugs, we mean not only alcohol or marijuana or pills, but anything that dulls the mind and makes us seek after it even when it doesn't feel right. It can be TV or talking too much or crossword puzzles. Always it is what numbs us, takes us out of the present, and prevents us from fully feeling what is happening right now and responding with appropriate action to *that*.

Not speaking against others

In every group of people—whether a family, a school, a neighborhood, a meditation center, a few friends—two things are needed: trust and what we might call "open problems." Open problems means stating openly any difficulty we're having to the other person—and being open to solving it together, each giving to the other some needed change. We all know that when we criticize another person behind their back, trust goes immediately. One reason we do it anyway is that "open problems" is scary. It's easier to complain to a third person, and if the trust is broken, open problems may become impossible. So we're off the hook—but at a terrible price.

Not speaking against others requires the willingness to see our part in our difficulty with other people, to speak our experience honestly, and to negotiate mutual change. The reward is the trust that keeps love growing.

Not praising yourself while abusing others

For our own self-esteem and the well-being of our friends and family, it is important that we remember that each of us is special. So we don't brag and we don't put other people down. We give up the easy gratification of "mine is better than yours"—and the insecurity that "yours is better than mine." No one is more important than you. You are no more important than any other being. Just like the seed in each compartment of the lotus pod, we are all equal. We want to cultivate the mindfulness that sees that equality all the time, throughout all our hours and actions. Then we can live happily together, enjoying each other's skills and achievements, benefiting from each other's goodness.

Not sparing the Dharma assets

This means a willingness to share. Whatever good life brings us, we gladly pass on to others. Maybe we give a certain percentage of our income to the hungry and homeless. Maybe we give a few hours a week to help the sick or the elderly. Maybe we help the forests by recycling and the rivers by writing letters in support of conservation laws. Not everything of value that life gives us is sunny and bright—sometimes our pain can be a gift too. We are called on to share not only material wealth, but also whatever helps us to understand and act rightly. We share our compassion and wisdom, our ideas and skills.

Not indulging in anger

Anger can be a great energy, giving the light to see what needs changing and the heat to change. But without great mindfulness, it is a destroyer. Everything in the universe has a building up phase, a static phase, and a breaking down phase. Anger can be taken as a signal for a breaking down stage. But what do we do with this signal? When anger uses us, we are destructive, sending waves of bad karma in all directions. When we befriend our anger carefully, our compassion and insight enable us to transmute bad karma into lovingkindness. Whatever we say or do to another, is said and done to us. Be very, very careful.

Not defaming the Three Treasures

Even if we are not Buddhists, we cannot live happily without honoring those who can show us how to live wisely. All people do not agree on the best way to live—indeed, we each must find our own path, unique to ourselves. But whoever and whatever teaches us and helps us follow our path in truth and integrity—that we each must honor. And we must offer respect to what helps others find their way, whether similar of different from our own. The great and vast truth of the universe in all its manifestations—how could we defame this? Look carefully to each thought, each word, each action—and grow the blossom of understanding. Enjoy the growing and blossoming of all the diverse beings around you, without whom you do not even exist.

❀

There is a formal ceremony in which we are asked, after the reading of each precept, "Have you made an effort to study and practice this during the past two weeks?" To have the opportunity to do this ceremony with others is a great help. We can also make the same review on our own. Some people do this as a family ritual on each full moon night.

The precepts tell us how not to cause suffering. Always, suffering is related to being not fully present—clutching at an idea, rushing ahead to the future, lingering in the past. Not being awake to the needs of the present moment, which are completely unique, always changing, never repeated. When we're totally in the present, suffering disappears.

So the precepts are reminders of how to stay in the present—both self and others. How to keep yourself in the present, and how not to push anyone else out of it. How to enable yourself and all other beings to open up completely, not hiding anything anywhere. How you and all other beings can see and treat each other as absolutely sacred—as all the god there is. They're simply Buddha's Helpful Hints for Being Buddha.

But don't worry. Nobody's perfect.

Julie Quinn

❀

Falling Off the Precepts

One of the ways I share my practice with my children, Sara, age four, and Trenton, age two, is to start the day with a chanting service. This is something we do at the monthly family service at the Minnesota Zen Meditation Center. We chant five precepts three times each:

> No Killing Life.
> No Being Angry.
> No Blaming Others.
> No Lying.
> No Stealing.

We take turns striking our bell, a crystal wineglass from my wedding set, after each repetition. When we are done chanting, we sit zazen for a few minutes, then bow to each other, put away our cushions, and go eat breakfast.

The whole business takes about five minutes, and at first I didn't think such a short amount of time would influence the kids very much. Then one day I heard Sara explaining to her father that we shouldn't get angry because it not only made everyone else unhappy, it made him unhappy as well. Great! She wasn't just saying the precepts, she was thinking about them, too.

A few weeks later she came to me asking how she could fix the precepts once she had broken them. She was pretty worried about this, and I realized that I had been talking and thinking about the precepts in the same way I grew up talking and thinking about the

Ten Commandments, as laws that once broken required harsh punishment to set matters right.

After a long discussion, we decided together that the precepts were really like a big bridge over a stream. If you walk on the bridge, it supports you and makes your path easier. But if you fall off the bridge, or even jump off the bridge, you get all wet and miserable, and have a tough time crawling over the rocks.

The nice thing about this analogy is that it makes living a "good" life so much easier. Fixing a broken precept seems like a nearly impossible task, but climbing back onto something you've just fallen off of seems pretty simple, especially to children. They do it every day.

Ryo Imamura

❧

Good and Evil Are One

During my years of experience working as a psychological counselor, I was fortunate to be able to work with teenagers who had run afoul of the law (now called "youth at risk"). Usually they came in for counseling only because it was required by the justice system. Some seemed to benefit from counseling and to make positive changes in their attitudes and behaviors. Others were resistant to counseling and left relatively unchanged in attitude. Among all the factors that seemed to make a difference, the central determinant was whether they had substantial contact with religious education in their childhood or were raised by religiously devout parents. If they had learned one of the many versions of the Golden Rule (to be kind to and avoid hurting others) in their childhood, they appeared to retain the lesson and be able to distinguish between good and bad thoughts and behavior: the seed of morality existed and could be nourished and cultivated. If they had no exposure to such ethical training in their childhood, they seemed to have no strong sense of the difference between good and bad, and made their decisions based on situational ethics: they would choose actions that were most beneficial to themselves without regard for the welfare of others. In these cases, the prognosis for change seemed very poor.

Most parents know at a gut level that their children need religious education, if only to be exposed on a consistent basis to the Golden Rule. Recognizing this undeniable reality, the adult members of our Jodo Shin temples place tremendous importance on the Dharma Schools and temple recreational programs for their children. The programs and training for adults certainly take a back seat to the children's activities. This is probably a central reason why most adult American Buddhists, who usually come to the temple alone and seeking their own liberation, have not been attracted to Jodo Shin, which is the most popular form of Buddhism in Japan and in America among those of Japanese descent.

From a very early age, we teach our children to recite the "Golden Chain":

> I am a link in Amida Buddha's golden chain of love that stretches around the world. I must keep my link bright and strong.

> I will try to be kind and gentle to every living thing and protect all who are weaker than myself.

> I will try to think pure and beautiful thoughts, to say pure and beautiful words, and to do pure and beautiful deeds, knowing that on what I do now depends not only my happiness or unhappiness but also those of others.

> May every link in the Buddha's golden chain of love become bright and strong, and may we all attain Perfect Peace.

We teach our children the ethical guidelines of Buddhism, called the Precepts, which originated from the Gautama Buddha. I might try to explain them to children and parents alike in the following manner:

The five basic precepts that all Buddhist are urged to try to practice are the following:

1. It is better not to kill.
2. It is better not to lie.
3. It is better not to steal.
4. It is better not to be unfaithful.
5. It is better not to take intoxicants.

The Theravada bhikkus (monks) are still required to keep some 253 precepts in their daily practice, and the bhikkunis (nuns) have even more to keep. Even though we lay Buddhists have only five precepts to keep, we gradually come to realize that even keeping five precepts is a most difficult, if not impossible, task.

Upon first perusal, the Five Precepts read very much like the Ten Commandments of Christianity. In actuality, they differ quite a bit. The Commandments, as the word suggests, must be followed without exception or serious consequences follow. The precepts, on the other hand, are gentle and kindly advice from the Gautama Buddha, who through his life experience found that trying to follow the precepts leads to a happier and more sincere life that otherwise.

As a parent of a very sociable teenager, I can command him to "be home by midnight or else. . . ." Or I can gently and calmly advise him to be home at a reasonable hour because of the healthful benefits I have found from such a habit. Of course, as good Japanese parents, we would be remiss in not reminding him that, as parents, we cannot help but stay up and worry about his welfare and safety.

We understand and appreciate the precepts according to our individual levels of spiritual maturity. The Gautama Buddha noted three basic groupings of people, which he explained through the analogy of lotuses growing from the bottom of a muddy pond. He described lotuses that grew in the murky depth far below the surface of the pond, those that were just breaking through the surface, and finally those that rose magnificently and freely above the surface. In a similar vein, he spoke of people who are unawakened spiritually, who take everything at face value, never questioning and never seeking deeper meaning. He continued to speak of those at the next level, who have begun their spiritual quest, seeing the relative and impermanent nature of things, and becoming disillusioned with the blind ego. At the third level are those who have awakened to things-as-they-are, life-as-it-is, true and real, who have realized true freedom in this life. These are the people of shinjin, satori, enlightenment.

At the first level (the unawakened), we find the so-called good people, who see themselves as good and virtuous and are quick to label others as evil. They are convinced that they do not kill, lie, steal, act unfaithfully, or take intoxicants for the most part. If they do violate a precept or commandment, they can easily rationalize the cause to be someone or something other than themselves. They might make comments like, "I got drunk because I didn't want to be unfriendly," "I got involved with the other woman because you were ignoring me," or "I dropped the bombs because I received orders."

At the second level (the partially awakened), people see themselves as partially good, partially evil. They begin to see that those whom they formerly labeled as Commies, Reaganites, gooks, liberals, spics, and so forth, are not evil but rather just different from themselves. They begin to realize that morality is in the sphere of not only action but also thought and intention. They see themselves much more deeply and perceptively than the good people. Their understanding of the Five Precepts is much broader and inclusive to the point where they become difficult, if not impossible, to practice perfectly.

1. Not to kill means not killing indirectly as well as directly. This can include not paying taxes that fund the military, not adding pollutants to the environment, not wasting resources, and not remaining silent against the death penalty. It means not killing all forms of life, including plants and animals. It means not killing psychologically and always encouraging the potential and talents of children and adults.

2. Not to lie means more than telling the truth in a legal sense. It also means being true to one's heart even if it means telling a lie in a legal sense. For instance, if an angry and armed person asks you where a potential victim is hiding, it would be a lie to tell the legal truth. Not to lie means being honest, but in a compassionate way. As you can sense, this precept is exceptionally difficult to keep because of its complexity. One can even correctly argue that every statement contains both truth and falsehood and therefore is technically a lie.

3. Not to steal means more than the theft of material property. Depriving others of their rights and dignity is stealing. Littering is stealing the rights of others to a clean environment. Academic work is largely "borrowing" the ideas of others. And one can steal the happiness of others through cruel and unthinking words and actions.

4. Not to be unfaithful means more than abstaining from improper sex relations. As a former president properly pointed out, it could take the form of "lust in one's heart." Being unfaithful could mean using others to fulfill our selfish desires at their expense. And it is easy to recognize when one can be unfaithful to one's own principles and beliefs.

5. Not to take intoxicants means more than avoiding alcohol and illegal drugs. It can be expanded to include all chemical substances, because they are all mind-altering. Taking it further, all human activities carried to excess, such as watching TV, exercising, playing golf, reading, meditating, socializing, working, studying, and traveling can be intoxicating and lead us away from enlightenment.

Partially awakened people still see themselves as basically good. But they have awakened to the great difficulty in living a truly virtuous life. And they have begun to realize that there are mysterious and wonderful dimensions of life, those of an absolute, timeless reality, which they have yet to experience fully.

The truly awakened one (at the third level) sees him- or herself as being absolutely Evil.[1] In contrast, the ignorant and bland see themselves as good people. How can this be? To shed light on this confusing paradox, let me relate a Buddhist story, which is typically baffling to linear Western thinking:

> One day a Japanese college student began learning kendo under a master teacher. Feeling quite proud of himself after several days of vigorous sparring, he approached the master teacher and asked how long it would take him to become a master if he came to the dojo once a week. The master teacher replied, "Two years." Encouraged by the answer, the student asked how long it would take if he came to the dojo three times a week. He was surprised when the master teacher replied, "Five years." Wondering if the master teacher had misunderstood his question, he asked how long it would take if he lived at the dojo and devoted his every waking minute to the practice of kendo. The master teacher laughed and said, "Then you will never become a master," and walked away.

If one is truly sincere about being virtuous, one must see one's true nature in comparison to the absolute Good of the Buddha, and thereby awaken to one's absolute Evil. This can lead only to absolute and profound despair, which is the very opening in one's ego defense that makes possible the awakening to the wisdom and compassionate heart of the Buddha. Absolute Good and absolute Evil are One.

> Even though I have returned to the truth of the Pure Land
> The mind true and real is impossible.
> This self is a being of vanity, falsehood, and untruth
> Without a trace of purity of mind.

> The appearance of goodness and diligence
> Is for everyone a matter of external form;
> Because of the abundance of greed, anger, and falsehood,
> Deceit and lies fill this self.

> Difficult is it to be free of evil nature—
> The heart is like a snake and scorpion;
> Good acts also are mixed with poison—
> They are but vain and false deeds.

> Although within this shameless, unrepenting self
> No genuine, sincere heart exists,
> By virtue of the Name-That-Calls granted by Amida
> Virtues permeate the universe in all directions.

> Lacking the smallest bit of love or compassion
> How can I bring benefits to sentient beings?
> Without the vessel of Tathagata's vow
> How could I possibly cross the ocean of pain?

> Shinran Shonin
> founder of the Jodo Shin sect

Notes

[1] Editor's note: This use of the word "Evil" may be disturbing to some readers of Judeo-Christian upbringing. Further reading of Jodo Shinshu teachings may clarify the depth of this concept. See Education Department, Buddhist Churches of America in *Resources*.

Robert Aitken

The Wise Words of Birdsnest

Long ago in China, there was a teacher who would climb up in a tree every day and sit there. Because of this, he was nicknamed "Birdsnest." His real name is not so well known.

After a while, Birdsnest became famous, and people would come to ask him questions and listen to his wise answers. One day, the Governor heard about him and decided to go and ask him a question. He went to the forest, and sure enough, there was Birdsnest in his tree. Looking up, he said, "O Birdsnest, you don't look very safe to me up there."

Of course, the Governor was just teasing Birdsnest, who had a solid perch up in his tree. Birdsnest smiled and looked down at the Governor and said, "O Governor, you don't look very safe to me down there." The Governor was standing on the solid ground under the tree. Why should Birdsnest say that didn't look safe? Please think about this for a moment before we go on with the story.

Then the Governor remembered that he had a question. Looking up at Birdsnest, he asked, "What is it that all the Buddhas taught?" In other words, What can we learn from the wise people of the world?

> Birdsnest answered,
> Don't do bad things;
> always do good things;
> keep your mind pure —
> that's what all the Buddhas taught.

Birdsnest is repeating a poem from an old Buddhist book called the *Dhammapada*. But the Governor was like you and me. He had been hearing about good and bad and being pure all his life. So he said, "Don't do bad things; always do good things; keep your mind pure —I knew that when I was three years old."

Birdsnest said, "Yes, the three-year-old child knows it, but the eighty-year-old person can't do it."

This answer must have been surprising to the Governor. Why can't the eighty-year-old person be good and be pure? Maybe the Governor began to think again about the poem Birdsnest had repeated. But we don't know, because that's the end of the story.

But the story doesn't really have to end. It can go on in our minds. Think about the poem. When is a thing bad? When is a thing good? Pretend that you never heard the words "bad" and "good" before, and those questions can get quite interesting.

Then think about the next line: "Keep your mind pure." Does this mean that we should be goody-goody? I am reminded of pouring sweet tea over the Baby Buddha on his birthday. I think that when you and I pour sweet tea over the Baby Buddha, we are pouring it over ourselves. We are remembering to be fresh and clean, not just our bodies, but also our minds.

Sometimes you get muddy, and then it feels nice to take a bath. Sometimes you get angry with somebody, and then it feels nice to make up. Pouring sweet tea over the Baby Buddha is a reminder about making up with your friends and staying fresh and clean. How about when you wash your hands? Could that be a reminder too?

That still isn't the end of the story. Why did Birdsnest say that even an eighty-year-old person can't help doing bad things, and can't do good things, and can't keep a mind that is pure and fresh and clean? Surely by the time people get old they will know how to be good and pure. What does Birdsnest mean?

So you see, sometimes when you ask questions, you get questions back. Then *you* have to be the wise person who finds the answers after all.

Benares Valerie Lofell

※

Children's Paramitas

Young children enjoy choosing one of these, drawing a picture about it, and focusing on it for a week.

1
I will try to be kind to everything.

2
I will try to help wherever I can.

3
I will try to be patient and not get angry.

4
I will try to do my best work and finish my work.

5
I will try to be calm and careful in whatever I do.

6
I will try to do what helps us all to be happy
so we can feel like one family.

Gregory Kramer

❦

Lovingkindness Practice with Children

Ever since my first child was just about old enough to understand speech, I have practiced lovingkindness meditation with him at bedtime every evening. I've done the same with my other two children. It's been about thirteen years now. I would be happy to pass along some of what I've learned.

Lovingkindness is a meditation practice taught by the Buddha to develop the mental habit of selfless, or altruistic, love. By arousing within ourselves feelings of good will towards ourselves, those near to us, and all beings, we make it likely that these feelings will arise rather than other, less desirable feelings. Hatred cannot coexist with lovingkindness; it dissipates and is not replenished if we supplant thoughts rooted in anger with thoughts rooted in love.

Lovingkindness makes the mind more pliable, counteracts the judgments that arise as we become more perceptive about ourselves and others, and brings us beyond our selfishness. This outward movement is very important to balance the inner focus of meditation practice. The benefits of lovingkindness practice extend far beyond those who meditate. It offers to all the opportunity to find selflessness, joy, adaptability, and expansiveness. It is a truly universal practice and need not be associated with any particular religious concept.

I've always given my three sons a choice. Most evenings they're feeling all right and clearly want to do this. If, however, one of them is cranky or upset, I'll say, "Would you like to do lovingkindness tonight?" and if the answer is no, then I'll say, "OK, honey," give him a kiss (through the blanket if necessary), and say goodnight. So they know it is for *them*. If they see it is OK with me not to do it—it won't hurt my feelings—then it is alive and part of their lives. It prevents it from becoming a ritual with little meaning.

Feeling good about doing this meditation is what brings it into their lives. They associate their own happiness and peace with a meditation that wishes happiness and peace for themselves *and* others.

It also feels good that the practice has become part of our evening, just as the story and my lying down with them. It is a special time of attention, gentleness, fantasy, mind opening, and familial love.

I keep expecting the day when my teenager (now fourteen) won't want to do this. But so far the associations he has with the practice make him want it. I'm hoping that, even as the wedge of teenagerdom drives him further into his independence from me, this can remain a link, a place of emotional connection, or at least neutrality, to the issues of the everyday world.

Now, I have to point out, this can all take a lot of time. The stories (usually made up, rather than read), the lovingkindness, meditation, and the "be with" time can add up to twenty or thirty minutes. I have the two younger kids in one room and the older one in a different room. This adds up to nearly an hour each evening. As wonderful as it can be, sometimes I can't do it.

Here is how we do the lovingkindness practice. I ask them to close their eyes and relax. Then, they think along with me as I say the following:

> Send lovingkindness to yourself. Really love yourself.
> Want yourself to be happy. Think:

> I love myself.
> May I be free from anger.
> May I be free from sadness.
> May I be free from pain.
> (I really want to be free from pain.)
> May I be free from difficulties.
> May I be free from all suffering.

211

May I be healthy.
May my body be healthy and strong.
May I be filled with lovingkindness.
May I know the joy of generosity and love.
May I be happy.
May I really be happy.
May I be at peace.

I spread this lovingkindness out. I send love to Dad and Mom.
May Mom and Dad be free from difficulties.
May they be free from pain and sadness.
May they be free from attachment,
Free from anger and ill will.
May they be free from all suffering.
May Mom and Dad be healthy and happy.
Completely healthy and happy.
May they be at peace.

I send lovingkindness to both my brothers.
May they be free from sadness and anger.
May they be free from sickness.
May they be free from all suffering.
May they be happy and free.
Free from suffering, free from difficulties.
May they be well and happy.
May they be at peace.

I send lovingkindness to my teachers and the kids at school
(Even the ones I don't know).
May they all be free from sorrow and suffering.
May they be free from anger and difficulties.
May they be happy.
Free from all difficulties and sadness.
May they be well and happy.
May they be at peace.

I send love now to all the people I don't know
everywhere on the earth.
May all beings on the planet be free from suffering.
May they be free from pain, grief, and despair.
May they be happy,
Truly happy.
May they be at peace.

May all beings in the universe be free from suffering.
May all beings in all universes, everywhere,
be free from suffering.
May they be well and happy.
May they be at peace.

May all beings of all kinds, in all directions
be happy and at peace.
Above and below,
Near and far,
High and low.
All types of beings.
Humans and non-humans.
Seen and unseen.
All the animals, birds, and fish.
All beings and creatures,
With no exceptions,
May they all be happy.
May they be free.

I open my heart
And accept the lovingkindness
of every being and creature in return.
I let that love into my heart.
And I share the benefits of this meditation with every one.

May all beings be well and happy.
May all beings be well and happy.
May all beings be well and happy.

May there be peace.
May there be peace.
May there be peace.

Following the meditation, each child gets a kiss and an "I love you." I lie there briefly, then leave.

This practice is slightly different from the one I do with my adult meditation students. There are nuances that I adjust with age and mood, to make the meditation something that kids can relate to directly and emotionally. As they mature and their world grows, the scope of the meditation can grow and still be congruent with that world.

By beginning with the instruction rather than the practice itself, I'm telling them to relax and think. I set the stage and the mood, creating a transition from listening to stories to focusing on their feelings and then growing those feelings towards love.

Another adjustment is that each person, group, or region towards whom the lovingkindness is sent has slightly different words. I do not want this practice to become rote. By avoiding repetition, we help the meditation stay alive and relevant.

Then, we grow the feelings of love in the most fertile soil: logically the closest and most loved people (or animals or plants). The children themselves get the most attention, based on the simple fact that we all want to be free from pain and difficulties. When we know how that feels for ourselves, we can, with identification and understanding, spread that feeling to others. After all, they are just like us and must also want to be free from pain, discomfort, and other suffering.

We extend lovingkindness toward ourselves, toward someone we love a great deal (Dad and Mom), toward others we love (the brothers), then toward those we like (our friends at school) or at least feel neutral toward (teachers, other kids), then toward all beings. With adults, the practice goes from oneself to a loved one, then to a neutral one, than to one towards whom we feel anger, then on out geographically. With children, we slowly grow the world; we are not "pushing the river." When they are ready, we extend the lovingkindness toward people they feel some agitation toward.

There is an element of improvisation in the way I conduct this practice. If I feel the kids are in a particularly loving place, I may focus more on sending love to their teachers. "May they really be free from difficulties and suffering." This would help them to see their teachers as regular humans, with pain, with lives outside the classroom, and not beyond error and emotion. I may also focus extra lovingkindness on someone in need, such as an ill grandmother. The child can then be helped to see that when there is need, you step outside yourself and you give extra.

In spreading the lovingkindness geographically, I try to walk the line between it becoming a mental exercise ("Where is that town?" "What is a continent?") and being so general as not to invoke feelings of expansiveness ("Oh, we're at that spreading thing that I don't really understand, I'll just lie here."). This grows in sophistication with age. But one must be careful not to turn it into a geography lesson, although a little intrigue doesn't hurt ("I send lovingkindness across all of Asia, Africa, Australia; across all the oceans to all the creatures in the sea"). The feeling of expansiveness is paramount here. From me, to them, to all on earth, to all in the universe, to all in all directions, with no exceptions. This helps the heart grow and soften. It takes children (or us) out of themselves in a gentle way.

Questions come up with kids that may not come up with adults, like the time my youngest wanted to send lovingkindness to "Yellow Blankie." First, I said to him that Yellow Blankie doesn't have a consciousness. This did not impress him. Then I said we'd send lovingkindness to Yellow Blankie, figuring that "all beings" could include his fabric friend if my son so chose. However, when we began the lovingkindness practice, it went like this:

Me: "I send lovingkindness to Dad and Mom . . ."

My son: ". . . and Yellow Blankie."

Me: "OK, and Yellow Blankie."

Now that my eldest is expanding his emotional understanding, the meditation we do before sleep is gently expanding with him. Compassion is an extension of love, further along this trajectory of going beyond ourselves to embrace others. So the eldest may, after sending lovingkindness to all beings, be instructed to let himself feel the suffering of others, to let his heart resonate with the pain of others. This will be done in a gentle and nondogmatic way. There is a sense of respect and maturity that he may feel, albeit subtly, for being able to grow in his practice in this way.

I can't say for certain, but it is my hope that this compassion will grow within my sons as they reach deeper into the rich and complex social world of young adulthood and thus act as counterbalance to the arrogance and judgment that comes with the territory. I particularly hope that they can develop a true compassion for those less fortunate than themselves, people without enough to eat, without adequate clothing or housing, people who are in war zones or are stricken by disease. In our privileged society, where many of us don't see the outer reaches of human suffering, I want actively to instill the *capacity* for compassion. The compassion itself will grow with their experience.

I try to do this without too much attachment to results or to the process itself. If my children decide they don't want to do this anymore, I hope I can let go of it lightly. But for now, as for the past thirteen years, they value this practice of lovingkindness.

China Galland

❀

Tara and the Man Afraid of Lions

Tara is often described as a Goddess and a Great Bodhisattva. She is also called the Great Saviouress. But what many people don't realize yet is that Tara is also Buddha, a fully and completely enlightened being in her own right. There is just no end of this Tara in sight! Having a fully enlightened image of the feminine, with emanations that are variously wise, compassionate, fierce, joyful, and peaceful, is a wonderful gift for young people to grow up with. Tara also has many manifestations and appears to us in different colors, just like people do. Some of her colors are Green, White, Red, Black, Gold, Orange, and Yellow. Tara vowed only to be enlightened in a woman's body, for all time, and until all suffering is ended. I encourage you to call her by her most venerable name, Buddha Tara.

One thing that people who know Tara particularly treasure is her ability to take away all fears. Here is a story about how she saved a man afraid of lions:

Once upon a time there was a man who lived deep in the forest. He loved the bird songs that rose in the morning with the sun, the chatter of monkeys, the softness of the ground beneath the great tall trees as they swayed gently, creaking softly, the leaves clattering in the morning breeze. But the one thing he did not like and had a great fear of was another forest dweller, the lions. Whenever he heard their roar in the distance, he trembled and said to himself, "My, what a terrible fate awaits whomever lion's going to eat today." His face would grow long, his brow furrow, his palms grow damp. He couldn't sit still and would stop whatever he was doing and race inside his little forest hut, shaking until the roaring stopped and he could collect himself.

His friend the monkey knew exactly what was wrong and would tease him whenever this happened. "See, if you were a monkey like me, you would take off into the trees. No lion could catch you, even if he is the King of Beasts. It's really the Queen you need to worry about anyway, she's a much better hunter," he always added, scampering up and away through the trees laughing and pelting the poor man's hut with betel nuts for good measure.

The poor man's garden would sit untended until he got over his frights. Seeds didn't get planted, forest vines and other plants would begin to creep across his carefully tilled ground, birds stole the seeds he'd left out in his fright.

The man's fear paralyzed him altogether as he lay in his bed with his head covered up, his eyes closed, trying to block out his fears. He was so intent on his fear of the lion and trying to hide himself and make himself invisible, that he didn't even hear the lion slowly pad her way into his forest hut until it was too late: "Roaarrrrr, grrrrrowllll, aarrgggh, YUM!" the lion had him in her jaws. The forest dweller hadn't even seen her coming! Now he would be dinner for her children!

Her breath was hot and smelled of her last meal, making him want to vomit. Her teeth began to sink into his neck when he suddenly remembered Tara like a flash of lightning streaking across the night sky.

"Tara!" he cried out as he began to lose consciousness, begging her with all his heart to save him, "Help!" And with that single cry from his heart, Tara appeared instantly, clothed in the leaves of the Khadiravani forest's trees, shimmering green-gold, laughing and smiling, leaves all at play with the breeze in them, commanding the lion to drop her prey and go back into the forest, which she did immediately.

The poor man fell out of the lion's jaws onto his knees, bowing his head to his dirt floor, throwing his arms around Tara's feet in gratitude, when she said, "Stop this nonsense."

"When you live in the forest with lions, learn to befriend them, don't run and hide in your bed trying to pretend they're not there. That's how the lion walked right into your hut, and you didn't even know it because you had your back to the door and your sheet over your head. That's no way to live in the forest! You must learn to be a good neighbor and have the lion over and tell her a story. She's lonely! That's the secret with her."

And before he knew it, Tara had disappeared into thin air, only the sweetness of flowers was left in the air where she'd stood before him. It filled the room, letting him know that yes, Tara was real, she had come to him when he needed her and called out for her help.

After this episode, the forest dweller built a little altar to Tara in the corner of his room and never forgot his prayers to her each morning and night. He did as she told him, inviting the lion and her cubs over—after dinner—to tell them stories and to hear theirs. The lions had never heard a human story and he'd never heard a lion's. Now when he heard the lions roar in the forest, he could distinguish among them, the mother, the father, the children. He knew them by name, and he knew that they were friends and that, thanks to Tara, he had no fear of lions any more.

Anaar Eastoak-Siletz, age seven

Turkey Tara

Once Tara was born as a turkey. She lived with six other turkeys, in a very small cage. They all badly wanted to be free from the terrible bars that kept them from the wonderful world. They were the king's turkeys, and they were raised to be eaten. Tara was their queen. She saw how they suffered: she wanted to help them. At last she found a way. It was like a chess game. She planned ahead, assuming that her plan would work. She told the five turkeys her plan. She said, "Stop eating and they will ask you why you do not eat. You will say that you must not eat until you are freed."

Then the feeder came. He gave the turkeys their food. But the next day, when he came to feed them, yesterday's food was still there!! The feeder blinked. He rubbed his eyes. He pinched himself—but it was true! He then called the King. The King said, "Why don't you eat?"

The turkeys replied, "We will not eat and NOT eat and NOT eat until we are freed."

The King thought. Finally he told the Queen of the turkeys he would release her flock if one of the flock gave itself to be eaten. She was fine indeed, so she could not be the one. But the turkey Queen could not send anyone but herself. So she sent herself. The King asked her why she had done this.

"O great King," the turkey Queen cried, "I cannot send anyone but myself, so that is what I did."

The King was so moved by the turkey Queen's words that he set them all free and stopped all hunting in his kingdom. But he liked

the turkey Queen's words so much that he usually called his kingdom "The Turkey Queendom," and the cruel terrible bars were no
longer there to keep them from the wide wonderful world. And
everyone was happy after that.

Deborah Hopkinson

❀

Rice Cakes

Long ago in a small village in Japan lived an old woman and man who were quite poor. Each day they sat in their tiny hut weaving large hats out of straw. Every so often, the man would take the hats into the next town to sell them so that they could buy some food.

One cold winter, just before the New Year celebration, the man said to his wife, "Oh, how I wish that this year we could have some rice cakes to celebrate the New Year."

The woman answered, "I think that once you sell the hats to buy the things we need there may be a little money left to buy one or two rice cakes for us."

It was a long walk to the nearest town. Early the next morning the old man started out with five new hats to sell. He was excited to think that this year he and his wife would have rice cakes to eat to celebrate the New Year.

It was a cold and snowy day. When he got to the town, nobody wanted to buy his big straw hats. Everyone was too busy preparing for their own New Year's festivities. The man began to walk back to his village along a lonely mountain path.

Suddenly he came upon six statues of Jizo. Jizo is the protector of children and travelers, and people often put statues of Jizo in gardens and along paths.

"How cold these stone statues of Jizo must be, standing here alone in the snow and bitter wind!" exclaimed the old man.

Forgetting completely his own sadness and disappointment, he thought of a way to help the statues. Taking the five new hats from his back, he began to fasten them upon the head of each Jizo. "There, this will at least protect Jizo a little from this snowy storm," he said.

He put a hat on each statue in turn, but there were six statues and only five new hats. "Oh dear!" the old man exclaimed. "There are not enough hats. This last statue will still be cold."

Then he remembered that on his own head there was also a hat. Taking it off, he fastened it upon the last statue of Jizo. When he reached his little hut, he was wet and cold.

"My dear husband, what has happened to your hat?" asked his wife.

"I am so sorry to disappoint you. But I was not able to sell any hats today. And then coming home along the mountain path I saw six statues of Jizo with their poor heads all snowy and cold. So I gave each statue a new hat. Except for the last statue, to whom I gave my own hat."

"What a wonderful thing to do," said his wife. "Although we will have no rice cakes to celebrate the New Year, it is far better to forget ourselves and do such a kind thing."

She felt happy that even though they were poor and had no rice cakes, they had one another. So the old man and old woman went to bed feeling happy after all.

The next day was New Year's Day. In the early dawn, the man and woman were awakened by the sound of soft voices, singing. The voices came closer and closer, and soon the old couple could hear the sound of footsteps crunching through the snow. Who could it be? they wondered. Then they heard the words of the song:

> Forgetting your own troubles, you kept us from the snow,
> Giving your love and all your hats to us the stone Jizo.
> On this New Year's morning, we ask that you awake
> So that we may give to you a beautiful rice cake!

The old man and woman jumped out of bed and ran to the door. When they opened it, they could hardly believe their eyes.

On the doorstep was a straw mat. And on the mat was the biggest rice cake they had ever seen. It was more beautiful and fresh than any rice cake in the world—and whiter than the snow falling from the sky. "Who could have brought us this extraordinary gift?" they wondered.

In the distance, walking away from their house through the deep snow, they saw the six stone Jizos wearing the big straw hats they had been given by the old man.

"Look!" said the old man in surprise. "The stone Jizo brought us this feast!"

The old woman clapped her hands in delight. "They have come in gratitude for your kindness to them. You gave away everything you had, and look what we have received in return!"

"Truly, it will be a wonderful celebration of the New Year," said her husband.

And so, after all, the old couple were able to eat rice cakes to celebrate the New Year.

The story of the stone Jizos that walked through the snow became known through the whole countryside. After this, everyone wanted to buy hats made by the old man and the old woman. It was said that such hats would always bring good luck to whoever wore them. The kind old couple never went hungry again.

Whenever he walked on the mountain path, the old man stopped to thank the six stone statues of Jizo, standing in a row wearing their hats.

Notes

Children may want to act out this story. Round hats can be made from paper. A gate and a mat for the doorstep can represent the hut. This story is adapted from "The Grateful Statues," in Florence Sakade, editor, *Japanese Children's Favorite Stories* (Rutland, VT and Tokyo: Tuttle, 1958).

Part Five

Honoring the Source

Thich Nhat Hanh

❀

Practicing Mindfulness at Mealtimes

Meals are a good time to practice mindfulness with your family. The whole family can help in preparing the meal, by cooking, setting the table, or putting food on the table. Make sure the television set or radio is turned off. Because you do not have much time together during the day, you should spend time together at meals. Talking, laughing, and smiling in the kitchen together is a very wonderful thing.

When you sit around a table, you can practice breathing in and out three times. This is very important, because you recover yourself and become yourself—you become your best.

When you are your best, you take a look at everyone around the table. You look at your child and you see him or her, really see them, like Mahakashyapa seeing the flower. You see deeply, and it does not take a long time, just one or two seconds is enough. You look at your husband or wife in full awareness. This kind of awareness makes you happy, and you look at the food for a few seconds.

While eating, you observe some silence, because silence makes the food real and the people around the table real. If you talk, the talking should help to bring about happiness. You should not talk about mistakes made by the children, or the story of such-and-such a person. Just say things that have to do with dinner and with the happiness in the family.

Be aware that you are sitting here at the table together with other people, and hence you have a chance to see them more clearly. You have a chance to smile at each other, the authentic smile of friendship and understanding.

Suppose a child notices that tonight, there is a dish she likes very much and she enjoys it. She should learn how to say, "Mommy, I like this very much." If she sees that her daddy is absorbed in thinking, she will wake him up: "Daddy, don't you think this dish is wonderful?" Talking this way is simply the practice of mindfulness.

Eating a meal in silence helps us appreciate the food we eat and the presence of others at the meal. This awareness is possible only when we practice mindfulness while eating. Doing this will not tire your mind or your digestive system. It is not difficult. To the contrary, it gives us peace, strength, and enjoyment. Silence makes our meditation successful. The food we are eating can reveal the interconnections between the universe and us, the earth and us, and all other living species and us. Each bite of vegetable, each drop of soy sauce, each piece of tofu contains in itself the life of the sun and of the earth. We see the meaning and the value of life from those precious morsels of food. Your very first silent meal may cause you to feel embarrassed, but once you become used to it, you will realize that meals in silence bring much peace and happiness.

Here are some verses you may wish to share at your family meals. The images in the verses are all real and practical. We should be able to see them and use them in order to look deeply into things. Family members may also take turns creating their own verses to offer.

Looking at an Empty Plate

The plate is empty now
But I know
That it will soon be filled
With food for today's lunch.

When the Plate Is Filled with Food

My plate is now filled.
I see clearly the presence
Of the entire universe
And its contribution to my existence.

When Sitting Down

Sitting here is like sitting under the Bodhi tree
My body of mindfulness is upright.
I am not assailed by any disturbance.

While Looking at the Plate Filled with Food

All living beings are struggling for life.
May they all have enough food to eat today.

Just Before Eating

The plate is filled with food.
I am aware that each morsel is the fruit of much hard work
By those who produced it.

While Eating the First Four Mouthfuls

With the first mouthful, I promise to practice lovingkindness.
With the second, I promise to help relieve the suffering of
    others.
With the third, I promise to see others' joy as my own.
With the fourth, I promise to learn the way of non-attachment.

When the Plate is Empty

The plate is empty
And I am now satisfied.
The Four Gratitudes,
I vow to live up to them.

Holding a Cup of Tea

This cup of tea in my two hands
Mindfulness is held perfectly.
My mind and body dwell
In the very here and now.

Notes on the Verses, by *Michele Hill* and *Deborah Hopkinson*

Perhaps your children are old enough to use all the verses at a meal, perhaps at every meal, perhaps on a special occasion. Perhaps it will work better to use just one verse, or one at the beginning and another at the end. Perhaps these verses will be guides in creating your own verses to match the age, understanding, and attention span of your child.

Looking . . . The word *plate* can be replaced by the word *bowl* when appropriate. Likewise *lunch* can be replaced by *breakfast* or *dinner.*

When the Plate . . . This verse helps us see the principle of dependent co-arising through the image of food, and enables us to see that our lives and those of all species are interrelated.

When Sitting . . . This verse is a promise to oneself not to forget to practice mindfulness throughout the meal.

While Looking . . . This verse helps us nurture love and understanding, and to remember those who are unfortunate, including the tens of thousands of children who die every day of malnutrition, and the countless animals and plants whose encroached habitats no longer provide enough nourishment.

Just Before . . . This verse helps us see the hard work that the farmers put into the food, remember the contributions of many unknown people—migrant workers, truck drivers, food processors, grocers—in bringing it to us, and to appreciate the care that went into cooking and serving it.

While Eating . . . This verse is said during the first four mouthfuls of each meal, to remind us of the Four Immeasurables: lovingkindness, compassion, sympathetic joy, and non-attachment. They are the four abodes of Buddhas and Bodhisattvas.

When . . . Empty. This verse reminds us of the Four Gratitudes: to parents, teachers, friends, and all organic and inorganic species.

Holding . . . This verse brings us back to the present and helps us see the presence of the tea, of the people beside us, of the world around us, and of the small details that are important to life at this very moment.

Peter Levitt

❀

An Intimate View

There is a teaching in Buddhist tradition which tells us that each atom of the universe, at one time or another, has been our mother. And that we have been the mother of each atom as well. Each atom has brought us into being, given us life. Each atom has nourished us, and we have done the same for every atom in the neverending continuous moment we call our lives. To grasp even a little of this teaching makes quite a difference in how we move through the world; seeing what we see and hearing what we hear. It changes our touching and how we touch, our knowing and how we know.

Usually, when we think of where we came from, our human root, we think something like, Oh, my mother gave birth to me. We think that's where it starts, with birth. But recently I've been thinking something different: I used to live inside my mother. I lived there, inside her body for nine months. Can you imagine if somehow you were suddenly transported inside of somebody and lived there for nine months right now?

When I lived inside the body of my mother, she was the entire world to me. She was my Earth, and she was my sky. She was my rivers. She was the weather. She was the sun. She was my absolute physical world. And, of course, even more. But while I was living inside *her* body, she was living inside the body of the world. The body of the world was her Earth, and her sky. Her rivers. Her weather. Her sun. And, though I was me, living inside of her, two bodies, somehow there was one body there at the same time. When I look deeply I see that this very same thing was true for my mother,

233

living in the body of the world. There were also two bodies, but, at the same time, somehow there was only one.

The body of the world is living in the universe, just like a child inside its mother. And each thing of the universe, each of the many, countless things of the universe, sometimes called the 10,000 dharmas, form one body. When we practice slow walking meditation, we can get a feeling for this. There are many bodies walking, but we walk as one body, we breathe as one body, we act as one body. A kind of great intimacy is present. When we sit in meditation, that intimacy is there as well. We breathe in, we follow our breath, we stay with our breath, we know our breath. That means we know our life—we are intimate with it. And when we breathe out, we intimately know our death.

Think of the intimacy my mother and I shared during those first nine months. The kind of deep knowing of one another. Not intellectual knowing, but intimate knowing, in the same way a leaf on a maple tree knows it is autumn when the air has become a little cold and the leaf is turning red. Natural, intimate, immediate, direct knowing. A knowing so intimate that, really, we cannot say it is *knowing* at all—just naked mind.

But what is the naked mind, this mind that is at once the body of the universe, world, mother and child? It is the mind that cannot even be called by that name because, in its fecundity, it is so bare. It is the red of that leaf as autumn comes on, the smooth grey flank of a boulder we lean against during one of our mountain hikes, the sudden flash and dive of a red-tail over the deep-green scented ridge of pines.

It is the mind that knows, not because of anything it has learned, but because it is intimate and full, full each instant, as one constituent member of the universe, of the whole. That full. That fullness we call *empty* in Buddhism. The sound as Bashō's frog-plop!— enters the pond. The soundless sound that gives birth to all sound in our world.

It is the wind, transparent in the highest branches of aspen or oak, the wing of a calligrapher's brush flying across the page, the green of lettuce in your garden, the roar of the river as it flows in your arteries and veins, the warm moist look, borrowed from a spring morning, as you gaze into the eyes of a child—your child in this moment because it is the one you hold, knowing him, knowing her as the very substance, the stuff of galaxies and grasses, snowfalls, deer trails, right there in those little feet that, even as you hold them, walk around the world, taking the whole world with them in every step.

The whole thing is right there, right there in your hands, your intimate, knowing, empty-headed, capable hands. The hands you look into to see your fate, that same fate which we, all of us together, bring about on this planet. Every cell of each one of us, children and mothers, fathers, brother cedar, uncle mountain stream, sister arroyo, aunt snowfield, cousin grizzly, grandmother night sky, grandfather dew, one inside the other inside the other, which is no other than ourselves.

Ourselves, this intimate world.

Patrick McMahon

❀

Small Steps

The series of "Neighborhood Nature Walks" I conducted with my
fifth grade class this past autumn started with my own lunchtime
ambles. Usually, wherever I find myself teaching, I manage to scout
out a nearby park, grove of trees, pond, or stream, where I can shake
the chalk dust out of my cuffs, and where the all-too-human environment of the classroom can shrink back into perspective. But
here in South Vallejo I felt out of my element, a white teacher walking the depressed and depressing neighborhoods of my Black, His-
panic, and Polynesian students. Post-WWII stucco houses peeling
paint, junked cars collapsed on dead lawns, broken wine bottles in
empty lots—I clung to school as a sanctuary. But as the year wore
on, and I shuttled day after day between classroom and the teacher's
lounge, I could feel the dust accumulating.

Then, one breezy February day the outside world summoned,
and at lunch break I struck out into the wasteland. Just around the
corner I came upon a gloriously unpruned old plum tree, profusely
blossoming. I returned that afternoon a little pinker. Next day I was
back, and the next, until all the blossoms had blown away and the
old plum was glossy with new leaves. By that time I had overcome
my initial prejudices, and the neighborhood opened its treasure
chest—a crumbling retaining wall, crevices busy with spiders; a
family of sun-lounging cats; cornflowers turning blue against a
chain link fence; bees swarming in a hollow tree. When I found a
park within walking distance, I began taking my lunch there in
company with three Monterey pines.

Earth Day was coming up about this time, and a young environmental education teacher was piloting suitable lessons in my class. Sincere as he was, for some reason the material just didn't go over. My students couldn't care less about the rainforests, and recycling was for them just a scam for making candy money. After several agonizing weeks I intervened to suggest that the visiting teacher allow the kids to speak frankly. It quickly became clear that their pressing issues were social, not environmental: drug dealers, gangs, guns, and an often tumultuous homelife. Even if their personal well-being was not at risk, as burgeoning adolescents they had other concerns. As Rodney said, "I care about the environment, but I've got better things to do than worry about it." Was the environmental movement, indeed, as I'd suspected, the province of the educated, white, adult middle class?

In spite of my questioning, I was infected by the young teacher's mission, and when he moved on I reviewed the materials he left behind. Much of it required access to wilderness or semiwilderness. I schemed about how to get us to the Marin Headlands, or Mount Tamalpais, but in the end realized I was missing the point: *our* wilderness was just outside the door. I would simply take my class along on my noon outings!

The following September I initiated these walks, and most Fridays, from the equinox to the solstice, as it happened, we spent lunchtime exploring the nooks of our neighborhood. The following entries were selected from my journal of the time.

September 14

Still not ready to take kids off the grounds. Why am I so uneasy?— is it the wildness that comes up in them outside the fence? So went out to the playing field instead. Distributed hula hoops, and installed a pair of students in each, with instructions to take note of what was within those limits. "Bor-r-r-ing." But when they stopped doing the hula and paid attention to this small perimeter, the turf came alive. Jessie and Kevin zeroed in on a column of ants and followed them to the entrance of the colony. "They're carrying eggs!" Jajaira and Estella found the remains of a butterfly. ("How did it die, Mr. McMahon?" How, indeed, *do* butterflies die?) Rodney, always the fisherman, grubbed up some earthworms. He's going to start a worm ranch back in the room. Anthony found a nickel. Cesar and James got a lot of mileage out of some lime-white dog turds.

October 5

We're getting over initial uneasiness at being on the street as a class. It's sad that the kids feel so out of place. The neighbors look at us suspiciously—Why aren't you in school, learning? Children are institutionalized away from their community, as surely as criminals.

In the past few weeks, we've just been walking around the block, but today we ventured down the street that deadends on a pasture. I'm always surprised afresh to come upon this leftover rural patch. Curious about the noise, a pair of horses ambled over. What a panic. A few of our bravest touched their steamy noses. Warm animal breath. Barely managed to get us turned around for school How we crave that contact with our nonhuman brothers and sisters. On our return I read to them D. H. Lawrence's "The White Horse":

> The youth walks up to the white horse, to put its halter on,
> And the horse looks at him in silence.
> They are so silent, they are in another world.

October 26

Assignment today was to collect things autumnal. I expected leaves, and wasn't prepared for the inventiveness of their gathering instincts. Rock wanted to pull up a six-foot-high fennel, roots and all. The lunch bags we brought weren't nearly adequate. Back in the room, I had them do drawings. Some dashed them off, not seeing beyond the letter, but some, like Lisa, really let herself enter the spirit of her object. All afternoon she traced the bumps, cracks and lichens of her stone. Unique attached this note to her drawing—

> *On the nature walk I seen lots of things. I seen a funny looking leaf.*
> *It was pink and green. When it seen me it ran away. I ran after it,*

*then I got it. We went back to the class. Then I traced over it and
colored it pink and green.*

She and the leaf came alive together.

October 30

None of them want to part with their treasures of last Friday. In our
crowded room, I've given over a whole counter to display. What
had been taken for granted is now charged with attention and imagination. Today they wrote from the point of view of their object.
Tashia—

*One day I was laying on the ground when this big old black kid
picked me up and put me in his pocket and said, I got something.
Then he closed his pocket. It was hot in that pocket. I started
swelling.*

So the raging hormones of this age attach to whatever's at hand.
I'd prefer that what's at hand is a leaf, rather than a video game joy-
stick.

November 7

When I stroll around in the city,
I vow with all beings,
to notice how lichen and grasses
never give up in despair.[1]

I need Aitken Roshi's courageous gatha today. Nothing dispir-
its me more than seeing the deep-seated fear these kids have of the
natural world.

There was a great hubbub today toward the back of the line.
When I doubled back, I found several of the boys stomping on a
family of beetles, the girls shrieking in mock terror. What can I say
to turn their heads around? It's not just that they're snuffing out
life, it's that they're snuffing out what I think they also sense as their
own bugness. They are so vulnerable to being stomped on by an
adult foot, parent's or teacher's.

A little later we came upon a dead cat on the street. Their response?—stone it. Are they trying to cast away the fear they carry inside themselves? It would be a worthwhile experiment to bring it back to the classroom and observe it through all the stages of putrefaction, as in the Therevadin corpse meditation.

November 14

I've always wanted to take the kids all the way to the park, but I didn't believe they could make it. But the autumn wind blew us along like leaves today, and before we knew to complain, we were there. I felt curiously protective, as though I were exposing something to violations. This is, in Native American terms, my Secret Place. I should know by now that a teacher's "secrets" are all eventually revealed.

It was enough to let them play on the swings before heading back. Next week will lead them in one more small step to the world of my three pines.

November 16

Took our mindfulness bell with us to the park today. This is the first time I've sounded it outdoors; it carries well. The awareness we've cultivated with it stood us in good stead. After letting the kids disperse into groups, rang it once to signal our customary three breaths; a second to attend to the earth under us; a third, the sky; and a fourth, again three breaths. Some eyes opened.

Michael—

> *I saw a bird building a nest. It was in the tree. It was working very quietly. It was getting sticks and putting them neatly. It was the first time I've seen a bird making a nest.*

So meditation must have had its beginnings, in silence watching a bird make its nest.

Cesar stayed conscientiously with the format of earth and sky, then let his imagination fly—

I saw all the birds flying south for the winter. I saw frost on the ground, and I saw the sun and the blue sky. I would like to go down the Kiddie Walk and find some things, like trees, birds, and wild animals like a bear.

Time to read them *The Ohlone Way,* with the passages about grizzly bears wandering this area just 200 years ago.

December 7

Assignment today was "signs of winter."
Quanisha—

I seen a couple of winter signs like birds flying south, dead baby bugs in the grass, leaves falling off the trees, flowers dying, all kinds of things. But most of all is that the people who planted the flowers can grow some more, and the birds can come back, and the bugs can grow, and the grass can too. And the leaves.

A nine year old's grasp of the larger picture.

December 21

Shortest day of the year, still dark coming to school. And bitterly cold—the Northbay winds cut through my jacket as I stood yard duty, watching students arrive in huddles. Been planning a solstice walk to cap off our autumn ambles, but once in the cozy cave of the classroom, kids couldn't be coaxed out. Neighborhood walks ended for the year as they'd begun—with me on my own.

Paid a visit to the plum tree that had kept me coming back day after day last February. Wished the students could see those bare old branches, miraculously to blossom in another couple of months. Passed the tumble-down retaining wall, spider webs empty. Had lunch under the pines, watched a vee of wild geese cross the gray sky. So where, I reflect over my sandwich, have we gotten over the last months? No further than around the block. No expansive views like those we could have had from Mount Tam. And yet, we *do* know these streets now, fennel and corn flowers growing up around the junk cars, broken glass sparkling in the rough lots, beetles on the sidewalk and dead cats in the road, sky shifting overhead, earth rolling below. This environment is *ours,* welcomes us home as we attend to it in silent observation or active drawing, writing, discussing.

I unfolded my stiff legs and headed back to school. All I can say for sure, I realized, is that they've taken a few steps into the environment and perhaps into themselves. If environmental education is to make any headway with these kids, it will be by way of these small steps. I recall Aitken Roshi's gatha about the perseverance of lichens and grasses, and by the time I return to the warm classroom, I have this gift of the wind.

> As I walk around the block
> I vow with all my neighbors
> To discover the Secret Place
> Among wine bottles and wild geese.[2]

Notes

[1] Robert Aitken, *The Dragon Who Never Sleeps: Verses for Zen Buddhist Practice* (Berkeley: Parallax Press, 1992), p. 42.

[2] *Ibid.*

Michele Hill

❧

Earth Day Celebration

Earth Day presents a wonderful opportunity to celebrate the earth with children, and to create new traditions very much akin to old Buddhist teachings and practice. In April, 1990, adults and children at Koko An Zendo in Honolulu celebrated the community's first Earth Day together by holding an "Evolutionary Remembering" and "Council of All Beings," based on the work of Australian environmentalist John Seed.[1] For other ideas, you may wish to consult your local Earth Day coordinators.

We announced our Earth Day program in this way:

> Twenty years ago millions of people all over the world took part in the biggest demonstration ever seen—on behalf of the earth. Sunday, April 22, 1990 marks the twentieth anniversary of Earth Day and the Diamond Sangha will hold a special program to commemorate this event.
>
> The program will begin at 9 a.m. with one period of zazen. This will be followed by a guided visualization, "Evolutionary Remembering," and an introduction to the Council of All Beings. At about 10 a.m. there will be walking meditation during which children and others will select their "being." Then we will make masks to wear to the Council of All Beings.
>
> For those who wish to take part in the Council, it will be helpful if you can begin thinking about a plant, animal, or some form of life—endangered or not—for which you feel affinity. Bring any materials you think might enhance your mask.

At our Earth Day Celebration, one person read the "Evolutionary Remembering," encouraging each person to feel and act out the creatures in the stages of evolution. Needless to say, we had quite a few enthusiastic participants among the children, particularly when we got to monkeys and apes! This is how our guided meditation went:

OUR EARTH: Within the Milky Way, our sun was born about five billion years ago, near the edge of this galaxy, while the cosmic dust and gas spinning around it crystallized into planets. The third planet from the sun, our own earth, came into being about four and a half billion years ago.

The ground then was rock and crystal beneath which burned tremendous fires. Heavier matter like iron sank to the center; lighter elements floated to the surface, forming a granite center. Continuous volcanic activity brought up a rich supply of minerals and lifted up chains of mountains.

Then about four billion years ago, when the temperature fell below the boiling point of water, it began to rain. Hot rain slowly dissolved the rocks upon which it fell, and the seas became a salty soup containing the basic ingredients necessary for life.

Finally, a bolt of lightning fertilized this molecular soup and an adventure into biology began. The first cell was born. You were there, I was there. Every cell in our bodies is descended in an unbroken chain from that event.

Through this cell, our common ancestor, we are related to every plant and animal on earth.

EVOLUTION OF ORGANIC LIFE: Remember that cell awakening. BE that cell awakening (as indeed you are). We are all composed of that cell, which grew, diversified, multiplied, and evolved into all the life of the earth. What does it feel like to reproduce by dividing into two parts that were me and now *we* go our separate ways?

Now some hundreds of millions of years have passed. First we were algae, the original green plants, then the first simple plants. The algae started to produce oxygen as a byproduct of photosynthesis. Over a billion years or so, this created a membrane of ozone, filtering out some of the fiercest solar rays.

Now I am a creature in the water. For two and a half billion years, simple forms of life washed back and forth in the ocean currents. Imagine them as I speak their names: coral, snails, squid, worms, insects, spiders. Imagine yourself as a simple worm or an early coral living in the warm sea. Feel your existence at this time, for it remains within each of your cells, the memories of this period of your childhood.

FISH: This was followed by the evolution of fish and other animals with backbones. How does it feel to have a flexible backbone? How do you move through the water as a fish? Lying belly down, staying in one place, begin to experience gentle side-to-side rolling, with your head, torso, and lower body moving all as one. How does the world look, feel, sound? Be aware of your backbone, your head, and gills. What does it feel like to move through the ocean, to listen through the ocean?

AMPHIBIAN: Then about 450 million years ago the first plants emerged from the water and began to turn the rock into soil, preparing the ground for animals to follow. The first animals to emerge from the seas were the amphibians. Slowly raise your forearms to drag your body along. Pull with your left and right together. As amphibians we are still very dependent on the water, especially for our reproductive cycle.

REPTILE: It wasn't until the evolution of the reptilian amniotic egg that we were liberated from our dependence on water and able to move completely onto dry land. Still crawling on your belly, start to use legs coordinated with arms, alternating from one side to the other. Notice how our range of movement and perception changes. By 200 million years ago, we had successfully moved onto the land.

EARLY MAMMAL: As mammals we became warm-blooded. Remember how as a reptile you used to have to wait, sluggish, for the sun to warm you? The sun now fuels your metabolism in a more complex way. Feel how this helps you. Imagine yourself a lemur, or perhaps a small cat. Notice how your spine feels. Now with your belly off the floor, begin crawling on your hands and knees. How does this feel? How does your head move? Now our young need to be looked after until they can fend for themselves.

EARLY MONKEY: Begin moving on hands and feet with greater lightness, leaping and climbing. Discover more flexibility in movement of the spine, head, and neck. Make sounds. You can communicate easily with one another by shrieks and whistles. Notice your playfulness and curiosity. We move through the trees, running along branches and swinging through them, our strong opposable thumbs giving us the grip we need. Our sensitive fingertips (with nails instead of claws) are able to judge the ripeness of fruit or groom our fur. Agile balance and keen vision develop. We eat food on the spot where we find it.

GREAT APE: Our body becomes heavier and stronger. We can squat erect but use knuckles to walk. Experiment with balancing. How does the world look and feel? How do you communicate? How do you care for your young?

EARLY HUMAN: Ten million years ago a major climatic change began. The forests, home of the ape, began to retreat to the mountains and were replaced by woodland and the savannah. Here on the savannah we first learned to walk on two legs . . . standing on two feet with strong jaw thrust forward. How does it feel? Vulnerable, but inventive and adaptable. Able to look up and easily see the sky. We postpone eating food until it can be brought back to camp and shared. We live in families, discover language, learn to make fire, make art, music, tools . . . the complexities and subtleties of cooperating successfully with others in a group involved the development of language, the telling of stories, the use of tools, the making of fires.[2]

MODERN HUMAN: Developing farming, working on the land, in market places, moving to town, seeing houses, temples, skyscrapers, walking through busy streets, driving in cars— what do you see and hear and smell and feel? How does it feel to be dwelling more often in cities? How have you become separate from the earth? Now you are pushing your way through a crowded street, you are in a hurry, everyone is in your way.

FUTURE HUMAN: Sitting down quietly, your mind's eye open to any glimpses, images, forms that are waiting to emerge as future human life ... potential in us that is waiting to awaken a larger ecological Self, living fully as part of nature expressing our full potential in whatever way may occur to us ... becoming form.

At the end of this meditation we took turns with a partner going back over the stages we remembered, describing what we experienced in first person—"I am a single cell and I notice...." Then we went outside and did walking meditation while looking for natural materials to enhance the mask that we would wear to the Council of All Beings. As children and adults were ready, they gathered on the porch and began making masks, cutting and drawing eyes and facial features in paper plates, then adding construction paper, leaves, sticks, flowers, and sparkles.

In the original Council of All Beings workshops led by John Seed, the Council is a mourning process for the animals and plants we have lost and may still lose. But our Council was intentionally more hopeful and affirming: we were celebrating Earth Day and empowering ourselves and our children to action, even while we recognized with sadness the life forms we have lost.

We all sat in a circle. One person led the Council, and each being spoke about who we were and what we wanted to tell humans. We had a wide variety of Beings: several kittens, a koala bear, a mouse, the wind, viruses, plants, a coyote, the ocean, an elephant, a Bodhi Tree. At the end, a human arrived. She sat in the center while we told her what we wanted her to bring back to her fellow human beings: stop setting mouse traps, stop polluting, look around and notice the tremendous diversity of life.

We ended with songs—"Children's Precepts" and "Mother Earth" are good choices—and a potluck lunch. The children who participated, ages three to eight, enjoyed this Earth Day celebration very much. We presented the concepts of Earth Day and the interconnectedness of all beings in a way they could understand, and gave them an opportunity to create and participate fully with adults. Together we were able to deepen our practice of compassionate understanding, and to embrace the urgent needs of the earth.

Notes

[1] Our shortened version of the "Evolutionary Remembering" is taken from John Seed, Joanna Macy, Pat Fleming, and Arne Naess, *Thinking Like a Mountain* (Philadelphia: New Society Publishing, 1988) and is reprinted with permission of the publisher.

[2] Editor's note: Many characteristics cited as human development are shared by other creatures in varying degrees and styles—caring for young, language, cooperation, keen vision, tool use, building, adaptability. You may want to explore some of these in detail as a further antidote to our common misconception of humans as the "pinnacle of evolution."

Wendy Johnson

❀

At Home on the Earth—
Nature Practice with Children

In early spring I went at dusk with my four-year-old daughter down to the garden to harvest the first freesia flowers of the season. In the dying sun the red-cupped blossoms glowed with their own light. Alisa hung back in awe and respect, mesmerized by the flowers. When I bent to cut the freesias, she lunged forward in their defense: "Don't, Mama—don't take those flowers from their bed!" She was ardent, passionate, and undeniable. Seeing the chalice of the blossoms filled with rain water, I cut no more flowers and instead sat in the garden with Alisa, sipping a "high tea" of sweet rain from the vermillion flower cups. Satisfied and happy, we returned home through the dark garden.

I live in a Buddhist meditation center, Green Gulch Farm, in the coastal mountains of Northern California, on the edge of the Pacific Ocean. For the last fifteen years, my work has been in organic gardening and environmental restoration in our 115 acre watershed. This work is greatly enhanced by the participation of children and their families. About ten years ago, our huge organic farm was visited by a group of inner-city children from the San Francisco Bay area. Many of these children had never been out of the city before. Huddling together on the edge of a bed of gigantic, oriental poppies pulsating in full bloom, one young boy buried his face in the flowers, coming up only to ask, "Do they bite?" This child directly entered the majesty and mystery of the poppy kingdom, taking me with him in his question. Like little Alisa protecting the red freesias, this young boy helped me to listen and follow the voice of the garden.

In our meditation hall is a seated Buddha with his right hand extended in the earth-touching mudra. Just before his enlightenment, Prince Siddhartha was challenged by Mara, the lord of illusion—by what right was he able to sit still under the Tree of Enlightenment? The Buddha simply extended his hand and touched the Earth, calling on her to be his Witness. The Earth confirmed his call by rumbling in support, and Mara's elephant bowed down in response. This Buddha figure is a favorite among visiting children. They love to assume this calm and solid posture, and they have much to say about what the earth tells the Buddha.

In our quieter times it becomes very clear that we learn a great deal from our observant children. Since 1986, the Green Gulch Community, in cooperation with our local Buddhist Peace Fellowship, has hosted day-long retreats called Family Days of Mindfulness. Designed to offer us a chance to meditate with our children and enjoy a day of nature together, these days are organized in three seasons: spring, fall, and winter. For each season, we do work related to caring for the earth. In the spring we plant potatoes, in the fall we harvest the crop (being sure to collect many boxes for the soup kitchens in San Francisco), and in the winter we dedicate our mindfulness day to trees all over the world.

When Thich Nhat Hanh and friends founded the Plum Village Community in southwestern France a decade ago, the initial event for children and adults was planting a plum orchard. The trees were planted by Vietnamese children living in exile in Europe. The hope was that once the plum trees began to yield, the income from the fruit harvest would be donated to hungry children in Vietnam. "In this way we touch directly the suffering of our friends and loved ones in Vietnam," Thich Nhat Hanh reminded the young tree-planters. The children deeply understood this connection through their planting and care of the trees.

Aware that forests all over the world are being cut, we at Green Gulch Farm apply this same spirit to replanting forest trees in our watershed every winter. Our planting day begins with families sitting in meditation together and discussing what trees have meant to each member. Sometimes we will tell old stories from the life of the Buddha, but we always add modern stories of the good work being done to preserve our natural world. This winter, as we walked up into the hills, we sang our favorite tree song, written by local meditator and friend, Nina Wise:

> I am walking on sunshine,
> I am walking on rivers in the wind . . .
> I am breathing in, trees are breathing out—
> I am breathing out, trees are breathing in.

Our walking was slow and alert, each step dedicated to planting peace. In a beautiful meadow, facing north, with rich deep soil, we set out seventy-five seedlings of Douglas fir and coast redwoods. At the end of the morning, children were tired and very happy. We stopped and sat in the midst of our new trees. Fully aware of the loss of trees in our world, we imagined how our yearling "forest" would look when the children were ten years older. After a while we returned to Green Gulch to eat a vegetarian lunch prepared from the garden. Then the kids played soccer and drew pictures, while their parents talked together about family life. Our day closed by regathering in the meditation hall for hot tea and a treat and to sing together before everyone returned home.

Often we feel we must protect our children from the despair and pain in our world. Watching children meet the life of the natural world directly, unsentimentally, and with true freshness, I have learned that children are excellent meditation guides for adults. When children see a section of forest that has been cut down, they respond directly: What happened here? What can I do? How can I clean up this mess? Will these seeds grow new trees? Working with children on restoration gardening projects can be very inspiring: they remind us to be brave and to keep going.

Although children remind us how to be present with happiness and clarity in the natural world, they also have a real need for good

rituals to help them with extreme loss, such as the death of a pet or wild animal. In these rituals, a garden spot is essential. One young boy, Sam, discovered a dead newt on the way to a tree planting ceremony with his Mom. For their family, caring for the newt took priority. On the spot Sammy devised a perfect ritual—burying the young newt and planting a tree nearby.

We have devised a memorial service to express our sadness and grief for the animals and plants who have died in conjunction with our efforts in organic farming and gardening:

Plants and Animals in the Garden,

We welcome you—we invite you in—we ask your forgiveness and your understanding. Listen as we invoke your names, as we also listen for you:

Little *sparrows, quail, robins,* and *house finches* who have died in our strawberry nets;

Young *Cooper's Hawk* who flew into our sweet pea trellis and broke your neck;

Numerous *orange-bellied newts* who died in our shears, in our irrigation pipes, by our cars, and by our feet;

Slugs and snails whom we have pursued for years, feeding you to the ducks, crushing you, trapping you, picking you off and tossing you over our fences;

Gophers and *moles,* trapped and scorned by us, and also watched with love, admiration, and awe for your one-mindedness;

Sowbugs, spitbugs, earwigs, flea beetles, woolly aphids, rose-suckers, cutworms, millipedes, and other insects whom we have lured and stopped;

Snakes and *mice* who have been caught in our water system and killed by our mowers;

Families of *mice* who have died in irrigation pipes, by electricity in our pump boxes, and by predators while nesting in our greenhouses;

Manure worms and *earthworms,* severed by spades, and numerous microscopic lifeforms in our compost system who have been burned by sunlight;

Feral cats and *raccoons* whom we've steadily chased from the garden;

Rats whom we poisoned and trapped and drowned. *Deer,* chased at dawn and at midnight, routed by dogs, by farmers, by fences, and numerous barriers;

Plants: colored *lettuces,* young *broccoli,* ripe *strawberries* and sweet *apples,* all of you who have lured the animals to your sides, and all plants we have shunned: *poison hemlock, pokeweed, bindweed, stinging nettle, bull thistle;*

We call up plants we have removed by dividing you and sep-
arating you, and by deciding you no longer grow well here;

We invoke you and thank you and continue to learn from
you. We dedicate this ceremony to you. We will continue to
practice with you and for you.

When I consider the work of taking care of our Earth, I feel that
we are taking marriage vows: Know one another in every way. Love,
honor, and protect one another. And take risks together in order
to bring back into balance what has been disturbed. Fall in love
with the Earth, the land, the place you inhabit. Look deeply at where
you live. Know your place in every way, so that you understand
how to act. Notice when the trees on your street bud out and burst
into flower, when the birds arrive and depart, and when they sing
and fall silent. Notice how the rain runs away after a storm. Notice
how you feel when you slow down to give such attention.

During the Buddha's teaching lifetime, he encouraged his fol-
lowers to plant and see to the establishment of one tree every five
years. Over the years many trees were planted and tended during
the rainy season in northern India, and the country felt a true benefit. Over the years at Green Gulch we have planted thousands of
trees, and we now begin to see a change in our landscape, the green
band of saplings fanning out over the coastal mountains. The deeper
we go into this work of reforesting, the keener we have become to
gather and start seeds of native shrubs and trees, to nurture them
for a few years, and later to plant them in their best situation. So,
like the young trees, our work and commitment is also fanning out,
growing deeper and broader with every season.

While I plant trees at Green Gulch, I enjoy practicing this gatha
I learned from Thich Nhat Hanh:

> I entrust myself to Earth
> Earth entrusts herself to me.
> I entrust myself to Buddha
> Buddha entrusts herself to me.

Sometimes I abbreviate the words in irreverent Zen shorthand, saying to the little tree:

> You and me
> Inter-be
> For the long haul.

Please let these words encourage you to share good times in the natural world with your children. Family days do not depend on a meditation center. Set aside your own special times to cherish with your family. Learn from your children and enjoy with them what you observe and love. Let your children help you see the beauty and gifts of our world as they come alive in your time together.

Rafe Martin

❀

The Black Hound[1]

Shakra, king of the gods, arose from his golden throne and peered down towards the earth. There were shining seas and pearl-like clouds, snow-capped mountains and continents of many colors. It was beautiful, yet Shakra felt uneasy.

His luminous senses expanded through the heavens. He felt the heat of war. He heard the bawling of calves, the yelping of dogs, the cawing of crows. He heard children crying. He heard voices shouting in anger. He heard the weeping of the hungry, the lonely, the poor. Tears fell from his eyes, showering the earth like meteors.

"Something must be done!" said Shakra. And he changed himself into a forester with a great horn bow. By his side stood a black hound. The hound's fur was tangled. It's eyes glowed with crimson fire. Its teeth were like fangs. Its mouth and lolling tongue were blood red.

Shakra and the hound leaped, plummeting down down down from among the shining stars. At last they alighted on the earth beside a splendid city.

"Who are you, stranger?" called out an astonished soldier from atop the city's walls.

"I am a forester, and this," said Shakra, with a gesture toward the animal at his side, "is my hound."

The black hound opened its jaws. The soldier on the walls grew dizzy with terror. It was as if he was peering down into a great cauldron of fire and blood. Smoke curled from the hound's throat. Its jaws opened wide, wider still...

256

"Bar the gates!" shouted the soldier. "Bar them now!"

But Shakra and his hound vaulted over the barred gates. The people of the city fled in every direction, like waves flowing along a beach. The hound bounded after them, herding the people like sheep. Men, women, and children screamed in terror.

"Hold!" called Shakra. "Do not move!" The people stood still. "My hound is hungry. My hound shall feed."

The king of the city, quaking with fear, cried "Quick! Bring food for the hound! Bring it at once!"

Wagons soon rolled into the market loaded with meat, bread, corn, fruit and grain. The hound gobbled it all down in a single gulp.

"My hound must have more!" cried Shakra.

Again the wagons rolled. Again the hound gobbled the food down with one gulp. Then it howled a cry of anguish, like a howl from the belly of hell.

The people fell to the ground and covered their ears in fright. Shakra, the forester, plucked his great bow's string. Its sound was like crashing thunder on a story night.

"He is still hungry!" cried Shakra. "Feed my hound!"

The king wrung his hands and wept. "He has eaten all we have. There is nothing more!"

"Then," said Shakra, "my hound shall feed on grasses and mountains, on birds and beasts. He shall devour the rocks and gnaw the sun and moon. My hound shall feed on you!"

"No!" cried the people. "Have mercy! We beg you to spare us! Spare our world!"

"Cease war," said Shakra. "Feed the poor. Care for the sick, the homeless, the orphaned, the old. Teach your children kindness and courage. Respect the earth and all its creatures. Only then shall I leash my hound."

Then Shakra grew huge, and he blazed with light. He and his black hound leaped up, curling like smoke as together they rose through the air, higher and higher.

Down below, in the streets of the city, men and women looked up into the skies with dismay. They reached out their hands to one another and vowed to change their lives, vowed to do as the mighty forester had ordered.

From up above, Shakra looked down from his golden throne and smiled. He wiped his brow with a radiant arm. The countless stars blazed with light and the darkness between them slumbered like a dog by the fire.

Notes

[1]From *The Hungry Tigress*, p. 128–129.

Alexis Rotella[1]

❀

Pea Pod

It was doll Ruthie's birthday.
My best friend came to the party.
Each day to school she wore
the same plaid dress
but she brought a present—
a pea pod tied
with a piece of pink yarn
and in it, the tooth
she could have given
to the fairy.

[1]From *Middle City*, p. 5.

Jacqueline Mandell

❧

Cultivating Kindness
with Young Children

Living Our Kindness

Being healthy role models for our children is vital. Our children are imitative. All of our actions are important to them.

Manifesting true kindness to oneself as well as to others creates harmony in our lives and provides a balanced role model for our children. If we are only kind to others and not to ourselves, our children will imitate this self-negating pattern. If we are only indulgent of ourselves and not generous with others, our children will imitate our selfishness. The honesty of kindness within and without is essential for all generations.

Recognizing Children's Natural Kindness

Before my twin daughters, Chloe and Erica, could talk, they began comforting and caring for each other in times of illness or distress. One child would offer a special toy, blanket or bottle to her sister. They demonstrated a natural kindness toward one another. Recognizing children's natural tendencies toward kind actions reminds us that we need only to nourish and appreciate a quality that is already there.

Supporting Children's Natural Generosity

When my daughters offer bits of food to their dolls and stuffed animals, I tell them how kind they are. They enjoy offering real or imaginative food to all insects, mammals and reptiles. I praise the generous activity of my children.

Thank You

A favorite children's song by Raffi says, "Thanks a lot. Thanks for the sun and the moon."[1] He reminds us to be grateful for everything. Saying *thank you* to our children shows our true appreciation for them and helps to build their self-esteem. Saying *thank you* also reinforces helpfulness. As toddlers, my daughters would always bring their pink and purple brooms and mops to help me clean up after meals. I was grateful for their help and they understood this by my saying, "Thank you."

Mindful Activity

A calm and spacious mind allows for a compassionate heart. After the children go to sleep, I take time to concentrate on unfinished household tasks. Slowing down and focusing in a quiet environment clears tension. Mindful dishwashing, laundry folding or straightening rooms clears space in the house and the mind.

Mothers' Meditation Group

Several mothers and I formed a weekly mothers' meditation group when all of our children were about a year old. Each mother would take a turn for meditation while the other mothers watched the children. Our children played in the same room in which we meditated. In the beginning meetings, my children would climb all over me and try to capture my attention. Later they either sat quietly on my lap or played elsewhere. One day as one mother was sitting in meditation, Chloe sat across from her and watched. Erica sat next to the meditating mother and lined up several stuffed animals for quiet sitting. A few days later my husband noticed one of our daughters sitting in meditation posture for a few minutes. We don't need to exclude our children from our meditation. Our mothers' group discovered that our children could adapt to our discipline.

Patience

When our daughters were two months old, we took them to His Holiness Ganden Tri Rinpoche for blessings. He chanted, touched their heads with his scripture book, and gave them Tibetan Buddhist names. He also gave each of them a piece of Tsong Kapa's robe. For Allan and me, as parents, he emphasized the practice of patience.

Much of children's learning happens in a non-linear way. Since our children use repetition to explore their world, this requires great patience.

Patience requires us to:

Accept the present moment as it is.

Be flexible and calm.

Foster perseverance of inquiry without expectations and time constraints.

Rejoice in our children's small and great discoveries.

Respect the timelessness of children's play.

Remember and Reflect

It helps to reconnect with our feelings of loving kindness for our family by looking back on significant photos, writings or videos and remembering the source of our love. It is also helpful to read and reflect on inspiring books.

Remember what it is like to be served and how good it feels. Then we can appreciate the service we give to our children.

Forgiveness and Letting Go

Practicing forgiveness toward ourselves and our family is healing. Forgiveness allows us to let go of the fear and anger which hinder true compassion. Letting go of resentment and hurt clears the way to an open heart.

Loving Kindness

Joseph Campbell said that "Love is perfect kindness." When our girls are being exceptionally kind to one another, holding hands in their car seats, or offering a hug, we say "Loving." They look back at us and know.

Notes

[1]On the *Baby Beluga* album.

Robert Aitken

❀

How To Make Friends

The other day my son Tom and I were talking about how people want to be popular. He reminded me of a conversation we had when he was a little boy. He was about to go to a different school and was worried about making friends. I suggested that the way to make friends was not to talk about other people.

He didn't see how not talking about other people could make friends for him. I told him that when people notice that you don't gossip, they feel safe with you. They trust you. They like you because they know you could say or do hurtful things, but you don't.

I said this to Tom long ago. I had forgotten about it. So when he reminded me, I asked him, "Did you try not to gossip in your new school?"

"No," he said, "I could never hold back. It was such fun to talk about other people."

I asked, "Why was it fun to talk about other people?"

He said, "I guess it made me feel that I was better than they were. But there was a girl who never gossiped. She was the most popular person in the school. Everybody wanted to be with her."

Think of that person who never gossiped. She became popular because she held back. Instead of joining in the gossip and feeling important, she probably walked away.

Perhaps she didn't know those people who were being talked about. Or if she knew them, maybe she didn't feel that they were very attractive. But still she couln't bring herself to gossip about them. What was she thinking when she walked away? I guess she was probably not thinking about herself. She was probably feeling sorry about the people the others were laughing at.

It seems that everybody knew that the girl would not talk about them. So they felt that she protected them. I imagine that she was not just popular. I imagine that she was a leader. Her example probably made the whole school better.

I remember when I was in elementary school. I wore glasses and had very few friends. I admired a certain group of boys. One day I said something in front of them. I don't remember what I said, but I do remember how one of the big boys answered. He said, "Who put a nickle down your slot?" The other boys laughed. Maybe that made him feel important. It made me feel crushed. I hated him.

The other boys in the group probably felt important too. I hated them too. But I think one reason they laughed was because they were afraid of the big boy. He was dangerous. Someday he might be rude to them too. They needed to show him that they were on his side. Really, he was not their friend.

So there are two ways to be popular. One is the fake way and the other is the true way. The fake way is to make people afraid of you by talking about them and being rude to them. They will try to be nice to you so that you won't put them down.

Remember that what you say and do can be catching. Like a bad cold. When you try to be popular in this fake way, then people will copy you. Soon everybody in the school will be afraid of everybody else. Everybody will be watching everybody else. It will be all they can think about. The playground will have an uneasy spirit.

I think the true way is to make people like you by being decent to them. Being decent is also catching. When you remember to be decent, people will begin to copy you and be decent too. Even if they do not change right away, you can keep on being decent. You can believe that the whole school will get better, little by little. It can be your project. You can be a leader, just like the girl in Tom's school.

But it must be a secret project. You must be a secret leader. If you tell everybody that you are not gossiping or being rude, then you are showing off what a holy saint you are. Make it secret that you don't gossip. Make it secret that you say and do decent things. People will notice very quickly.

When you have a project like this, you can forget about making friends and being popular. What a great relief that can be!— just as though you suddenly recover from a sickness. You feel safe with everyone because everyone feels safe with you and they want to be with you.

All of this comes when you protect other people by being decent. Other people stop worrying about protecting themselves, and instead they protect you. This gives you a chance to be yourself.

Soon everybody is protecting everybody else and everybody has a chance to be themselves. The world suddenly becomes much bigger. You begin to like yourself and to trust yourself to do things on your own. For example, you don't have to depend on TV to take up your time. You're able to entertain yourself with your own interests and feel yourself develop. You get better and better at the things that interest you—maybe music or reading or writing or volleyball or swimming. You find friends who are interested in the same things and you do them together. You are popular but it doesn't seem to matter any more. You are growing up and liking it.

Sandy Eastoak

This, Sweet Food

Once a friend fed me
a steer whose ears I scratched
each time I fed him
apples. Shocked I returned
to silence and felt
his vast and willing
bounty, grateful
for a pleasant country
life, happily
gone beyond

The ducks feast on snails
that I may eat zucchini later on,
a pile of crabgrass dies in the sun
that lettuces and leeks might thrive
to become my dinner,
the blackberries defend
sweet fruit with merciless thorns,
the mint doesn't cringe
when I pour the boiling tea water—
"they know your intent" Ray said
"it's all right"

Vultures don't
kill to eat

yet the fire in their cells
like mine is fueled
by the patient capture of
solar rays turned green
the breath and pulse
of previous lives

I peel an orange
and the vastness of space
among the stars
falls open in my hands

in absolute silence
I might see it
smile

Richard Nelson

✿

The Island Within[1]

My dog Shungnak and I come across a familiar place, where blazes mark a trail that passes through a stretch of heavy forest. Inside the woods, I feel refreshed and secure. I've walked through here so many times that certain trees are like friends, to be greeted or touched in passing.

The trail through this opaque, self-concealing forest was only a faint game path before I brushed it out a few years ago, making an easier route across this part of the island. Deer have taken it over since then, made it a thoroughfare for daily trips between the beach and the muskeg. Here, in the middle stretch of woods, it's always dark and wet; broad-trunked spruce and hemlock loom overhead, and the ground is matted with deep, feathery moss. An old fallen tree trunk beside the trail is nothing but a long mound beneath the cushion of moss; its stump rises above one end like a hunched man in a green cloak. The entire forest floor is hidden this way, under a thick, living shroud.

Looking off into the forest, I imagine that the moss and soil have magically become transparent, so I can crawl around like a kid on a frozen pond, peering into the clear earth. All the embedded things have become visible—the rotted tree trunk, the stump, and the knitted maze of living roots. Each root is revealed, from its thick beginnings at the base of the mother tree, snaking away and gradually becoming thin, branching and weaving through dozens of other roots like a single strand in an immense, sprawling net. The root becomes slender as a pencil, then a string, and finally a delicate thread with hairs so minute they're too small to see. At these

269

far extremities I can no longer tell where the root ends and the earth begins.

Then, I look at the trees and imagine that they've become transparent—tall columns of pure crystal. I see dark lines of dissolved minerals and water from the soil seeping through the roots, into the trunk and then upward, drawn by whatever mysterious force works in the veins of trees. I follow them to the high limbs, then out through the centers of branches and boughs, finally into the tips of crown needles a hundred feet above the ground. The once-dark soil becomes lighter along the way, then finally turns clear and vanishes as the tree absorbs it.

Tracing these metabolic pathways, I see that just as the tree fingers into the earth, the earth also fingers into the tree. Each encloses the other. The earth extends high above me within the tree, and the tree spreads out under me within the earth. Each flows inside the other and through it. "Where does the earth end and the tree begin?" I whisper. "Where does the tree end and the earth begin?"

Approaching a peninsula of timber, I spot a small deer grazing near the trees. He's already noticed us but stands there watching, fascinated and unperturbed, as we gently cross the meadow. Shungnak doesn't see the deer until we've come within thirty yards. Then he takes a few steps and, on an impulse, I make a soft bleat, like a fawn or a rutting buck. He stops short, peers at us, relaxes, and starts feeding again. Each time he gets nervous I make the bleating sound, and each time he seems reassured. Impetuous little deer, this summer's fawn, I wonder how he became separated from his mother.

When we're about fifty feet apart, Shungnak becomes so excited I'm afraid she'll charge after the deer, so I fasten a rope on her collar and tie it to a tree. Then I shake my finger at her nose to intimidate her into keeping quiet. Bent over to make myself small, still bleating at intervals, I inch closer. The orphan stares, blinks, lets me come within twenty feet, then frisks up an embankment toward the woods. I follow him to the edge of the trees, then get down on all fours, bleat softly, and move toward him again.

Over the past year, I've kept a secret dream, that I would some-day touch a full-grown deer on the island. But since the idea came, it's seemed harder than ever to get near them. Now it almost looks possible, if only with this delicate little fawn. He faces toward me, ten feet away, showing no inclination to leave.

Then Shungnak intervenes. Losing her self-restraint, she pours out a chorus of whines and yowls that frightens the deer but draws his attention away from me. Expecting that he'll dash off at any moment, I settle into the grass and take in whatever I can. Naive and innocent waif, forest dwarf, the living embodiment of an artist's fawn; feather-soft body wrapped in thick brown fuzz; wispy, flick-ing, long-furred tail; frail and supple legs with tiny black hooves; huge vitreous eyes; inordinately long, fluttering lashes. He works his little jaw back and forth, lifts his nose and gropes for a scent, looks toward us and away, telegraphing his anxiety. I can see the breaths pulsing in his chest, the parting of fur on his neck as he turns his head from side to side. Then Shungnak lets out a star-tling, protracted wail, and the deer child dances off into the forest.

If only Ethan had been along. I would gladly have stood aside to watch the meeting of fawn and boy, and especially to share the peculiar afterglow it's left in me. As Shungnak and I walk away, I feel an elation that illuminates my whole view of the surrounding forest. It seems vital, alive, filled with energy, as if autumn is sud-denly a season of birth rather than of dormancy and death. Look-ing through the woods where the deer vanished, I now see a radi-ant mosaic of leaves—the mottled green haze of alders, the tawny clouds of blueberry and menziesia, the fields of thick-bladed sedges, the remnant patches of deer cabbage and wild lily of the valley—sheltered by a canopy of needles and boughs. And I suddenly under-stand something I've only known intellectually before: that all of them are nothing more or less than the earth expressing itself in living form. The earth grown out from within and shaped into leaves.

The same is true for the other plants: every spruce and hemlock and shore pine; every creeping juniper and devil's club; every sprig of crowberry, labrador tea, and bracken fern; every skunk cabbage, twisted stalk, horsetail, and sundew. So far, it's a clear and easy observation, the earth drawn up through roots, transformed into stalks and branches, quivering as leaves and bursting into flower. In the case of animals, the connection is more subtle but just as absolute. The little buck is nothing more or less than earth, grown out from within to express itself as deer. The glaucous-winged gull, surf scoter, varied thrush, bald eagle, dark-eyed junco, and even the raven himself—all of them, earth shaped into birds, shaped into bright feathers and hot blood, shaped into morning songs, shaped into flight and flung out over the soil like molten lava.[2]

The quick edge of earth, shaped into every creature that grows and breathes; that creeps, flies, burrows, swims, slithers, leaps, or dances; that shudders in the surge, soars on the high winds, or sinks into the deep soil; that hides beneath rocks, flashes in the sun, trembles in the shadows, roars a warning at dawn, or throws its song up against the mountainsides; that laughs, plays, frolics, exalts, cries, or cringes; the powerful and the weak, the huge and the small, the clever and the slow, the ornate and the plain, the nimble and the clumsy, the prolific and the rare. Fleeting expressions of the earth, shaped for a moment to crawl up into the light, fall back onto the surface, and sink down inside. In such a world, where is the real separation between organic and inorganic, living and nonliving?

My thoughts drift away from the plants and animals, and focus inside myself. I become sharply conscious of my own breathing— a cool, fresh sensation rushing down inside my chest, and then warm, moist air brushing against my face as I exhale. A sudden *understanding* runs through me, that every breath I take draws the clear flesh of earth through my self, creates a never-ceasing flow of particles in and out of my body. During every moment, I fill myself this way, with air that is as much a part of earth as the soil and all that lives on it. This comes like an insight to me, though it might seem naively self-evident to native people, whose entire thought centers on an intuitive, almost instinctual awareness of being connected to the earth.

I breathe in the soft, saturated exhalations of cedar trees and salmonberry bushes, fireweed and wood fern, marsh hawks and meadow voles, marten and harbor seal and blacktail deer. I breathe the same particles of air that made songs in the throats of hermit thrushes and gave voices to humpback whales, the same particles of air that lifted the wings of bald eagles and buzzed in the flight of hummingbirds, the same particles of air that rushed over the sea in storms, whirled the high mountain snows, whistled across the poles, and whispered through lush equatorial gardens...air that has passed continually through life on earth. I breathe it in, pass it on, share it in equal measure with billions of other living things, endlessly, infinitely.

And like the alder and spruce, the brown bear and black oystercatcher, the mink and great horned owl, I bring the earth inside myself as food. The bedrock of this island becomes soil, feeds the skunk cabbage and marigold, then becomes deer bone and muscle...then becomes me. Storm driven rain that seeps down under the muskeg moss becomes the stream; I drink from the stream and it becomes me. Fiddleheads and cockles, lingcod and huckleberries, Dolly Varden trout and beach greens have all become me. I eat from this island; I eat from this ocean. The island and ocean flow through me.

There is nothing in me that is not of earth, no split instant of separateness, no particle that disunites me from the surroundings. I am no less than the earth itself. The rivers run through my veins, the winds blow in and out with my breath, the soil makes my flesh, the sun's heat smolders inside me. A sickness or injury that befalls the earth befalls me. A fouled molecule that runs through the earth runs through me. Where the earth is cleansed and nourished, its purity infuses me. The life of the earth is my own life. My eyes are the earth gazing at itself.

The croaks of a raven sweeping overhead bring me back to the muskeg. I look around and wonder aloud: "Where does the earth end; where do I begin?" My words puff out in ribbons of fog that wreathe over the moss. They lift up through the tree trunks and

high boughs, float over the forest, and vanish into a cloud that smokes from the distant ridge of Kluksa Mountain. The cloud whirls off, thickens and towers into the sky, fuses with a mass of cumulus, and drifts away on the wind far aloft.

Above the island, above the archipelago, above the western edge of the continent, above the sprawling back of the ocean, caught in the gyre of the atmosphere and the slow turning of the earth, my breath is carried into the stream of life.

I remember the orphan deer, and think: there are no boundaries; there is no separation; each of us is the other. I am the deer and the deer is me.

Recognizing this, I see a compelling reason to live as much as possible not only on the island but also *from* it—the meat and fish and fruit it provides. In this way, I can bring the island inside me, binding my body and my soul more closely with this place. Turning away from the artificial boundaries of physical separateness, I can strive to become a part of the island's life, just as it has become the center of mine.

Living from wild nature joins me with the island as no disconnected love ever could. The earth and sea flow in my blood; the free wind breathes through me; the clear sky gazes out from within my eyes. These eyes that see the island are also made from it; these hands that write of the island are also made from it; and the heart that loves the island has something of the island's heart inside. When I touch my self, I touch a part of the island. It lives within me as it also gives me life.

I am the island and the island is me.

I hope someday the children of my son Ethan's generation will understand their connection to the earth far better than I, in a way that transcends the mechanics of teaching and objective thought, as native people[3] must have come to know it in their childhood. And I hope I might live long enough to see Ethan recognize and celebrate the fact that he is the earth, expressing itself as a beloved, laughing boy.

Notes

[1]Excerpted from *The Island Within*, p. 244–50, ©1989 by Richard Nelson. Reprinted by permission of Susan Bergholz Literary Services, New York.

[2]You may want to read this story to your children, then work together to ennumerate the beings that are shaped by the earth where you live. You can create your own recognition ceremony to help make your place deeply home.

[3]Richard Nelson's experiences reflect years of learning with the elders of the Koyukon people, a Native American tribe living in interior Alaska.

Anaar Eastoak-Siletz, age seven

❀

Hungry Hawk?

Some people have destroyed yet another very large chunk of grass, brush, and trees. There used to be jackrabbits there. Now a hawk, sitting on a nearby tree is looking for any rustles in the tiny clump of brush that is left, but probably won't stay very long. We walk toward the brush. Five small quail scurry to another pile, this one of grass. We do not follow. I think of the hawk. Will she starve? Will he move? Do the quail know about the hawk? I would rather have the hawk eat a rabbit or a mouse than a quail. But with this field bulldozed bare, there are no jackrabbits or mice left.

A breeze rustles through the grass. "It's time to go," I feel some-one say. "Just a minute." The breeze blows again. I look over this wide, brown, dusty stretch of land, over to the next field. It's still covered with grass. The next field looks just like this one did before it was bulldozed. Jackrabbits who lived in the next field might have to share their homes with the jackrabbits who used to live in this field. It might be much too crowded.

There is a stronger breeze. "Hey!" I shout. "I saw a jackrab-bit!...or was that just the wind?" I think about the quail and the hawk and the brush as I run over the ditches, trying to catch up with everyone.

Jim Harrison[1]

✸

Dogen's Dream

What happens when the god of spring
meets spring? He thinks for a moment
of great whales travelling from the bottom
to the top of the earth, the day the voyage
began seven million years ago
when spring last changed its season.
He enters himself, emptiness
desiring emptiness. He sleeps
and his sleep is the dance of all the birds
on earth flying north.

[1]From *Beneath a Single Moon*, p. 128.

Sandy Eastoak

❀

Wider Family, Deeper Sangha

One morning, I was editing manuscripts in a lawn chair beneath two young pine trees. My interpretations of what I was reading had input from these fellow beings. I confess that there is no influence on earth, including the best Zen masters, whom I trust as completely as a good tree. It was no coincidence that the Buddha was enlightened beneath a Bo tree. The great wisdom of the tree-consciousness held him, and gave, in its tireless generosity, just that extra bit he needed to go the whole way. We must thank that tree, as well as that man, for these centuries of guidance.

In company with pines, all separation between Buddhist parenting and nature love vanished. I, or the pines, knew that today it is essential for parenting—and for Buddhism—to emerge from and express continuously our oneness with earth's manyness.

Buddhism, or any other practice of mindfulness, will take us to an understanding of the equality of life forms as tao, as dharma. Reverence for all life forms, and our supporting forms of rock, wind and water, is a profound and inevitable aspect of Buddhist practice. How could Buddhist parenting not make this very clear?

But how could any parenting not make this very clear? We, and all sentient beings with us, are currently undergoing a suffering peculiar to our time—total environmental peril. The enormity of suffering that extinguishes whole species every day can be seen in part as what comes with a long period of parenting that did not make this very clear.

The other day I saw a young mother and father fishing from a dock with their small son and daughter. The fish they were catching weren't good to eat, they said. They weren't going to cook them. Why then subject them to pain and death? What were they teaching their children? The wonder was there, hand-clapping delight at the beauty and mystery of these underwater beings as they were brought flapping to the dock. But the lesson was one of desensitization.

One can kill a fish in great reverence and gratitude in the process of sustaining one's body. But to impale it and rip its lip just for fun, just to see who can catch the most—even when the fish are eventually thrown back, possibly to recover and swim again—and to do this in the presence of young children, is to impart the wrong relationship. These parents were loving and enjoyed the sun, the salt air, the company of their family—no mean accomplishments these days. But they were also defaming the Three Treasures, particularly the third treasure of the Sangha, which includes those fish-beings so callously used and those children so blithely deceived.

We are raising children not only in an endangered environment, but also in a culture that views incidents like this as good family fun. The mainstream would view me as a little crazy—or perhaps as merely metaphorical—for attributing editorial decisions to pine trees. We are systematically cut off from belief in our own experience of communion with other species. Buddhist parenting must put considerable emphasis on nature awareness precisely to counteract the prevailing attitudes that other species are so unintelligent as to be essentially dead. To young children, every sentient being is alive and volitional. We will heal ourselves by refraining from changing their minds about this.

It helps to widen our notion of the family. Family practice is the family practicing together. There really is no other practice. It's like the Bodhisattva not entering nirvana until all beings are saved. I first took this as an ideal—one should be as generous as that. Then I saw it was a simple description of how things work—we are really as connected as that.

One member of a family does not practice outside the practice of the whole family. (That explains some of the peculiar miseries of parents at odds about spiritual practice.) Each member's practice is determined in part by each other member's practice. Even the baby has a way of practicing that affects mom's practice, dad's practice, the family dog's practice.

It is the dog's practice that I'm really getting at. Mu? No, bu wu.

When I was a child I was very proud of having a dog that was a whole year older than I. An elder dog, her elderness becoming more apparent each year as she aged "seven" to my one. She was an experienced mother before I could use a knife and fork, which of course, she never learned.

Being a somewhat unattended child, I was free to feel the respect her age and experience deserved. She felt rather like an aunt to me. As aunts go, she was quite a good one. Comparing my literal ethical sense with the more fluid maneuvers of other members of my family, I seem a little alien. Why this difference? Ah, my aunt, the dog. This was a dog you could lock in a car with a bag full of steaks and come back two hours later to find the steaks untouched and the dog cross-eyed with virtue.

She was normally gentle, with one exception—you must *not* touch her tail. One day I realized that my extreme fussiness about my good pen was very like that. I began to wonder how many people's characters derive from a nonhuman significant other in their childhood.

Even more influential in my departing the beliefs of my immediate family and seeking a path of wisdom and healing was a woods that adjoined the property where I lived from age six to eleven. At the knees of trees I learned love, nurturing, deep ecology, and respect.[1] The consciousness of these tree-beings endowed me with energy and direction out of the insanity of my human family. My practice was nurtured, saved, made possible by theirs.

I sense in the world today a movement toward extensive family practice. Australian deep ecologist John Seed, who experiences himself as "a part of the forest that can talk," was claimed by this movement.[2] There are signs and nuances of it wherever anything

feels good. The family as a whole, the global, all-species family, knows it is in trouble. We must practice together or perish together.

Buddhism is coming to America in earnest just as the ecological crisis is coming everywhere in earnest. The Council of All Beings, ecofeminism in its mystical forms, the revival of Native American spirituality, the renewal of European goddess religions—all seek and show a spiritual answer to this superficially material challenge. These are not coincidences. *These are the family stirring itself to practice.*

In our personal practice, our human family, whether nuclear or extended, is not enough. Our children need not only a grandfather to tell them stories of the old days and a grandmother to soothe them when mom's overwhelmed, they also need a pine to teach them rooting in the mysterious, a blackberry to teach protection of what we love[3], a turkey to teach unmediated generosity, a hawk to help them soar over distant visions.[4]

The characters of other species, both the species character and individual characters, are teachers, gifts of abundance, sources of joy and comfort. There are times when my younger daughter is sad and I can soothe her only partially. Some time spent holding her chicken is just what she needs to bring her back. Who is this chicken? A friend of my daughter. Her family. What my daughter gets from her is partly mysterious to me, which is good.

What she gets holding her chicken on the porch is different from what she gets holding her chicken among the grape vines. The grapevines also have things to tell, things neither I nor she understand in words, yet our understanding and behavior are influenced by these ones. The grapevine, too, is a unique eye of the cosmos seeing itself, its seeing communicated to us when we are openly awake in its presence.

When our world and our children's future is crumbling by human mistreatment of nonhumans, we need more than zafus and meditation bells to help our children on their spiritual journey. Perhaps we absolutely must surround them with significant others of the plant and animal kingdoms. We must believe their experiences of interspecies communication and we must demonstrate our own.

What do I feel in the presence of a maple that is different from what I feel in the presence of a redwood? What do I learn about right action watching a chicken or about right mindfulness watching a bee? How can I find a language without simile or metaphor to tell my children—to agree with my children!—that these experiences are real? How can I deepen these messages from other ways of being and share them plainly with family, friends, community?

We can view our family as including those nonhuman beings we live with, honoring them as we do human family members. We can "discuss" pruning with a tree before we take up saw and shears[5], just as we would discuss thinning our child's toy collection before making a trip to Goodwill. In the backyard we can make a brush pile as habitat for birds[6], as well as a swing set.

We also need to make explicit how many beings belong to our sangha. The trees at Sonoma Mountain Zen Center give spiritual support as tangible as that of the Roshi and senior members—there must be ways to demonstrate that we are aware of this. There must be ways to interweave our personal, family and sangha practice with all forms on earth—the animals, the plants, the stones, the waters, the winds.

I know children are acutely aware of earth's situation, even if many have been socialized to keep quiet about it. My older daughter Anaar, when she was about eighteen months old and barely learning to talk, went with me to the Department of Motor Vehicles. As we waited in the room so close to the busy freeway, she gazed out the window for a long time and then said sadly:

"Cars say no."

"What, honey?"

"Cars say no."

"Cars say no to who?"

"To trees."

"What do trees say?"

"Ari. Mommy. Rocks."

Deep in our animal hearts, we of any age cannot take as sincere a religious practice that fails to name our sadness and fear about the earth and to speak commonly our mystical experiences with nonhuman beings. Our children need this just to be their whole selves. Our whole earth family needs it just to survive. That such a practice deepen, strengthen and spread is the hope of everybody's future generations and the ground of all beings' enlightenment.

Notes

[1] Sandy Eastoak, "A Child of the Woods," unpublished manuscript.

[2] See "The Rainforest as Teacher," an interview with John Seed, *Inquiring Mind*, 8:2, Spring 1992.

[3] See Sandy Eastoak, "My Neighbors, the Blackberry," unpublished manuscript.

[4] For more on animals as teachers, see Jamie Sams and David Carson, *Medicine Cards*, in Resouces.

[5] See The Findhorn Community, *The Findhorn Garden: Pioneering a New Vision of Man and Nature in Cooperation* (New York: Harper & Row, 1975).

[6] See Noble Proctor, *Garden Birds: How to Attract Birds to Your Garden* (Emmaus, PA: Rodale Press, 1985).

Jerry Davis[1]

❀

The Faraway Sangha

I live in a city near a river. Every morning and evening I walk my dogs. At these times I practice walking meditation and breathing. I try to be aware of everything around me. Sometimes as I breathe outward, I chant, "Om mani padme hum." This is a very ancient chant which means, "the jewel in the lotus," a saying used to remind us about the treasure of great wisdom that appears in ordinary life. One morning I was chanting when suddenly, without even the tiniest thought about it, I felt an incredible sensation.

I felt—just as clearly as I felt the cool breeze and the tugging of the dogs on their leashes—I *felt* that I was right that moment being loved by Buddhist monks who were a long, long way away in space and time. The feeling was so real, I could sense their arms around me in a loving embrace.

The feeling was so wonderful that I began to weep. As I stood in the street, in the midst of my tears, I returned the love to the universe. I shone that love back out into the universe with the intention that those monks receive it, no matter where they might be.

I don't know how or why this happened to me. I only know that it now has a special meaning. I'm not a monk. I don't belong to a sangha near my home. But now, even though I practice alone, I feel connected to a sangha somewhere. As I told my friend Richard, Now I take refuge in them, and I ask them to take refuge in me.

Notes
[1]This story was adapted from a letter to Thich Nhat Hanh that appeared as "Simply Being Present" in *Mindfulness Bell*, Spring, 1991, p. 18.

OM MANE PADME HUM

This mantra means: "God resides in the lotus of my heart." From Anna Keoloha, *Songs of the Earth*, p. 29.

OM NAMAH AMITABIYAH

KWANSEUM

Calypso

All day All night All
day All night While
walk - ing While stand - ing While
sit - ting While ly -ing down Be - yond
wrong Ee - yond right Be - yond
Dark - ness Be - yond light No
sound No sight All
day All night.

Descant

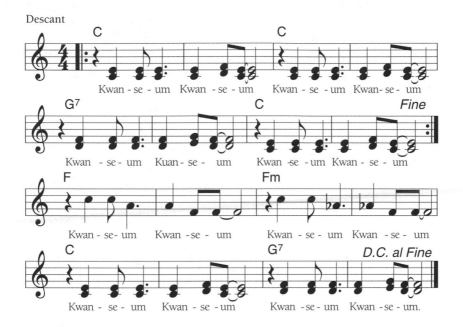

From Nathaniel Needle, *Dharma Moon*.

BUDDHA AND THE CHARIOTEER

words and music by Nathaniel Needle

Oh Bud-dha rode out from the pal-ace one day where his fa-ther the king kept him out of the way did-n't want him to see a-ny suf-frin' or pain but Bud-dha made his char-i-o-teer ex-plain. "Chan-na, Why He said, is that wo-man's face all wrin-kled why is that wo-man's face all wrin-kled why is that wo-man's face all wrin-kled?" The char-i-o-teer re-plied, "That's an old wo-man with her face all wrin-kled, an old wo-man with her face all wrin-kled that's an o-old wo-man with her

face all wrin-kled," and Bud-dha's eyes o-pened wide. He said, "Im-per-ma-nence sur-rounds us, ex-is-tence does-n't stay, The old ones of to-mor-row are young e-nough to day" So he Sat in med-i-ta-tion, he did-n't dream or doze, and he found lib-er-a-tion, which nei-ther comes or goes!

2. "Why is that man all cold and sweaty?
   "That's a sick man all cold and sweaty, a sick man all cold and sweaty, that's a sick man all cold and sweaty."
   "The sick ones of tomorrow are well enough today."

3. "Why has that man got sheets around him?"
   "That's a dead man with sheets around him, a dead man with sheets around him, that's a dead man with sheets around him.
   The dead ones of tomorrow are live enough today."

HAPPY BIRTHDAY BUDDHA

words and music by Nathaniel Needle

Does a dog have Bud-dha Na-ture? Bud-dha

Na-ture? Bud-dha Na-ture?

(Be a dog) (Be a dog)

Hap-py Birth-day Bud-dha Hap-py Birth-day Bud-dha

Hap-py Birth-day Bud-dha 'cause

Bud-dha's Birth-day's al-ways ev-ery day 'cause

Bud-dha's Birth-day's al-ways ev-ery day. Ev-en

(Shout)

now. Ev-en now. Now!

Repeat song with a pig, a rock, or anything else that occurs to you!

LONG AGO IN INDIA

Kimi Hisatsune, Jane Imamura

Long a-go in In-di-a, A lit-tle babe was born And all a-round were pret-ty flowers, to greet the glo-ri-ous morn.

2. Far away in India, This babe began to grow, And all around were happy sights, So pain he did not know.

3. Long ago in India, He studied hard from all, He learned so well he soon became The greatest Prince of all.

4. Far away in India, The Prince went out to see, The city and its habitants, And felt deep sympathy.

5. Long ago in India, The Prince decided to go, And seek the way to save us all, From pain of birth and death.

6. Far away in India, The Prince had found the truth, And now he's Buddha wise and kind, Who shows the way to peace.

THREE TREASURES (I TAKE REFUGE)

Thich Nhat Hanh (based on a traditional Buddhist chant), music by Betsy Rose

I take refuge in the Dharma, The way of understanding and light, Namo Dharmhiya, Namo Dharmhiya, Namo Dharmhiya

I take refuge in the Sangha, The community of mindful harmony, Namo Sanghiya, Namo Sanghiya, Namo Sanghiya

BREATHING IN, BREATHING OUT

Betsy Rose

Breath-ing in   Breath-ing out   Breath-ing

in   Breath-ing out   I am bloom-ing   like a

flow - er   I am fresh   as the dew   I am

sol - id   as a   moun -tain   I am firm   as the

earth   I am   free.................

Breathing in, breathing out
Breathing in, breathing out
I am water reflecting
What is real, what is true
And I find I have space
Deep inside of me
I am free

I am free, I am free
Breathing in, breathing out...

293

CHILDREN'S PRECEPTS

Thich Nhat Hanh and Betsy Rose

COMPASSIONATE UNDERSTANDING

Anaar Eastoak-Siletz, age 7

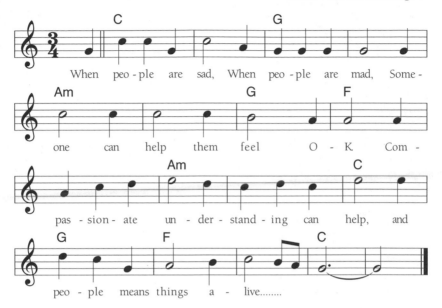

When peo-ple are sad, When peo-ple are mad, Some-one can help them feel O - K. Com-pas-sion-ate un - der-stand-ing can help, and peo-ple means things a - live........

If you want to, you can make up your own verses, for example:

When redwoods are sad,
When redwoods are mad,
Someone can help them feel ok.
Compassionate understanding can help,
And redwoods are things alive.

OM TARA

Om Ta - ra, tu Ta - ra Om Ta - ra, tu Ta - ra

From Anna Keoloha, *Songs of the Earth*, p. 30.

SANGHA ROUND THE CAMPFIRE

words from the Metta Sutta, four part round music by Nathaniel Needle

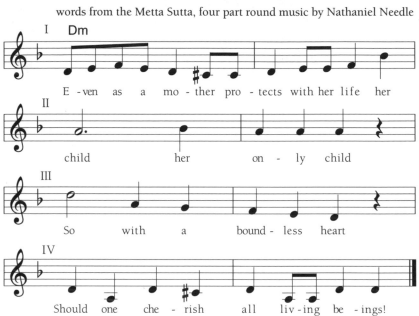

E -ven as a mo -ther pro -tects with her life her

child her on - ly child

So with a bound - less heart

Should one che - rish all liv -ing be - ings!

REMEMBER?

Jane Imamura

What are the things to re-mem-ber? Re-mem-ber?

Think, think, think, of pure and beautiful thoughts, say, say, say, -

pure and beautiful words and do, do, do - pure and beautiful deeds,

1. Those are the things to re-mem-ber.

2. most beau-ti-ful!

What are the purest and most beautiful? Most beautiful?
Think, think, think, of boundless life and light, say, say, Namu
Amidabutsu, and put our hands together in thanks,
Those are the purest and most beautiful!

LOVE OF A LOTUS

Baba Hari Dass/Shankar Heinrich

The lo-tus blooms in the wa-ter to see the sun's face. The
sun turns a-round, and the lo-tus turns in place. The
lo-tus blooms in the wa-ter to show love to the sun. They
talk with their eyes, the lo-tus cha-ses for fun. The
lo-tus blooms in the wa-ter, the lo-tus fades a-way.
Love is shown by the heart, not by the words you say.
Love is shown by the heart, not by the words you say. The
lo-tus blooms in the wa-ter. Stars twin-kle in the sky.
An-i-mals dance in jung-les. The birds sing when they fly.

From *A Child's Garden of Yoga*, pp. 99–103. Hand movements to accompany the song are illustrated in the book—see *Resources*.

Contributors

Robert Aitkin, Roshi and Director of Diamond Sangha in Honolulu, has written many books, including *Taking the Path of Zen* and *The Practice of Perfection*.

Jaymz Asher studies theater and relishes the natural environment.

Allan Hunt Badiner is a writer living in Big Sur, California, and editor of *Dharma Gaia*.

Dhyana Cabarga, ten years old, used to live a door away from San Francisco Zen Center. She has a cat named Grace.

Jerry Davis, Vice President of Research at Pennsylvania Higher Education Assistance Agency, practices independently "the best he can."

Amie Diller, the mother of a three-and-a-half year old daughter, was ordained a priest by Maureen Stuart Roshi in 1987.

Diana Diprima, author of thirty-two books of poetry and prose and mother of five grown children, studies alchemy and Tibetan Buddhism in California.

Sandy Eastoak, artist and student of John Tarrant Roshi, home-schools her two daughters with her Iranian husband.

Anaar Eastoak-Siletz raises ducks and trees. Her favorite part of Sonoma Mountain Zen Center is the pond.

Sahel Eastoak-Siletz, a Brownie Girl Scout, has five goldfish, a rabbit, and a black chicken.

Christina Feldman, teacher at Insight Meditation Socieity in Barre, MA, has led retreats around the world for 18 years. She lives in Totnes, Devon, with her partner and two children.

Eliot Fintushel, who studied with Philip Kapleau and Toni Packer, makes his living as a mask theater and mime performer for children.

Norman Fischer, a Zen Buddhist priest since 1980, is author of six volumes of poetry. He lives at Green Gulch Farm with his wife, Kathie, and their twin sons.

China Galland, long-time student of Buddhism and Christianity and mother of three grown children, is the author of *Longing for Darkness: Tara and the Black Madonna*.

Barbara Gates, a writer and co-editor of *Inquiring Mind*, lives in Berkeley, California, with her husband and four-year-old daughter.

Ari Gervon-Kessler participated in an early Family Mindfulness Retreat with Thich Nhat Hanh.

Maggie Glueck lives in Mount Colah, Australia, and practices Zen at Gorrick's Run.

Sam Hamill, editor at Copper Canyon Press for 20 years, is contributing editor for *American Poetry Review* and *Tricycle: the Buddhist Review*.

Thich Nhat Hanh, Zen master and prolific author, conducts retreats in Europe and North America for veterans, helping professionals, artists, environmentalists and children.

Susan Hansen lives and grows with her two children in Ann Arbor, Michigan. Her practice is focused on chanting and mindfulness in everyday life.

Jim Harrison is a poet and novelist living in Northern Michigan.

Michele Hill, Director of the University of Hawaii Chidren's Center, has developed curriculum and presented workshops on sex abuse prevention for children.

Deborah Hopkinson co-founded *Kahawai*, the first journal on Western women in Buddhism. Her children's stories include *Sweet Clara and the Freedom Quilt* (Alfred A. Knopf, 1993).

Mushim Ikeda has traveled widely to Buddhist centers in North America and South Korea, and lives in Oakland, California, with her partner and their son.

Jane Imamura has served the Jodo Shin community as a *bomori* (priest's wife) for most of her adult life. An accomplished musician and composer, she is devoted to the cultivation of Buddhist music.

Ryo Imamura, professor of psychology at Evergreen State College, represents the 18th generation of Jodo Shin priests in his family, and is a past national president of the Buddhist Peace Fellowship.

Laurie Jackson, a nurse with degrees in Chinese traditional medicine, spent three years working and studying in Asia, and now works part-time in a health program for low-income Asian women and children.

Wendy Johnson is a lay disciple of Zen Master Thich Nhat Hanh. She lives with her family at Green Gulch Farm Zen Center, where her work is in organic horticulture.

Grace Karr lived with her parents at Berkeley Zen Center from age eight to fourteen. A Phi Beta Kappa graduate of University of California, Santa Cruz, she now lives in Mexico City.

Anna Kealoha is a mother, musician, writer, and homeschool teacher who lives in Occidental, California. Her book on homeschooling, *Trust the Children*, is forthcoming from Celestial Arts.

Lee Klinger-Lesser, whose family is now her primary practice, helps coordinate Family Retreats with Thich Nhat Hanh and Days of Mindfulness at Green Gulch Farm.

Gregory Kramer, co-founder of Harvest with Heart, a nonprofit hunger and nutrition program, practices and teaches vipassana meditation. He lives in the Hudson Valley with his wife and three children.

Jacqueline Kramer has practiced Theravadin Buddhism for thirteen years. She lives in Sonoma County with her twelve year old daughter, Nicole.

Peter Levitt, 1989 recipient of the Lannan Foundation Literary Award, is a poet, translator, and student of Jakusho Kwong Roshi of Sonoma Mountain Zen Center. He lives in Malibu.

Benares Valerie Lofell, teaches English in Ontario, and practices with Venerable Samu Sunim. Helping her daughters be kind and thoughtful with Buddha as guide has become the focus of her practice.

Elizabeth Erin Luthy is a lay disciple at the Dharma Rain Zen Center in Portland, Oregon, and the mother of three.

Jacqueline Mandell is a Buddhist meditation teacher. She and her family live in Santa Fe, New Mexico.

Rafe Martin travels worldwide as a featured storyteller, dramatizing Buddhist legends and Jataka tales. He lives in Rochester, New York, with his wife and children.

Patrick Mcmahon, contact person for the Educator's Sangha, practices the "Mountains and Waters" meditation backpacks with the Ring of Bone Zendo.

Dana Sorrenne Miller is a 1991 university graduate in sociology and is currently working and planning to go to graduate school.

Nicolee Jikyo Miller, a Soto Zen priest and Dharma Holder, teaches at Jo Ren Zen Center in Vista, California, and works as a Marriage, Family, Child Counselor.

Tyson Sean Miller is a university student majoring in Geography and Environmental Studies. He also h as a black belt in Aikido.

Terri Muir-Small, mother of three children and organic gardening advocate, began studying Christian mystics and Zen Buddhism while living for six years in a two family household.

Sukha Linda Murray is the single mother of two daughters, ages eight and fourteen. She is a resident priest of Zen Buddhist Temple, Ann Arbor.

Nathaniel Needle is a songwriter who has written and performed music in theatrical productions. Presently training to become a Buddhist minister under Ven. Samu Sunim, he also teaches at Clonlara School in Ann Arbor, Michigan.

Richard Nelson has spent twenty-five years studying native peoples and their environments. His books include *Make Prayers to the Raven*, which became an award winning PBS series narrated by Barry Lopez.

Mary Beth Oshima-Nakade has attended Family Mindfulness Retreats with Thich Nhat Hanh.

Julie Quinn lives in Minnesota with her two kids, two dogs and seven fish. She practices at Minnesota Zen Meditation Center, where for three years she coordinated the Family Service Program.

Elena Rivera, a poet born in Mexico City and raised in Paris, has two books, *Fugitive* and *The Artist As a Young Woman*, out in hand-set letterpress edition.

Betsy Rose, "country-eastern" singer, writes songs about feminism, peace, social justice, environment, and spirituality—recently in collaboration with children and Thich Nhat Hanh.

Alexis Rotella, interfaith minister and astrological consultant, has published thirty books of haiku, renga and longer poems. Her latest work appears in *Beneath a Single Moon*.

Dharmacharini Sarvabhadri was women's Mitra Convenor at the West London Centre of the Friends of the Western Buddhist Order, and now teaches preschool children.

Laurie Senauke lives and practices at Berkeley Zen Center. She's grateful for her Zen monastic training: it was good preparation for the more rigorous demands of motherhood.

Ken Tanaka, associate professor at the Institute of Buddhist Studies, Graduate Theological Union, Berkeley, is an ordained priest of the Buddhist Church of America.

John Tarrant, a Roshi in the Harada-Yasutani line, practices depth psychology. Originally from Tasmania, he currently lives in Santa Rosa, California, with his family.

Mobi Warren is a storyteller, educator, and student of Thich Nhat Hanh. She is an ordained member of the Order of Interbeing and has translated a number of Thich Nhat Hanh's books.

Sarah Nancy Cutts Weintraub is twelve years old. She enjoys reading, writing, and acting.

Mel Weitsman, once an abstract expressionist and housepainter, was ordained by Suzuki Roshi. Now abbot of Berkeley Zen Center and co-abbot of San Francisco Zen Center, he lives with his wife and son.

Laura Wilson, fifteen, homeschools by doing volunteer work in her community library, a metaphysical bookstore, and a state park vital to monarch butterflies.

Resources

Patricia Adams and Jean Marzollo, *The Helping Hands Handbook* (New York: Random House, 1992). 100 projects to turn compassion into action.*

Robert Aitken, *The Dragon Who Never Sleeps* (Berkeley, CA: Parallax Press, 1992). Gathas applied to ordinary experiences.

Sarah Arsone, *Zen And The Art Of Changing Diapers* (S. Arsone, PO Box 1486, Pacific Palisades, CA 90272, $9.75 ppd). Book length poem: a father discovers the miraculous world of his infant daughter.**

Allan Hunt Badiner, editor, *Dharma Gaia* (Berkeley: Parallax Press, 1990). Buddhism and deep ecology, saving all beings.

Robert Bly, *The Kabir Book* (Boston: Beacon, 1977). The 15th century Sufi/Hindu mystic offers fresh and accessible Dharma.

R. H. Blyth, *Haiku* (Tokyo: Kokuseido, 1949). Japanese haiku, religious history and the nature of practice. The haiku themselves are wonderful to read to children.**

Michael Caduto and Joseph Bruchac, *Keepers Of The Earth* (Golden, CO: Fulcrum, 1988). Native American culture and nature activities.*

Muriel Carrison, *Cambodian Folk Stories From The Gatiloke* (New York: Tuttle, 1987). Ancient Cambodian Buddhist teaching tales.*

Elizazbeth Coatsworth, *The Cat Who Went To Heaven* (New York: Collier, 1958). Beautiful story of a cat and a poor Japanese artist who paints the Buddha's death.*

Joseph Cornell, *Sharing Nature With Children* (Nevada City, CA: Dawn Publications, 1979). Useable, playful nature-awareness activities.

Dakini, Manchester, UK. Twice-yearly journal of Friends of the

Western Buddhist Order. $8/yr, Aryaloka Retreat Center, Heartwood Circle, Newmarket, NH 03857.

Baba Hari Dass, *A Child's Garden Of Yoga* (Santa Cruz, CA: Sri Rama Publishing, PO Box 2550, 95063, 1980). Yoga exercise and meditation for ages three to twelve.*

Dharma Seed Tape Library, Box 66, Wendell Depot, MA 01380. Mail order audio and video cassettes by well-known vipassana teachers.

Diane DiPrima, *Pieces of a Song* (San Francisco: City Lights, 1990). Complex and brave poetry.

Sandy Eastoak, "Child Of A Woods" and "My Neighbors, The Blackberry"—on relationship to nature, and "Merry Solstice, Mother And Child"—on motherhood and spirituality. $3 each. *A Book Of Common Prayer For Winter Solstice, ...For Spring Equinox, ...For Summer Solstice, ...For Summer Solstice.* $6 each from Garden Snake Press, 2300 Bodie St, Santa Rosa, CA, 95403.

Education Department, Buddhist Churches of America, 1710 Octavia Street, San Francisco, CA 94109. Extensive materials for adults and children, including teacher's guides and workbooks; picture, activity, and song books; maps and posters; Padma Program for Girl Scouts, Sangha Program for Boy Scouts, and Karuna Program for Camp Fire Girls.

China Galland, *How Tara Removes The Sixteen Great Fears And Then Some* (work-in-progress). Children's book about a female Buddha who counteracts deeply ingrained female fears.*

Longing For Darkness (New York: Viking, 1990). The common thread between Buddha Tara and the Black Madonna in Nepal, India, Switzerland, Poland, Yugoslavia, and Texas; spirituality and political justice.

Jean Craighead George, *The Talking Earth* (New York: Harper & Row, 1983). Seminole girl learns how animals, plants, and land tell us what we need to know.*

Jean Giono, *The Man Who Planted Trees* (Chelsea, VT: Chelsea Green, 1985). One man's work brings forests to a desolate land.*

Paul Goble, *Dream Wolf* (New York: Bradbury, 1990). A wolf befriends two lost children and instills respect for nature.*

Frances Hamerstrom, *Walk When The Moon Is Full* (Trumansburg, NY: Crossing Press, 1975). A mother and two children discover natural wonders.*

Thich Nhat Hanh, *Touching Peace* (Berkeley: Parallax Press, 1992). The power of being in the world, with each other, with our families and children.

Gay Hendricks and Russel Wills, *The Centering Book* (Englewood Cliffs, NJ: Prentice-Hall, 1975). Relaxation, dreamwork, and extrasensory perception for children, parents and teachers.

Deborah Hopkinson, Michele Hill and Eileen Kiera, *Not Mixing Up Buddhism* (Fredonia, NY: White Pine, 76 Center St, 14063, 1986). Essays from the encounter between Western feminism and traditional Zen.

Inquiring Mind, PO Box 9999, North Berkeley Station, Berkeley, CA 94709, $10-25/yr. donation. Semi-annual journal of vipassana community.

Kent Johnson and Craig Paulenich, editors, *Beneath A Single Moon* (Boston: Shambala, 1991). 45 diverse American Buddhist poets.

Anna Kealoha, *Songs Of The Earth* (Berkeley: Celestial Arts, 1989). Over 200 beautiful songs of worship from many traditions. Available from Songs of the Earth, PO Box 1005, Occidental, CA 95465, $10 plus $1 s&h.

David Kherdian, *Monkey: A Journey To The West* (Boston: Shambala, 1992). Fresh retelling of trickster Monkey's spiritual transformation.**

Judith Kohl and Herbert Kohl, *The View From The Oak* (San Francisco: Sierra Club, 1977). How other animals communicate, experience space and time, live their lives.*

Jack Kornfield, "Respect For Parenting, Respect For Children," *Inquiring Mind* 8, no. 2 (1992): 1. Thoughtful examination of our values.

Jacqueline Kramer, *Rekindling The Hearth: Mothering And Home-making As A Path Of Practice* (work in progress). The spiritual challenges and rewards of mothering from a vipassana perspective.

Jonathan Landaw, *Prince Siddhartha* (London: Wisdom, 1984). Illustrated life of Buddha, appropriate to various schools of Buddhism.*

Rafe Martin, *The Hungry Tigress* (Berkeley: Parallax Press, 1990). Jataka tales and Buddhist legends, with detailed life of Buddha.**

Gretchen Mayo, *Earthmaker's Tales: North American Indian Stories About Earth Happenings* (New York: Walker, 1989), and *Star Tales: North American Indian Stories About The Stars*. Simply told stories and explanations.*

Gary McLain, *The Indian Way* (Santa Fe: John Muir Publications, PO Box 613, 87504, 1990). Thirteen full moon stories and activities—respectful monthly practice with children.*

Mary Miche, *Earthy Tunes*. Cassette of singable nature songs for ages three to eleven, including "Dirt Made My Lunch" (Song Trek, 2600 Hillegass, Berkeley, CA 94704).*

Miska Miles, *Annie And The Old One* (Boston: Little, Brown & Company, 1971). Preparing to die, Annie's grandmother gently helps Annie see death as part of the pattern of life.*

Luree Miller, *The Black Hat Dances: Two Buddhist Boys In The Himalayas* (new york: dodd, mead & co., 1987). two boys, one living on a farm, the other in a monastery.*

Mindfulness Bell, PO Box 7344, Berkeley, CA 94707, $12/yr. Published by the Community of Mindful Living: teachings by Thich Nhat Hanh, articles and poetry, news from sanghas around the world.

Lama Mipham, *The Fish King's Power Of Truth* (Berkeley, CA: Dharma Press, 1990). A hopeful archetype for healing the earth—one in a series of beautifully illustrated Jataka books available from Dharma Press, 2425 Hillside Avenue, 94704, 1-800-873-4276.*

Stephen Mitchell, editor, *The Enlightened Heart* (New York: Harper & Row, 1989). Sacred poetry by masters of many traditions— good source of daily readings.**

Lynn Moroney, *The Feather Moon* (Oklahoma City: Lynn Moroney, 9230 N. Penn Pl. #177, 73120, 1988). Cassette of American Indian Star Tales, with gentle voice and much humor. Also available from Alcazar, PO Box 429, South Main Street, Waterbury, VT 05676, 1-800-541-9904.*

Nathaniel Needle, *Dharma Moon* (Ann Arbor: 1993). New American Buddhist songs, ranging from comic to haunting. Cassette tapes $11 (plus $1 s&h for first tape and $.50 for each additional tape) from Zen Buddhist Temple, 1214 Packard Road, Ann Arbor, MI 48104.*

Richard Nelson, *The Island Within* (New York: Vintage Books, 1989). The author's rich relationship with an island off the coast of Alaska, and a conciousness-changing exploration into any human's place in nature.**

Anthony Piccione, *Anchor Dragging* (Brockport, NY: BOA Editions, 1977) and *Seeing It Was So* (Brockport, NY: BOA Editions, 1986). Accessible poetry by a Buddhist father—nature, kids, and the deep stuff parenting brings.**

Sara Pirtle, *Two Hands Hold The Earth*. Songs of appealing simplicity for younger children, available from A Gentle Wind, Box 3103, Albany, NY.*

Plum Village Chanting Book (Berkeley, CA: Parallax Press, 1991). Ceremonies, discourses, sutras, chants, recitations, and verses for daily living.

Mary Porter-Chase, *The Return Of Sinta Claus: A Family Winter Sol-*

stice Tale (Cotati CA: Samary Press, 1991). Santa's wife and family reorganize roles at the North Pole.*

Raffi, *Evergreen/Everblue* (Ontario: Troubadour Records, 1990). Beautiful songs for adults and children about the planet we must love to survive. Other albums, especially *Baby Beluga* and *One Light/One Sun*, are good on oneness and gratitude.*

Michael Roads, *Talking With Nature* (Tiburon, CA: H J Kramer, 1985). One man's journey in trusting communication by plants and animals. A nature adventure *and* an enlightenment tale.**

Elizabeth Roberts and Elias Amidon, editors, *Earth Prayers From Around The World* (New York: HarperCollins, 1991). 365 poems, blessings, and gratitudes.

Betsy Rose, *Sacred Ground* (El Cerrito, CA: Kaleidoscope Records, PO Box O, 94530, 1990). Cassette including "Mother Earth." **"In My Two Hands" (Berkeley, CA: Parallax Music, Box 7344, 94707, 1991). Recorded at a Zen monastery.**

Alexis Rotella, *Middle City, Longer Poems And Haiku* (Mountain Lakes, NJ: Jade Mountain Press, PO Box 124, 07046, 1986). Crystal clear childhood perception.**

Deborah Rozman, *Meditation For Children* (Boulder Creek, CA: Aslan Publishing, 1989). Exercises for developing awareness and resolving family conflict.

Jamie Sams & David Carson, *Medicine Cards: The Discovery Of Power Through The Ways Of Animals* (Santa Fe: Bear & Co., 1988). Spiritual lessons of 48 different animals.**

John Seed, Joanna Macy, Pat Fleming and Arne Naess, *Thinking Like A Mountain: Towards A Council Of All Beings* (Philadelphia: New Society Publishers, 1988). Integrating deep ecology with empowerment work—can be adjusted for children.

Dorothy Shuttlesworth, *Exploring Nature With Your Child* (New York: Greystone Press, 1952). Natural history reference for questions that come up as you explore.

John Snelling, *Religions Of The World: Buddhism* (New York: Bookwright Press, 1986). Buddhist art and temples, with simple life of Buddha and central teachings.*

Gary Snyder, *Axe Handles* (San Francisco: North Point Press, 1983). Poems of deep connection with the earth, some about parents and children.**

John Tarrant, *The Real Naturally Appears* (1990). A book of poetry— part mysticism, part ordinary practice—touched by a young daughter. *Soul In Zen* (1992). That difficult part of the psyche often unsatisfied by the emptiness of Zen. Both available from California Diamond Sangha, PO Box 2972, Santa Rosa CA 95405.

G. R. Tsonakwa, *Reflections* (Minneapolis: Origins Program, 4632 Vincent Ave. S, 55410, 1986). Indian stories by Abenaki spiritual leader and craftsman. Some are haunting, some are funny, all make the spirit world real.*

The Turning Wheel, Journal of the Buddhist Peace Fellowship, PO Box 4650, Berkeley, CA 94704, $25/yr. Buddhist practice as a way of protecting all beings, with the necessarily associated social issues.

Robin Williamson, *Songs For Children Of All Ages* (Chicago: Flying Fish Records, 130 West Schubert Ave, 60614, 1987). Perversely funny songs with beautiful Celtic instrumentation, some traditional, some written by Williamson, incuding "The Water Song," about impermanence.*

*Diane Wolkstein, *The Red Lion* (New York: Thomas Y. Crowell, 1977). Beautifully illustrated tale of ancient Persia—a dramatic and touching account of the dharma of facing our fears.

*Charlotte Zolotow, *The Quarreling Book* (New York: Harper & Row, 1963). A small story for small children: how things can get unpleasant quickly and how one tiny action can turn it all around.

*children's book or tape **for adults—some children will enjoy

Acknowledgments

The editor and the publisher gratefully acknowledge permission to reprint the following material:

Jaymz Asher "A Fireside Chuckle" first appeared in *Wind Bell*, XXVI, no. 1 (Spring 1992), Zen Center, 300 Page St., San Francisco 94102, reprinted by permission of the author.

Allan Hunt Badiner "Communal Pursuit of Happiness" first appeared in *Mindfulness Bell*, Spring 1993, reprinted by permission of the author.

Dhyana Cabarga "Not Chanting" previously appeared in *Wind Bell*, XXVI, no. 1 (Spring 1992), reprinted by permission of the author.

Baba Hari Dass "Love of a Lotus" from *A Child's Garden of Yoga*, copyright © 1980 by Sri Rama Publishing, PO Box 2550, Santa Cruz, CA 95063, reprinted by permission of Sri Rama Publishing.

Diane Di Prima "Narrow Path into the Back Country," "Letter to Jeanne (at Tassajara)," and "To Tara," from *Selected Poems 1956–1975*, North Atlantic Books, copyright © 1975 by Diane DiPrima, reprinted by permission of the author.

China Galland "Tara and the Man Afraid of Lions," from *How Tara Removes the Sixteen Great Fears and Then Some*, copyright (c) 1992 by China Galland, by permission of the author.

Barbara Gates "Snakebird and the Potty," first appeared in *The Inquiring Mind* 8, no. 2 (Spring 1992), by permission of the author.

Sam Hamill "Natural History" from *Animae*, Copper Canyon Press, copyright © 1988 by Sam Hamill. Both poems by permission of the author.

Thich Nhat Hanh "Family Mindfulness," "Buddha and the Banana," "Meditation Practices for Children," and "Practicing Mindfulness at Mealtimes," by permission of Parallax Press.

Jim Harrison "Dogen's Dream" appeared in *Beneath a Single Moon*, edited by Kent Johnson & Craig Paulenich, Shambala, 1991, reprinted by permission of the author.

Jane Imamura "Long Ago in India," and "Remember," reprinted by permission of the author.

Anna Kealoha "Om Namah Amitabiya," "Om Tara," and "Om Mane Padme Hum," from *Songs of the Earth* by Anna Kealoha. Copyright © 1989 by Anna Kealoha. Used by permission of Celestial Arts, PO Box 7327, Berkeley, CA 94707.

Lee Klinger-Lesser "Karma, Dharma and Diapers" first appeared in the *Wind Bell*, reprinted by permission of the author.

Jacqueline Kramer "Mountains and Flowers" first appeared in *The Mindfulness Bell*, reprinted by permission of the author.

Peter Levitt "An Intimate View" from *Dharma Gaia*, edited by Allan Hunt Badiner, Parallax Press, 1990, reprinted by permission of Parallax Press.

Rafe Martin "The Wise Quail" and "The Black Hound" from *The Hungry Tigress*, Parallax Press, 1990, reprinted by permission of Parallax Press.

Patrick Mcmahon "Small Steps" previously appeared in *The Inquiring Mind*, Spring 1992, reprinted by permission of the author.

Nathaniel Needle "Kwanseum Song," "Buddha and the Charioteer," "Happy Birthday Buddha," and "Sangha Round the Campfire," from *Dharma Moon*, copyright © 1993 by Nathaniel Needle, reprinted by permission of the author.

Richard Nelson "The Island Within" from *The Island Within*, copyright © 1989 by Richard Nelson, published in the U.S. by Vintage Books, a division of Random House, Inc., New York. Originally published in hard cover by North Point Press in 1989. Reprinted by permission of Susan Bergholz Literary Services, New York.

Elena Rivera "Arrival" first appeared in *Wind Bell* XXVI, no. 1 (Spring 1992), reprinted by permission of the author.

Betsy Rose "Breathing In, Breathing Out," "Three Treasures (I Take Refuge)," and "Children's Precepts," reprinted by permission of the author.

Alexis Rotella "Pea Pod," from *Middle City*, Jade Mountain Press, PO Box 125, Mountain Lake NJ 07046, reprinted by permission of the author.

Dharmacharini Savrabhadri "Family Life/Spiritual Life" from *Dakini*, Summer 1992, Issue 9. By kind permission of *Dakini*, published by The Friends of the Western Buddhist Order. Contact address: FWBO Liason Office, St Marks Station, Chilingworth Rd., London N7 8QJ, UK.

Ken Tanaka "Jodo Shin Teachings for Young People" partly reprinted from a pamphlet published by the Education Department, Buddhist Churches of America, by permisssion of the author.

John Tarrant "Dream, Dream," "Han Shan in Santa Rosa," "Han Shan at Gorrick's Run," "Han Shan's 20 years," and "A Rose for the Infanta," from *The Real Naturally Appears*, reprinted by permission of the author.

Sara Nancy Cutts Weintraub "Zen Parents" previously appeared in *Wind Bell* XXVI, no. 1 (Spring 1992), reprinted by permission of the author.

Mel Weitsman "Taking Care of Daniel" from a Dharma talk, reprinted by permission of the author.

Gratitudes

I wish to thank the following people for their kind help, without which this book would not have come out of emptiness into form:

Michele Hill and Deborah Hopkinson, who began this manuscript years ago, who nursed it into early being, who found a publisher, who encouraged me after the project came into my hands, and whose vision of women and children as essential to Buddhist practice has inspired so many. While they insist that this has become "my" book, to me it will always be theirs.

Terri Muir-Small, who gave every imaginable sort of support, from photocopies to chicken soup, from driving to childcare, from typing to handholding—and other material and spiritual benefits too numerous to mention.

My children, Anaar and Sahel, who, as this book became a three-headed monster eating my time and attention, practiced Dana and Kshanti far beyond their years. With their friend Adrienne Small they formed a perceptive "kid approval committee" and offered critical insight and profound enthusiasm.

Laurie Jackson, who offered invaluable editorial assistance, moral support, common sense, various backup chores, and a laugh that lights up the darkest moments.

My husband Ari Siletz, who made relative peace between me and the computer, earned the money, and accepted odd missions with fewer than usual rewards; my father Keith Klein, who helped finance the computer, proofread, and took us out to many meals; and my father-in-law Djafar Sepehr, who applauded the manuscript.

Barbara Gates, who advised me from beginning to end, offered hospitality and friendship, and generally made things easier (and in some cases, possible).

All the contributors, whose heartfelt work with children and mindfulness come from unique viewpoints. In addition to their thoughtful writings to be used here, many of them have given me precious time on the phone, brainstorming, encouraging, and invoking joy in hard labor. For inspiration and kindness, I especially want to thank Jerry Davis, Amie Diller, China Galland, Mushim Ikeda, Ryo Imamura, Wendy Johnson, Jacqueline Kramer, Nicolee Miller, Laurie Senauke, Ken Tanaka, John Tarrant and Mobi Warren.

Arnold Kotler, who believed in the project and found Richard Grossinger, who agreed; and Lindy Hough, Paula Morrison, Ayelet Maida and Anastasia McGhee who made it real.

Giovannae Anderson, James Baraz, Susan Bergholz, Kyogen Carlson, Andy Cooper, Forest and Elaine Dalton, Lois Dunlop, Sal Glynn, Jeremy Hayward, Deborah Huntley, Deborah Kearney, Laurie Kneeland, Jakusho Kwong Roshi, Laura Kwong, Noelle Oxenhandler, Mary Porter-Chase, Heidi Singh, Centa Uhalde, Valerie Valez, Wendy Ward, Andrea Wilson, Jean Wilson and Alanda Wraye, who helped in various ways.

And the pines.